MONOGRAPHS AND BIBLIOGRAPHIES
IN
AMERICAN MUSIC

Editor
James R. Heintze, The American University

Editorial Board
Michael J. Budds, University of Missouri-Columbia
Elise K. Kirk, Catholic University of America
David W. Music, Southwestern Baptist Theological Seminary
Katherine Preston, College of William and Mary
Deane L. Root, University of Pittsburgh

SOURCE READINGS IN AMERICAN CHORAL MUSIC
Michael J. Budds, Editor

The College Music Society
202 West Spruce Street
Missoula, Montana 59802

Source Readings
in American Choral Music

David P. DeVenney

Monographs and Bibliographies in American Music

Number 15

Published by The College Music Society

International Standard Book Number 0-9650647-0-0
International Standard Book Number 0-9650647-1-9 *paperback*

Printed and Bound in the United States of America

Published by
The College Music Society
202 West Spruce Street
Missoula, Montana 59802

To DGW
teacher, mentor, and friend

and to RDH and JJS
students and friends

Table of Contents

Preface

The history of almost any subject can be told, at least in part, through an examination of the documents that have helped to shape that history. In the literature on music are several lengthy, annotated volumes that reproduce documents from past eras, along with commentaries and introductions to historical figures and issues. The study of American music, admittedly short-lived by comparison to the historical study of many other musicological topics, has so far produced few of these anthologies. Indeed, American music history reaches back less than three hundred years into the past, and most of the writings concerning it until now have been devoted to the music itself, stylistic periods, individual composers, or well-circumscribed subjects. An intensive study of its documents has usually taken place as a by-product of other research. This volume shares that raison d'etre, as I have gathered these articles and essays over the past decade during the course of my own research into American choral music. What is different is that I have sought to publish them, with appropriate commentary, in order to shed light on this particular field and, hopefully, to inform a wider public.

This text is not a history of American choirs and choral organizations. Rather, this compilation is the first attempt to present important documents relating to the history and performance of choral literature written in the United States. The topics addressed in these selections, which are widely varied, may be grouped in three categories: reflections on the nature and purposes of choral music by major contributors to the repertory, critical responses to landmark works, and instructions on performance practice. Since much of the choral literature written in America was connected with churches and since the churches in the United States fostered as much as any other institution the growth of amateur — and sometimes professional-calibre — choirs, many of the writings deal with sacred music. The public schools in this country are the second largest purveyors of choral music, and have been since the middle of the nineteenth century. So there is much recorded here that deals with the practical needs of choral music in that situation. Finally, the contents may be divided into historical periods, as indeed I have done in laying out this volume.

The publication date of each essay is given following the title. Full bibliographic citations and publishers' copyright permissions are given at the conclusion of each essay. Some may consider the selection of essays eccentric, and others may wonder why an article on a composer or work of interest to them has not been included. While I have tried to include writings that are important — if not pivotal — to the history of American choral music, inevitably my own biases have surfaced in the process. Sometimes important writings can be found elsewhere, and I felt no need to reproduce them here. One example: I have included no writings by Robert Shaw or Howard Swan, two leaders in twentieth-century American choral music. Neither man is primarily a composer (although Shaw's many arrangements for chorus may qualify him), and secondly, their writings are collected (or are currently being collected) elsewhere. A second example: while the music of the Moravian church is of primary importance in the history of choral music in this country, there are few important writings by composers to be found, although there is a wealth of secondary literature, both from the period and from later. Therefore, there is no representative essay included here for them. Information on Shaw, Swan, and the Moravians may be found, however, by perusing the Select Bibliography at the end of this volume.

I have generally followed the source material exactly when reprinting it and have not changed antiquated grammar or spelling. I have sometimes corrected some obvious typographical errors without notation, but have labeled [*sic*] other, more questionable typographical errors or errors of fact. I have reprinted nearly all of these essays in full, except where indicated in the annotation following each.

It is my hope that the brief historical overviews introducing each section of this book, as well as the individual commentaries preceding each selection, will help to place these collected writings in perspective for the reader or teacher not familiar with this literature or its historical signifi-

xii

cance. As a further aid, I have compiled immediately following this Preface a Chronology of American Choral Music, highlighting publications, movements, and compositions that have helped to shape and form the history and literature of the choral art in the United States. Toward the same end, the reader will find a lengthy (but hardly exhaustive) bibliography of further writings at the end of the book, divided by historical period.

American choral literature, except for its first fifty years or so, has not been widely studied or discussed. Most of the major works and the circumstances surrounding their composition have escaped the notice of all but a few specialists in the field; much less have frequent performances of this great literature been given. Even the well-educated collegiate or university choral conductor may know little about this music, and its full history has yet to be written. It is my hope that, in the end, this compilation will serve to engage a larger public, intriguing conductors and others to survey and perform the music of this important aspect of our musical heritage.

* * * * *

I am grateful to the many publishers and journals who have graciously granted permission, usually free of charge, to reprint the essays included in this volume. Their credits are listed immediately following each essay. I am also grateful to the Otterbein Humanities Committee and the Sears/White Family Foundation at Otterbein for their generous support of my research into American choral music over the past ten years. Finally, I would like to thank the College Music Society, James Heintze, chair of the publications committee, and Michael Budds, who edited this volume for the Society, for their willingness to bring this volume to print, disseminating it to the CMS membership and to the scholarly, musical community at large.

A Chronology of
American Choral Music

Frontispiece to Supply Belcher, *The Harmony of Maine*.
Boston, Mass., 1794.

A Chronology of American Choral Music

1640   *The Bay Psalm Book* first published in Cambridge,
        Massachusetts

1698   *The Bay Psalm Book*, ninth edition: first known to
        contain music

1721   *An Introduction to the Singing of Psalm Tunes* (John
        Tufts)
        The Grounds and Rules of Musick Explained (Thomas
        Walter)

1741   Moravians establish permanent settlement in Bethlehem,
        Pennsylvania

1761   *Urania* (James Lyon)

1770   *The New England Psalm Singer* (William Billings)
        First American (partial) performance of Handel's
        Messiah takes place in New York City

1778   *The Singing Master's Assistant* (Billings)

1781   *The Psalm Singer's Amusement* (Billings)

1794   *The Art of Singing* (Andrew Law)
        The Harmony of Maine (Supply Belcher)

1800   *Sacred Dirges, Hymns and Anthems* (Oliver Holden)

1802   *The Columbian Repository of Sacred Music* (Samuel
          Holyoke)

1803   *The American Compiler of Sacred Harmony* (Stephen
          Jenks)

1805   *Masses, Vespers, Litanies, Hymns, Psalms, Anthems, and
          Motets* "for the use of Catholic Churches in the
          United States" (Benjamin Carr), published in
          Philadelphia; includes Carr's Masses in Two and
          Three Parts

1813   *Repository of Sacred Music* (John Wyeth)

1815   Handel and Haydn Society founded in Boston

1816   *Musica Sacra* (Thomas Hastings)

1820   *The Dawning of Music in Kentucky* and *The Western
          Minstrel* (Anthony Philip Heinrich)

1822   *The Boston Handel and Haydn Society Collection of
          Church Music* (Lowell Mason)

1831   First complete American performance of Handel's
          Messiah takes place in New York City

1834   *Manual of the Boston Academy of Music*, for Instruction
          in the Elements of Vocal Music, on the System of
          Pestalozzi (Lowell Mason)

1835   *Thanksgiving Anthem* (Oliver Shaw)

1838   Music instruction begins in the Boston Public Schools

1842	First concert by New York Philharmonic Society
1844	*The Boston Glee Book* (published by Mason and George Webb), including madrigals by Wilbye and Morley *Original Sacred Harp* (Benjamin Franklin White and E.J. King)
1845	Theodore Thomas arrives in New York from Germany
1852	*Journal of Music* (John Sullivan Dwight) begins publication in Boston (ceased 1881)
1855	*Stabat Mater* (William Henry Fry)
1856	*Esther* (William Bradbury)
1857	*The Haymakers* (George Frederick Root) *The Jubilee*: An Extensive Collection of Church Music for the Choir, the Congregation, and the Singing-School (Bradbury)
1860	*Daniel; or, The Captivity and Restoration* (Bradbury) Oberlin (Ohio) Musical Union formed, the first choral society sponsored by an academic institution
1866	*Daniel* (George F. Bristow) *Mass in D* (John Knowles Paine) Mendelssohn Glee Club founded in New York City
1868	*The Triumph* (Root)
1869	Great National Peace Festival in Boston, organized by Patrick Gilmore to celebrate end of Civil War; included chorus of 10,000
1871	Apollo Club founded in Boston

5

1872   World's Peace Jubilee in Boston; chorus of 20,000
                St. Peter (Paine)
                The Forty-sixth Psalm (Dudley Buck)
                First American performance of Beethoven's *Missa
                    solemnis* takes place in New York City
                Apollo Musical Club founded in Chicago

1873   First Cincinnati May Festival, followed by similar
                    festivals in Philadelphia, Ann Arbor, and other cities
                The Legend of Don Munio (Buck)

1874   Founding of New York Oratorio Society
                Mendelssohn Club founded in Philadelphia

1875   Paine appointed first professor of music in United States,
                    at Harvard

1876   Philadelphia Centennial Exhibition; choral works
                    included *Centennial Hymn* (Paine)

1882   *David, the Shepherd Boy* (Root)

1885   *Mass in C* (Bristow)

1886   First American performance of Bach's *B Minor Mass*
                    takes place in Cincinnati, Ohio

1887   *The Wreck of the Hesperus* (Arthur Foote)

1891   *St. John* (J.C.D. Parker)

1892   *Mass in E-flat* (Amy Beach)
                Phoenix expirans (George W. Chadwick)

1893   Chicago Columbian Exhibition; choral works included

Columbus March and Hymn (Paine) and *Festival Jubilate* (Beach)

1894   *The Life of Man* (J.C.D. Parker)

1897   *Hora novissima* (Horatio Parker)

1898   Bethlehem (Pennsylvania) Bach Choir founded,
        beginning annual performances of Bach's *B Minor Mass*
        The Celestial Country (Charles Ives)

1899   *Hora novissima* (H. Parker), first American work to be
        performed at Three Choirs Festival in Worcester,
        England

1901   *Judith* (Chadwick)

1906   *Job* (Frederick Converse), first American oratorio to be
        heard in Germany

1907   *The Chambered Nautilus* (Beach)
        Psalm 137 (Charles Martin Loeffler)

1912   St. Olaf Choir founded by F. Melius Christiansen

1916   Fred Waring's "Pennsylvanians" formed

1921   Westminster Choir founded in Dayton, Ohio by John
        Finley Williamson; moved in 1932 to Princeton, New
        Jersey

1925   *Lament for Beowulf* (Howard Hanson)

1932   National Convention of Gospel Choirs and Choruses
        founded

1934	*Advodath Hakodesh [Sacred Service]* (Ernest Bloch)
1936	*The Peaceable Kingdom* (Randall Thompson)
1939	*Folk Song Symphony* (Roy Harris)
1940	*And They Lynched Him on a Tree* (William Grant Still)
1941	Robert Shaw forms Collegiate Chorale
1942	*Cantata No. 2, A Free Song* (William Schuman) *The Prairie* (Lukas Foss)
1943	*The Mystic Trumpeter* (Norman Dello Joio)
1947	*In the Beginning* (Aaron Copland)
1952	*A Parable of Death* (Foss)
1954	*The Prayers of Kierkegaard* (Samuel Barber)
1956	*The Unicorn, the Gorgon and the Manticore* (Gian Carlo Menotti)
1959	American Choral Directors Association founded Margaret Hillis becomes conductor of the Chicago Symphony Orchestra Chorus
1960s	First doctoral programs in choral conducting formed at the University of Southern California and the University of Illinois
1965	*Chichester Psalms* (Leonard Bernstein)
1970	*When Lilacs Last in the Dooryard Bloom'd* (Roger Sessions)

1971   *Mass* (Bernstein)

1977   Association of Professional Vocal Ensembles founded

1988   *Te Deum* (Argento)

Part I
Music Before 1830

"Wake Every Breath," from *The New England Psalm Singer* by William Billings,
Engraved in Boston by Paul Revere, 1770.

INTRODUCTION: MUSIC BEFORE 1830

*C*horal music in the colonial years of this country was inextricably linked to the church. The early books that the Puritans and other settlers brought with them usually contained the words to familiar hymns and psalm tunes that they remembered from their home churches in Europe. Not until 1698 was a volume published in America, The Bay Psalm Book, which in its ninth edition finally contained a few hymns with music. Usually books like these began with instructions to the singer: in the absence of training institutions the authors or compilers of these books attempted to outline the rudiments of reading music and to teach beginning vocal techniques to the amateur. The singer could then apply his or her new knowledge to the performance of service music, for that was the principal reason behind the publication of these volumes. The ministers and musicians who wrote these "tunebooks" were concerned about the poor performance of music in their services, for those who might have accurately remembered the tunes from their home churches across the Atlantic could no longer do so, or had been succeeded with "American" singers who had neither the training to read music nor the memory of how to sing the tunes by rote. Two such early tunebooks were John Tufts's An Introduction to the Singing of Psalm Tunes and Thomas Walters's The Grounds and Rules of Musick Explained, both printed in 1721. The Preface to Walters's book is reproduced here, and it is useful for perspective on the needs of these ministers and others who with the publication of these didactic tools offered a solution to the problem.

By the end of the eighteenth century, especially in and around Boston, this didactic movement gained momentum. Often known as the singing school movement, the efforts to educate the church-going public in the reading and correct vocal performance of music literally exploded. In the course of the next fifty years or so, hundreds of tunebooks were printed and reprinted, and the people of the Northeast gathered frequently (it seems) to attend a singing school, where an acknowledged master would lead them through exercises and songs designed to make them musically literate. One of the most famous of these masters was William Billings, a Boston tanner by trade but who kept fingers in a number of pies. His many publications are filled with rather *elementary fuging tunes and hymns. In most of these collections, there are a number of anthems included, usually toward the end of the book. The anthems tend to be longer and somewhat more sophisticated than the rest of the music, and continue to be performed frequently in choral concerts today, while the fuging tunes and hymns have largely fallen into the historical dust bin. I have excerpted three of Billings's writings here, dealing with various problems related to the art of singing, with an additional selection by his contemporary Supply Belcher.*

New England churches were not the only ones concerned with poor vocal renditions of service music. I have also selected an essay on good eating habits for the singer by Conrad Beissel, the leader of the utopian Ephrata Cloister, and an essay from an early publication of the Episcopal Church in America.

THOMAS WALTER

THE GROUNDS AND RULES OF MUSICK EXPLAINED (1721)

THOMAS WALTER (1696-1725) was born in Boston, and studied for the ministry at Harvard, graduating in 1713. His instruction book in music, from which this preface is taken, was written and published in reaction to the decline of psalm singing. While earlier settlers had been able to remember the psalm tunes, successive generations could not, and the same tune could be sung quite differently from congregation to congregation. Walter was one of the principal forces behind a movement, largely led from the pulpit, that encouraged congregants to learn to sing by note. This idea of "regular singing" eventually gained momentum, resulting in the widespread and influential singing school movement. In the "Preface" below, fifteen important ministers, including both Cotton and Increase Mather, collectively outline the situation, while Walter, in his "Brief Introduction," explains the advantages of music literacy.

A Recommendatory PREFACE

An ingenious Hand having prepared Instructions to direct them that would Learn to Sing PSALMS after a Regular Manner; and it being thought proper that we should signify unto the publick some of our Sentiments on this Occasion; We do declare, that we rejoice in *Good Helps* for a Beautiful and Laudable performance of that holy Service, wherein we are to Glorify God, and edify one another with the *Spiritual Songs*, wherewith he has enriched us.

And we would encourage all, more particularly our *Young People*, to accomplish themselves with Skill to *Sing the Songs of the Lord,* according to the *Good Rules* of Psalmody: Hoping that the Consequence of it will be, that not only the *Assemblies* of *Zion* will *Decently & in order* carry on this Exercise of PIETY, but also it will be the more introduced into private *Families*, and become a part of our *Family-Sacrifice.*

At the same time we would above all Exhort, that the *main Concern* of all may be to make it not a meer [*sic*] *Bodily Exercise* but *Sing with Grace in their Hearts*, with Minds attentive to the *Truths* in the PSALMS which they sing and affected with them, so that in their *Hearts they may make a Melody to the LORD*.

SOME BRIEF

And very plain INSTRUCTIONS for *Singing* by NOTE

Musick is the Art of Modulating Sounds, wither with the Voice, or with an Instrument. And as there are Rules for the right Management of an Instrument, so there are no less for the well ordering of the Voice. And tho' Nature itself suggests unto us a Notion of Harmony, and many Men, without any other Tutor, may be able to strike upon a few Notes tolerably useful; yet this bears no more proportion to a Tune composed and sung by the Rules of Art than the vulgar Hedge-Notes of every Rustic does to the Harp of David. Witness the modern Performances both in the Theatres and the Temple.

Singing is reducible to the *Rules of Art*; and he who has made himself Mother of a few of these Rules, is able at *first Sight* to sing Hundreds of New Tunes, which he never saw or heard of before, and this by the bare Inspection of the Notes, without hearing them from the Mouth of a Singer. Just as a Person who has learned all the Rules of *Reading*, is able to read any new Book, without any further Help or Instruction. This is a Truth, altho' known to, and proved by many of us, yet very hardly to be received and credited in the Country.

What a Recommendation is this then to the following Essay, that our Instructions will give you that knowledge in Vocal Musick, whereby you will be able to sing all the Tunes in the World, without hearing of them sung by another, and being constrained to get them by heart from any other Voice than your own? We don't call him a *Reader*, who can recite *Memorized* a few Pieces of the Bible, and other Authors, but put him to read in those Places where he is a Stranger, cannot tell *ten Words in a Page.* So is not he worthy of the Name of a Singer, who has gotten eight or ten Tunes in his Head, and can sing them like a *Parrot by Rote*, and knows nothing more about them, than he has heard from the Voices of others; and show him a Tune that is new and unknown to him, can't strike two Notes of it.

These Rules then will be serviceable upon a *Threefold* Account. First, they will instruct us in the right and true singing of the Tunes that are already in use in our Churches; which, when they first came out of the Hands of the Composers of them, were sung according to the Rules of the *Scale of Musick*, but are not miserably tortured, and twisted, and quavered, in some Churches, into an horrid Medly [*sic*] of confused and disorderly Noises. This must necessarily create a most disagreeable Jar in the Ears of all that can judge better of Singing, than these Men, who please themselves with their own ill-sounding *Echoes*. For to compare small things with great, our *Psalm*[*ody*] has suffered the like Inconveniences which our *Faith* had laboured under, in case it had been committed and trusted to the uncertain and doubtful Conveyance of Oral Tradition. Our Tunes are, for want of a Standard to appeal to in all our Singing, left to the Mercy of every unskillful Throat to chop and alter, twist and change, according to the infinitely divers and no less odd Humours and Fancies. That this is most true, I appeal to the Experience of those who have happened to be present in many of our Congregations, who will grant me, that there are no two Churches that sing alike. Yea, I have my self heard (for Instance) *Oxford* Tune sung in *three* Churches (which I purposely forbear to mention) with as much difference as there can possibly be between *York* and *Oxford*, or any two other different Tunes. Therefore any man that pleads with me for what they call the *Old Way*, I can confute him only by making this Demand, *What is the* OLD WAY? Which I am sure they cannot tell. For, one Town says, theirs is the true *Old Way*, another Town thinks the same of theirs, and so does a third of their Way of Tuning it. But let such men know from the Writer of this Pamphlet (who can sing all the various Twistings of the old Way, and that too according to the *Genius* of most of the Congregations as well as they can any one Way; which must therefore make him a better Judge than they are or can be,) affirms, that the Notes sung according to the *Scale and Rules of Musick*, are the true *old Way*. For some body or other did compose our Tunes, and did they (think ye) compose them by Rule or by Rote? If the latter, how came they pricked down in our *Psalm Books*? And this I am sure of, we sing them as they are there pricked down, and I am as sure the Country People do not. Judge ye then, who is in the right. Nay, I am sure, if you would once be at the pains to learn our Way of Singing, you could not but be convinced of what I now affirm. But our Tunes have passed thro' strange *Metamorphoses* (beyond those of *Ovid*) since their first Introduction into the World. But to return to the Standard from which we have so long departed cannot fail to set all to rights, and to reduce the Sacred Songs to the primitive Form and Composition.

Again, It will serve for the Introduction of more Tunes into the Divine Service; and these, Tunes of no small Pleasancy and Variety, which will in a great Measure render this Part of Worship still more delightfull to us. For at present we are confined to *eight or ten Tunes*, and in some Congregations to little more than half that Number, which being so often sung over, are too apt, if not to create a Distaste, yet at least mightily to lessen the Relish of them.

There is one more advantage which will accrue from the Introductions of this little Book; and that is this, that by the just and equal *Timing* of the Notes, our Singing will be reduc'd to an exact length, so as not to fatigue the Singer with a tedious Protraction of the Notes beyond the compass of a Man's Breath, and the Power of his Spirit: A Fault very frequent in the Country, where I my self have twice in one Note paused to take Breath. This *keeping of Time* in Singing will have this Natural effect also upon us, that the whole Assembly shall begin and end every single Note, and every Line exactly together, to an Instant, which is a wonderful Beauty in Singing, when a great Number of Voices are together sounding forth the Divine Praises. But for want of this, I have observed in many Places, one Man is upon this Note, while another is a Note before him, which produces something so hideous and disorderly, as is beyond Experience bad. And then the even, unaffected, and smooth sounding the Notes, and the Omission of those unnatural Quaverings and Turnings, will serve to prevent all that Discord and lengthy Tediousness which is so much a Fault in our singing of Psalms. For much time is taken up in shaking out these Turns and Quavers; and besides, no two Men in the Congregation quaver alike, or together; which sounds in the Ears of a good Judge, like *Five Hundred* different Tunes roared out at the same time, whose perpetual interferings with one another, perplexed Jars, and unmeasured Periods, would make a

Man wonder at the false Pleasure which they conceive in that which good Judges of Musick and Sounds, cannot bear to hear.

These are the good Effects, which [some] skill in the *Gamut* will produce. We shall then without any further Preamble, proceed to give the Reader some brief and plain Instructions for singing by Note and Rule.

Thomas Walters. *The Grounds and Rules of Musick Explained: Or, An Introduction to the Art of Singing by Note, Fitted to the Meanest Capacities.* Boston: printed by J. F. Franklin for S. Gerrip, 1721, i-iii, 1-5.

CONRAD BEISSEL
INSTRUCTIONS ON THE VOICE (1747)

CONRAD BEISSEL (1690-1768), born in Eberbach, Germany, immigrated to the United States when he was thirty. He settled first in Boston, but in 1732 moved to Eastern Pennsylvania, where he founded a religious community at Ephrata, near Lancaster, devoted to the beliefs of the Seventh-Day Baptists (the Dunkards). Beissel was not only the religious leader of the Cloister, but also composed much of the music vital to its worship services and its daily life. He was largely self-taught in music, and his compositions are sometimes rather clumsy and thick sounding. Beissel attempted to create a utopian community and gave much thought to the elements of daily life that might contribute to harmonious communal living. His instructions for singing are reprinted below, taken from the preface to the Turtel Taube *of 1747, a book that explained various practices to the Cloister members and provided rules for living.*

Let us now proceed directly to the subject, and show, as briefly as possible, by what means and opportunities we may, both spiritually and physically, attain to this art of high degree, and then consider further whatsoever things the circumstances of the case may require. In the first place, be it observed, that divine virtue must be viewed from the summit of perfection, and occupy the first place, if one would become the right kind of pupil and thereafter a master of this exalted and divine art.

Furthermore, both pupil and master ought to know how necessary it is, in addition to all other circumstances, to embrace every opportunity to make oneself agreeable and acceptable to the spirit of this exalted and divine virtue, inasmuch as according to our experience and knowledge it has within itself the purest and chastest spirit of eternal and celestial virginity.

This naturally requires compliance with the demands of an angelic and heavenly life. Care must be taken of the body, and its requirements reduced to a minimum, so that the voice may become angelic, heavenly, pure and clear, and not rough and harsh through the use of coarse food, and therefore unfit to produce the proper quality of tone, but on the contrary, in place of genuine song, only an unseemly grunting and gasping.

At the same time it is especially necessary to know what kinds of food will make the spirit teachable, and the voice flexible and clear; as also what kinds make it coarse, dull, lazy and heavy. For it is certain that all meat dishes, by whatever name known, quite discommode us, and bring no small injury to the pilgrim on his way to the silent beyond. Then there are those other articles of food which we improperly derive from animals, *e.g., milk*, which causes heaviness and uneasiness; *cheese*, which produces heat and begets desire for other and forbidden things; *butter*, which makes indolent and dull, and satiates to such an extent that one no longer feels the need of singing or praying; *eggs*, which arouse numerous capricious cravings; *honey*, which brings bright eyes and a cheerful spirit, but not a clear voice.

Of bread and cooked dishes none are better for producing cheerfulness of disposition and buoyancy of spirit than *wheat* and after this *buckwheat*, which, though externally different, have the same virtues in their uses, whether used in bread or in cooked dishes.

As regards the other common vegetables, none are more useful than the ordinary *potato*, the *beet*, and other *tubers*. *Beans* are too heavy, satiate too much, and are liable to arouse impure desires. Above all must it be remembered that the spirit of this exalted art, because it is a pure, chaste and virtuous spirit, suffers no unclean, polluted and sinful love for woman, which so inflames and agitates the blood of the young as completely to undo them in mind, heart, voice and soul; whilst in the more mature it awakens excessive desire after the dark things of this world, and consequently closes heart, mind and voice to this pure spirit as its haven.

As concerns *drink*, it has long been settled that nothing is better than pure, clear water, just as it comes from the well, or as made into soup to which a little bread is added. Every other manner of cooking, however, whereby the water is deprived of its healthgiving properties and turned into an unnatural sort of delicacy, is to be considered as a vain and sinful abuse; just as other articles of diet, which we do not deem worthy of mention in this place, have, through many and diverse lusts, been turned from their natural and harmless use into delicacies. Of those who gormandize we cannot here speak, for we are concerned only with those who are already engaged in the spiritual warfare, and who in all respects strive lawfully. With those who walk disorderly and unlawfully we, therefore, have nothing to do. It of course stands to reason that the power to exercise divine virtue is not to be sought in the selection of this or that particular diet; for, were this the case, we would wish, if it were possible, to be entirely relieved of eating, so that we might lead an Enochian, supernatural and supersensual life. Then this heavenly wonder-song would of itself break forth, without the addition of any of those things that are only transient and never reach eternity.

Julius Friedrich Sachse. *The Music of the Ephrata Cloister; also Conrad Beissel's Treatise on Music, as Set Forth in a Preface to the "Turtel Taube" of 1747.* Lancaster, Penn.: printed for the Author, 1903; reprint, New York: American Musicological Society, n.d., 66-68.

WILLIAM BILLINGS
ON VOCAL MUSIC (1764)

Easily the most famous of the early singing school leaders, WILLIAM BILLINGS (1746-1800) was an enigmatic character. Short, with a withered arm and only one eye, and rather negligent personal habits, Billings nonetheless possessed an extraordinary energy and charisma. Self-tutored in music, Billings created tunes full of life and freshness, vitality, and rhythmic drive. Each of his six volumes of music consisted of tunes he wrote as well as those he gathered and collected from his contemporaries, in addition to instructions to the reader at the beginning of each volume.

The first of the following three readings is taken from The Massachusetts Gazette *and Boston* News-Letter Supplement *(12 July 1764), in which Billings extols the virtues of the human voice and its artistic possibilities. The second reading, from* The New England Psalm Singer *(1770), discusses his ideas on balance and intonation in the choir. The last excerpt, from* The Singing Master's Assistant *(1778), gives "how to" advice for the conductor on performance practice, tempo, and tone quality in the choral ensemble. In the latter, Billings also sets forth rules of order for establishing a singing school and for running efficient rehearsals.*

Nature has given to Man the first and finest of all instruments in his own Frame: Who is he then that shall pretend to say, when and in what Country Music first saw its Origin? It is doubtless coeval with the human Fabric, and native of all Countries where Men have lived: Art in all Things will improve what Nature has bestowed upon us: Art is the Offspring of our Understanding, and she who gave them designed them for this Purpose. There is no one of Nature's Endowments which may be more improved by Art than Music; nor hath there been an Age in which that improvement seemed to promise a greater Height than in the present; but yet the Rudiments are in Nature. We have only to correct some Errors in our Taste, in order to arrive at this perfection in the most delightful of all the Sciences. In order to [accomplish] this let us trace it from its Origin, not in remote and idle History, but in our own Breasts, and in the Works of those who have left us Proof of their Abilities, and we shall not fail to discover all our Mistakes, and to profit of the Discovery.

As the sweetness of all musical Sounds is the human Voice, so the highest Glory of the Art is the directing and accompanying it, the following [of] its Modulations and expressing the Sense of those Words in which it adds Meaning to Melody. The introducing this into Music is the Triumph of the human Voice alone: The Music of the Birds; the Notes of the sweetest Instruments, are but dead Sounds; they tinkle in the Ear, but they convey no appropriated Idea. The Voice gives Sentiments with its harmony, and on a double Score awakens every Passion of which the Heart is capable. It was on this Principle, that the immortalized Musicians of Antiquity acquired that Fame which has traveled down to us, and which will live to all posterity. The Harp of *Orpheus*, and the Shell of *Linus* were but Accompaniments to that Voice, which poured forth under all the Charms of Melody, Lessons that moved and that instructed the savage Inhabitants: It is on this Principle, that they are said to have tamed the Beasts of the Desarts [*sic*], and to have made the Lions and the Tygers follow them.

Amphion sung the pleasures and the Profits of Society, the Dangers of a War, and the Advantages of early Security: the Hearers of the Music gathered into a People, and it was thus (though Critics have not found it) his Music built the Walls. It was on this principle that the Performers and Composers of all Nations in old Time acquired their Fame, and it is on this that true Honor is to be attained at present. Concertos and Sonatas have their Praise, and they deserve it; but it is to the Appropriation of Sounds to Sense, that the supreme Honors of the Science always have been and always will be paid.

The Massachusetts Gazette and Boston News-Letter Supplement. Boston, July 12, 1764. Reprinted in Hans Nathan, *William Billings: Data and Documents*. © 1976 by The College Music Society, 17. Used by permission.

WILLIAM BILLINGS
THOUGHTS ON MUSIC (1770)

Thoughts on MUSIC

In order to make good Music, there is great Judgment required in dividing the Parts properly, so that one shall not over-power the other. In most Singing Companies I ever heard, the greatest Failure was in the Bass, for let the Three upper Parts be Sung by the Best Voices upon Earth, and after the Best Manner, yet without a sufficient Quantity of Bass, they are no better than a Scream, because the Bass is the Foundation, and if it be well laid, you may build upon it at Pleasure. Therefore in order to have good Music, there must be Three Bass to one of the upper Parts. So that for Instance, suppose a Company of Forty People, Twenty of them should sing the Bass, the other Twenty should be divided according to the Descretion of the Company into the upper Parts, six or seven of the deepest Voices should sing the Ground Bass which I have set to most of the Tunes in the following Work, and have taken Care to set it chiefly in the compass of the Human Voice, which if well sung together with the upper Parts, is most Majestic, and so exceeding Grand as to cause the floor to tremble, as I myself have often experienced. Great Care should also be taken to Pitch a Tune on or near the Letter it is set, though sometimes it will bear to be set a little above and sometimes a little below the Key, according to the Descretion of the Performer, but I would recommend a Pitch Pipe, which will give the Sound even to the nicety of a half a tone.

Much caution should be used in singing a Solo, in my Opinion Two or Three at most are enough to sing it well, it should be sung as Soft as an Echo, in order to keep the Hearers in an agreeable Suspense till all the parts join together in a full Chorus, as smart and strong as possible. Let all Parts close in a proper Key, and a full Organ, which will yield great delight to the Performers and Hearers.

William Billings. *New England Psalm Singer: or American Chorister, Containing a Number of Psalm-Tunes and Anthems and Canons In Four and Five Parts, Never Before Published*. Boston: printed by Edes and Gill, 1770, 18.

WILLIAM BILLINGS
LESSONS (1780)

LESSON VI.
An Explanation of the several Moods of Time

THE first, or slowest Mood of Time, is called Adagio, each Bar containing to the amount of one Semibreve: Four seconds of time are required to perform each Bar [♩ = 60]; I recommend crotchet [quarter-note] beating in this Mood, performed in the following manner, viz. first strike the ends of the fingers, secondly the heel of the hand, then thirdly, raise your hand a little and shut it up, and fourthly, raise your hand still higher and throw it open at the same time. These motions are called two down and two up, or crotchet beating. A Pendulum to beat Crotchets in this Mood, should be thirty nine inches, and two tenths.

THE second Mood is called Largo, which is in proportion to the Adagio as 5 is to 4 [♩ = 80], you may beat this two several ways, either once down and once up, in every Bar, which is called Minim [half-note] beating, or twice down and twice up, which is called Crotchet beating; the same way you beat Adagio. Where the tune consists chiefly of Minims, I recommend Minim beating; but where it is made up of less Notes, I recommend Crotchet beating: The length of the Pendulum to beat Minims in this Mood, must be seven feet, four inches, and two tenths; and the Pendulum to beat Crotchets, must be twenty two inches, and one twentieth of an inch.

N.B. When I think it advisable to beat Largo in Minim beating, I write "Minim beating" over the top of the tune, and where these words are not wrote, you may beat Crotchet beating.

THE third Mood is called Aliegro [*sic*], it is as quick again as Adagio, so that Minims are sung, to the time of seconds [♩ = 60]. This is performed in Minim beating, viz. one down and one up; the Pendulum to beat Minims must be thirty-nine inches and two tenths.

THE fourth Mood is called two from four, marked thus 2/4, each Bar containing two Crotchets, a Crotchet is performed in the time of half a second [♩ = 120]; this is performed in Crotchet beating, viz. one down and one up. The Pendulum to beat Crotchets in this Mood must be nine inches and eight tenths long.

N.B. The four above-mentioned moods are all Common-time.

THE next Mood is called six to four marked thus 6/4, each Bar containing six Crotchets, three beat down, and three up. The Pendulum to beat three Crotchets in this Mood, must be thirty-nine inches and two tenths long [♩. = 60].

THE next Mood is called six from eight, marked thus 6/8, each Bar containing six Quavers [eighth notes], three beat down, and three up. The Pendulum to beat three Quavers, in this Mood, must be twenty-two inches and one twentieth [♩. = 80].

N.B. The two last Moods are neither Common, nor Triple time; but compounded of both, and in my opinion, they are very beautiful movements.

THE next Mood is called three to two, marked thus 3/2, each Bar containing three Minims, two to be beat down, and one up; the motions are made after the following manner, viz. Let your hand fall, and observe first to strike the ends of your fingers, then secondly the heel of your hand, and thirdly, raise your hand up, which finishes the Bar: These motions, must be made in equal times, not allowing more time to one motion than another. The Pendulum that will beat Minims in this Mood, must be thirty-nine inches and two tenths long [♩ = 60].

THE next Mood is called three from four, marked thus 3/4, each Bar containing three Crotchets, two beat down, and one up. The Pendulum to beat Crotchets in this Mood, must be twenty-two inches and one twentieth long [♩ = 80].

THE same motion is used in this mood, that was laid down in 3/2, only quicker, according to the Pendulum.

THE next Mood is called three from eight, marked thus 3/8, each Bar containing three Quavers, two beat down, and one up. The Pendulum to beat whole Bars in this Mood must be four feet, two inches, and two tenths of an inch long [♩. = 52]. The same motion is used for three from eight, as for 3/4 only quicker; and in this Mood you must make three motions of the hand, for every swing of the Pendulum. N.B. This is but an indifferent Mood, and almost out of use.

N.B. The three last mentioned Moods, are all in Triple Time, and the reason why they are called Triple, is because they are three fold, or measured by threes; for the meaning of the word Triple is threefold: And Common Time, is measured by Numbers, as 2—4—8—16—32,—viz. 2 Minims, 4 Crotchets, 8 Quavers, 16 Semiquavers, or 32 Demisemiquavers, are included in each Bar, either of which amounts to but one Semibreve; therefore the Semibreve is called the Measure Note; because all Moods are measured by it, in the following manner, viz. the fourth Mood in Common Time, is called two from four, and why is it called so? I answer; because the upper figure implies that there are two Notes of some kind included in each Bar, and the lower figure informs you how many of the same sort it takes to make one Semibreve. And in 3/8 the upper figure tells you, that there are three Notes contained in a Bar, and the lower figure will determine them to be Quavers; because it takes eight Quavers to make one Semibreve.

N.B. This Rule will hold good in all Moods of Time.

Observe, that when you meet with three Notes tied together with the figure 3 over, or under them, you must sound them in the time you would two of the same sort of Notes, without the figure. Note, that this Character is in direct opposition to the point of addition; for as that adds one third of the Time to the Note which is pointed, so this diminishes one third of the Time of the Notes over which it is placed; therefore I think this Character may with much propriety be called the Character of Diminution.

Likewise, you will often meet with the Figures 1, 2, the Figure one standing over one Bar, and Figure two standing over the next Bar, which signifies a Repeat; and observe, that in singing that strain the first time you perform the Bar under Figure 1, and omit the Bar under Figure 2, and in repeating you perform the Bar under figure 2, omit the Bar under Figure 1, which is so contrived to fill out the Bars; for the Bar under figure 1 is not always full, without borrowing a beat, or half Beat, &c. from the first Bar which is repeated, whereas the Bar under Figure 2. is, or ought to be full, without borrowing from any other but the first Bar in the Tune, and, if the first Bar is full, the Bar under Figure 2 must be full likewise. Be very careful to strike in proper upon a half Beat, but this is much easier obtained by Practice than Precept, provided you have an able Teacher.

LESSON XI. Concerning SLURS.

In turning [singing] a chain of Notes under a Slur, you must keep your lips asunder, from the first Note to the last; for every time you bring your lips together you break the Slur, and spoil the Syllable, which is very disagreeable to the Ears of all good Judges; because it destroys the Pronounciation; but to avoid that, you must keep your lips and teeth asunder [*sic*], till the Slur is finished, and if it be possible, hold your breath to the end of the Slur; because stopping for breath, makes great breach in Pronounciation. And in order to do that more effectually, I advise you to take breath just before you get to a Slur; and then you may go through with ease; and I think it is ornamental to sing a Chain of Notes something softer than you do where they are plain.

Be sure not to force the Sound thro' your Nose; but warble the Notes in your Throat; and by following these directions, you may presently become expert in the practice; and in performing *Pieces* where your part is sometimes silent, after you have beat your empty Bars, you must fall in with *spirit* because that gives the Audience to understand another part is added, which perhaps they would not be so sensible of, if you struck in soft.

LESSON XIII.

Sing that part which gives you least pain, otherwise you make it a toil, instead of pleasure; for if you attempt to sing a part which is (almost or quite) out of your reach, it is not only very laborious to the performer; but often very disagreeable to the hearer, by reason of many wry faces and uncouth postures, which rather resemble a person in extreme pain, than one who is supposed to be pleasantly employed. And it has been observed, that those persons, who sing with most ease, are in general the most musical; for easy singing is a distinguishing mark of a natural Singer, and it is vastly more agreeable (at least to me) to hear a few wild uncultivated sounds from a natural Singer, than a Concert of Music performed by the most refined artificial singers upon earth; provided the latter have little or not [*sic*] assistance from nature.

One very essential thing in Music, is to have the parts properly proportioned; and here I think we ought to take a greatful notice, that the Author of harmony has so curiously constructed our Organs, that there are about three or four deep voices suitable for the Bass to one for the upper parts, which is about the proportion required in the laws of Harmony; for the voices on the Bass should be *majestic, deep* and *solemn*; the tenor *full, bold* and *manly*; the Counter [alto] *loud, clear* and *lofty*; the Treble *soft, shrill,* and *sonorous*; and if suitable voices cannot be had, to sing each part properly, some of the parts had better be omitted; for it is a maxim with me, that two parts well sung, are better than four parts indifferently sung; and I had rather hear four people sing well, than four hundred almost well.

LESSON XIV.

Good singing is not confined to great singing, nor is it entirely dependent on small singing. I have heard many great voices, that never struck a harsh Note, and many small voices that never struck a pleasant one; therefore if the Tones be Musical, it is not material whether the voices be greater, or less; yet I allow there are but few voices, but what want restraining, or softening upon high notes, to take off the harshness, which is as disagreeable to a delicate ear, as a wire-edged raisor to a tender face, or a smoaky [*sic*] House to tender eyes. It is an essential thing in a master, to propagate soft singing in the school; because soft musick, has a great tendency to refine the ears of the performers, and I know by experience, that a new piece may be learned with more ease to the master and scholars, where they practice soft singing, and in less than half the time, it would otherwise require. Here take a few hints, viz.

1. Let the low notes in the bass be struck full, and the high notes soft.

2. Let not the upper parts overpower the lower ones.

3. Let each performer attend critically to the strength of his own voice, and not strive to sing louder than the rest of the company; unless he is in the place of a leader.

4. Let each performer sing the part that is most suitable to his voice; and never stretch it beyond its proper bearing.

5. If you are so unhappy, as to set a piece too high, it is best to worry through without lowering the pitch; because that has a tendency to take away the *spirit* of the performers; but if you set a piece too low you may raise it according to your judgment, and that will serve to *animate* the performers.

6. Do not set the pieces so high as to strain the voices; for that takes away all pleasure in the performance, and all music from the composition.

7. Finally let every performer be fully qualified for a leader.

I would take this opportunity, to acquaint my younger Pupils, that it is deemed a point of ill manners to invade the province of another, by singing a Solo, which does not belong to your part, for it will admit of these two constructions, viz. that the persons to whom it is assigned, are not capable of doing justice to the piece, or at least, that you are more capable than they. It is also very degrading to the author to sing, when he (for reasons perhaps unknown to you) by presenting a number of empty Bars, tacitly forbids your singing, and no doubt this intention of his, is to illustrate some grand point, in the plan of the composition; when, by your ill-timed interruption, you not only destroy the sense, intended to be conveyed in the composition; but convey a very different sense to the audience: therefore for you to sing, when the author forbids your singing, is both unmannerly and ostentatious.

It is also well worth your observation, that the grand contention with us, is, not who shall sing *loudest*; but who shall sing *best* ....

Observe these Rules for regulating a Singing-School.

As the well being of every society depends in a great measure upon GOOD ORDER, I here present you with some general rules, to be observed in a Singing-School.

Ist. Let the society be first formed, and the articles signed by every individual; and all those who are under age, should apply to their parents, masters, or guardians to sign for them; the house should be provided, and every necessary for the school should be procured, before the arrival of the Master, to prevent his being unnecessarily detained.

2d. The Members should be very punctual in attending at a certain hour, or minute, as the master shall direct, under the penalty of a small fine, and if the master should be delinquent, his fine to be double the sum laid upon the scholars — Said fines to be appropriated to the use of the school, in procuring *wood, candles, &c.* N.B. The fines to be collected by the Clerk, so chosen for that purpose.

3d. All the scholars should submit to the judgment of the master, respecting the part they are to sing; and if he should think fit to remove them from one part to another, they are not to contradict, or cross him in his judgment; but they would do well to suppose it is to answer some special purpose; because it is morally impossible for him to proportion the parts properly, until he has made himself acquainted with the strength and fitness of the pupil's [*sic*] voices.

4th. No unnecessary conversation, whispering, or laughing, to be practised; for it is not only indecent, but very impolitic; it being a needless expense of time, and instead of acquiring to themselves respect, they render themselves ridiculous and contemptible in the eyes of all serious people; and above all, I enjoin it upon you to refrain from all levity, both in conduct and conversation, while singing sacred words; for where the words *God, Christ, Redeemer, &c.* occur, you would do well to remember the third Commandment, the profanation of which, is a heinous crime, and God has expressly declared he will not hold them guiltness [-less] who take his name in vain; and remember that in so doing, you not only dishonor God and sin against your own souls; but you give occasion, and very just ground to the adversaries or enemies of music, to speak reproachfully. Much more might be said; but the rest I shall leave to the Master's direction, and your own discretion, heartily wishing you may reap both pleasure and profit, in this your laudable undertaking.

William Billings. *The Singing Master's Assistant: or Key To Practical Music, Being An Abridgement from the New England Psalm Singer; together with several other Tunes never before published.* Boston: printed by Drape and Folsom, 1798, 7-11, 13-17. (Excerpts)

SUPPLY BELCHER
CONCLUSION TO THE HARMONY OF MAINE (1794)

A contemporary of Billings and another leader in the singing school movement, SUPPLY BELCHER (1751-1836) was a hymn writer, violinist, school teacher, and choir master, who also served under General Washington in the War of Independence. These remarks are taken from his single published collection of music and show the result of Thomas Walter's campaign for "regular" singing. Here, after giving the obligatory rules for reading music found in all of these period tunebooks, Belcher discusses the artistic results of this study, repeating some of the ideas seen earlier in Billings' writings, while adding his own observations and information on choral performance practice.

This part of the work will be concluded with some observations on singing, and general directions to learners, which are as follows, viz.

"When a tune is well learnt by note it may be sung in words, and every word should not only be pronunced [*sic*] according to the best rules of grammar, but spoken plain and distinct. Singers often fail in this point, by which means half the beauty of the musick is lost, the words not being understood.

"Notwithstanding all that has been said or can be said with regard to graces, the best way is to sing with ease and freedom, and without confining yourself to any certain rules for gracing music, any further than can be adapted in a natural and easy manner, there being nothing forced or unnatural in good music. — Every singer should sing that part which is most suitable to his voice, in which case learners should submit to the judgment of their master. Care should be taken, in singing companies, to have the parts properly proportioned; one half the strength of the voices should be upon the bass, the other half divided upon the other parts. — A solo should generally be sung softer, and a chorus which follows a solo, louder than the rest of the musick. When the words soft, loud, &c. are placed over the musick, some regard should be paid to them. When words are repeated in musick, the strength of the voices should increase every time they are repeated, and when the musick is repeated it may be well to sing it louder the second time than the first. Low notes in the bass should generally be sounded full, and the high notes in any part, not full, but clear. In fuging musick the strength of the voices should increase as the parts fall in, and the pronunciation in such cases should be very distinct and emphatical."

Supply Belcher. *The Harmony of Maine: being An Original Composition of Psalm and Hymn Tunes, of various Metres, suitable for Divine Worship. With a Number of Fuging Pieces and Anthems. Together with A Concise Introduction to the Grounds of Musick, and Rules for Learners. For the Use of Singing Schools and Musical Societies.* Boston: printed by Isaiah Thomas and Ebenezer T. Andrews, 1794, 16.

ANONYMOUS
GENERAL DIRECTIONS
FOR THE PERFORMANCE OF SACRED MUSIC (1828)

Tunebooks and other collections of anthems, particularly those compiled for sacred services and those for didactic purposes, continued to be common in the early nineteenth century. These "Directions" are taken from a publication entitled Music of the Church: A Collection of Psalm, Hymn, and Chant Tunes, *adapted to the worship of the Protestant Episcopal Church in the United States. The author, perhaps Peter C. Smith who printed the volume, describes common practices for the performance of sacred music, critiques those he finds inappropriate, and then proposes his own rules and methods for correcting them. While his writings specifically concern only the Episcopal Church, they can by extension serve to illustrate the musical practices of other Protestant denominations from this time period as well.*

PSALMODY

Sacred Music is the application of sweet sounds to celebrating the praise and glory of God. In order then, to render this service acceptable to him, as well as edifying to ourselves, it should ever be remembered that preparation of heart is the first and most essential step. Without this, the finest strains of melody or harmony are no better than mockery, "a solemn sound upon a thoughtless tongue." But if the voice responds to devout affections of the soul, *sounds coarse and inharmonious* will be acceptable in the ears of the God of Sabbaoth; and even those whom nature has deprived both of ear and voice, and who cannot therefore, without great discomfort to their fellow worshippers, be vocal in their praise, may thus "sing and make melody in their hearts unto the Lord."

The true design of Sacred Music then, being to excite and to express devotional feeling; this design should be kept in constant view, both in a selection of tunes for the use of the Church, and in the manner of performing them. As the tunes should be simple, dignified, and solemn, so also should the style of singing them exhibit the same characteristics. In this collection will be found tunes of every variety of character, from those which speak the highest sentiments of praise, to those suitable to the expression of the deepest penitence. Care has been taken to adapt appropriate words to these tunes. But as portions of Psalms or Hymns may be appointed to be sung which have no tune assigned to them, or as the *tune assigned* may not be known, or may not be approved, and another must be sought for; in such cases particular attention should be given by the person whose duty it is to select the tunes. He should first study the general character of the words, that he may avoid the error of setting a jubilant tune to penitential words, or vice versa, a tune in the minor moved to words of joyful praise.

Having thus adapted together the tune and the portions of words, according to the *general* character, he should next look at the distinct verses, and prepare to make slight alterations in the performance, as respects faster or slower, *piano or forte, crescendo or diminuendo*, as the sentiment may require. This is the only way by which a proper musical effect can be given, when the same notes are to be repeated to words varying in expression. And by a little attention to this point, and a little explanation and illustration, a choir or congregation will soon feel the propriety and beauty of thus making the sound an echo to the sense; and they will learn to do it without any particular direction. Besides the advantage thus gained in point of musical expression, there will be a much greater one in keeping the singers constantly attentive to the meaning of the words they are uttering.

As a general rule it may be observed, that, in single tunes or tunes which carry through one verse only, the piano or diminuendo may fall upon the third line, and in double tunes upon the two first lines of the second verse; the forte and crescendo may, in most instances succeed to the next lines. But no rule can be given of uniform application. As an illustration of the above observations, we will take the 100th Psalm, and the well known tune Old Hundred, page 3. The singing of the first verse should be commenced moderately forte. In this manner should the first two lines be sung. The third line, "Glad homage pay with awful mirth," should be piano, and the last line should be forte. The second verse should be piano throughout. The third verse should begin moderately, it should gradually increase, till the last line, which should be double forte. The last verse should commence rather piano, the third line should be crescendo, and the last forte. The Gloria Patri should always be full. As a farther illustration, take the 165th Hymn, and the tune St. George's, page 14. The first verse should be animated, and moderately loud. The second verse should be sung in slower time, and more piano. In the third verse, the first two lines should be piano, the last two crescendo. In the fourth verse there is a greater contrast, the first two lines should be rather slow and soft, the last two should have a decided and strong utterance. The last verse should be animated and forte. To the careful reader who will turn to the above mentioned tunes and words, and compare them with the explanations thus given, the observations made, in regard to varying the expressions of the tune in conformity with the sentiment contained in the words, will be sufficiently obvious.

Attention should be paid to another point which has been much neglected in Psalmody, viz. accentuation. The different verses of our Psalms and Hymns vary so much in this particular — the first verse commencing, perhaps, with an unaccented syllable, while the second begins with a strongly accented word, that when the same notes are used in both cases the correct ear is greatly offended. Wherever it is practicable, if the poetry commences with an accented syllable, the tune should begin with a full bar; on the contrary, when the Psalm or Hymn begins with an unaccented syllable, the tune should commence with part of a bar. But, as in succeeding verses there is often a change in this respect, we must give some attention to remedy the difficulty. It is to be done with much greater ease than may at first be apprehended. As an illustration, let the reader take the 97th Psalm, and the tune German Air, on the 109th page. Here the tune begins with a full bar; but the first syllable of the first verse is unaccented. To sing correctly then, begin the word "Jehovah" on part of a bar, and slur the two first notes of the tune to the 2d syllable "ho-." At the end of the tune the notes, as they should be sung, are printed in full. The next verse begins with a strongly accented word, "darkness"; and here the accent of the tune and of the words coincides. Verse 10, also, "Ye who to serve," &c. accords with the tune; but verse 12, "Rejoice," &c. must be commenced with what may be termed a starting note, as above. Another illustration may be found in the Evening Hymn, page 181, "Glory to thee, my God," &c. Here the first syllable is strongly accented, and yet as the tune is usually arranged the accent is made to come on the second syllable, "ry," which is unquestionably wrong. In this book, then, the tune begins with a full bar. But, as in the next verse, "Forgive me, Lord," &c. the first syllable is unaccented, the tune should have the starting note, which is expressed by small notes. By a little attention to these observations, the rhetorical and the musical accent need not, in any case, be permitted to clash. Take an example not marked in the book — Hymn 67, and a beautiful tune, Darley, on the 147th page. — The tune begins with a full bar, as is correct; the first syllable of the words being strongly accented, "High on the bending willows hung." But in the next verse the accent is entirely different, "Awake! thy loudest raptures raise," and, unless we would produce a most disagreeable effect, the beginning of the tune must be changed. Suppose, then, we introduce part of a bar, a quaver on F in the treble, for the first syllable "A-." The next syllable, "wake," we sing to the first note of the tune; then slur the two quavers, for the word "thy." The tune and words then proceed regularly. Thus with a little attention and judgment, the principal inconvenience, arising from using the same tune for many verses, may be avoided. To make the time correct, it may be added to, or taken from the last bar of the tune. Still, however, perfect accuracy in regard to accentuation should not be anticipated or sought for. Nor is any attention to the above rules to be considered as absolutely essential to congregational singing. Perhaps the object cannot be effected, except when there is a good choir. Unquestionably the perfection of Psalmody, *considering its great design*, is when the whole body of a congregation unites, as with one heart, and one voice, to sing the praises of God. Then, faults of accent and occasional discords are overwhelmed in the general effect; even a musical ear will be affected with its majesty and power, and the devout worshipper will desire nothing more refined, to stir up the affections of his heart, and to open his mouth with praises to God.

ANTHEM SINGING

As the proper execution of Psalmody requires the voices of all in the congregation who can sing; the singing of Anthems should be confined to the choir. In the ancient Jewish Church, persons were expressly appointed by God to conduct his praises, and the assembled congregation occasionally united in the loud chorus. So also in the primitive Church, and in the Church of England, Anthems are performed by a choir, to which the congregation are supposed to listen, with devout sentiments. The form of the Anthem is naturally derived from the structure of some of the Psalms, in which we frequently find the soliloquy, the dialogue, and the chorus. Thus, as has been observed, "The Lord hear thee in the day of trouble," is the voice of a company encouraging a Priest in his intercession. He then expresses his confidence in these words, "Now know that I the Lord helpeth his anointed." Then all join together in supplication. "Save Lord, and hear us when we call upon thee." The solo, the verse, and the chorus, in church music express all those turns of the sacred poetry when properly applied. But as Anthems are not often introduced in the service of our churches, and as it is presumed they will only be attempted when there is an able and well instructed choir, no farther observations are requisite in this place.

CHANTING

Although Chants are in themselves the most simple of all kinds of musical composition, yet to execute them with propriety and effect requires much practice. The single chant consists of two strains, the first containing three, and the last, four bars; the double chant, consists of four strains, of three and four bars arranged alternately. The first bar of each strain is the chanting note; and to this, the principal part of each half verse of the prose Psalms is recited; the remaining bars in each strain, form a species of cadence, and are to be expressed in the singing voice. The principal object to be attended to in chanting, is a distinct and forcible articulation of the words. They must be correctly accented, and where a stop occurs, it may be marked by a short rest. The recited part of the verse must occupy no longer time than a good reader would require to pronounce it, and the cadence must be given in correct time, the beat of which can be felt. A great difficulty in arranging the words of a chant, is to know when to break off from the words of the recitative, and to begin the cadence. There are two errors to be avoided. The first, is the drawling effect, produced by giving in every instance only single syllables to each note of the cadence; the second is the hurrying and confused effect, produced by taking too many syllables from the recitative, and crowding them into the cadence. The latter error, however, is by far most injurious, as it always destroys musical rhythm, and produces a light and trifling manner of singing, very inconsistent with sacred words.

In the adaptation of the words to the Chants contained in this book, an attempt has been made, and it is hoped successfully, to avoid both these errors. The general rules of adaptation are as follows: by following these rules any portions of the Psalter, or prose psalms, may be chanted.

It is to be observed in the first place, that every verse is divided into two parts, which division in the old prayer books and to this day, in all English editions, is marked with a colon stop for this very purpose. In the later editions of the Liturgy of our Church, this dividing point has been omitted, whether by design, or through ignorance of its use, we cannot say. But certainly, while our rubrics direct that certain prose portions of the service may be "sung or said," this great facility for singing, and one of such ancient standing should not be done away.

Suppose then, the verse to be divided at the semicolon or the comma, which most nearly separates it into two parts, always taking into consideration the sense. Then, to the first bar of the chant is chanted the first half of the verse, excepting the three last syllables, which are sung to the minims and semi-breve of the two next bars respectively. If any small word, or article should occur in the three last syllables, it is generally to be sung to one of the minims of the second bar, without being reckoned as a principle syllable; and if the word immediately preceding the division of the verse consists of two syllables, or if it be a longer word having a strong accent on the penult, or last syllable but one, as the word "salvation" — in these cases two syllables are sung to the first bar of the second strain of the chant, except the five last syllables, which are sung to the four minims and the semibreve of the second strain respectively. And as above, if any small words or articles occur in the five last syllables, they may be sung on one

41

of the minims where the effect will be best. And if the verse ends with a word of two syllables, or with a polysyllabic word having its accent on the penult, the last word of the chant is to have these syllables. This describes the manner of singing a single chant, but as a double chant is merely a repetition of the same number of bars, no farther direction is needed.

The great variety of sublime expressions in the verse psalms, renders it impossible to make any general rules, which can meet every case in applying them to the chants. And indeed, this style of singing is so peculiar, that perhaps no rules will be of much benefit. A truly good manner of chanting cannot be acquired, without the assistance of some person competent to teach it. As regards the division of the words, this book furnishes it, for all the ordinary services of the church. But no book can teach the tone and utterance which constitute the great beauty of chanting, and which render it, when well performed, the most devotional of all kinds of music, and of course the best adapted to the worship of the Church of God. We could wish that it were more general, and that instead of the metre version, which is often very feeble, compared with the Psalter, we could use portions of the prose psalms and have them sung to chants instead of psalm tunes. A proposition was made to this effect, and a selection from the prose psalms was published in reference to it, some years ago by the Rev. Dr. Smith of Connecticut.

Could we have chanting in perfection, it should be as it was designed, and as it is practised in the Cathedral Churches of England, a *responsive service.* When there are large choirs they might be divided into two equal parts, and be placed on each side of the organ. One side corresponding to what in the Cathedrals is termed "Decani," should sing the chant through once, taking one verse if a single chant, and two if a double one. The other side, called "Cantoris," should respond in the same manner. The Gloria Patri should be sung by the whole unitedly. And in congregations, where the singing is, as it should ever be, general, where would be the difficulty of having the portion of the congregation on one side of the broadaisle to respond in its chanting the other? Where the vocal worshippers of God are, as is unhappily too much the case in our churches, few in number, such an arrangement should not be attempted. But may we not hope that sacred music will be more cultivated than heretofore. There is no want of attention to the music of the world, and no sparing of expense in acquiring a knowledge of it.

Before 1830: Anonymous

Why should not religious persons, and above all religious parents, take some interest in the music that appropriately belongs to God, and learn themselves, and have their children taught, how to give a correct and melodious expression to the sacred songs of Zion. Then would the services of the sanctuary appear in their full beauty and solemnity. And while confessing our sins with heartfelt penitence, praying and giving thanks with earnest devotion, hearing the sacred word with attention and willing minds, we should also most delightfully and profitably "speak to ourselves in psalms and hymns, and spiritual songs, singing and making melody in our hearts to the Lord."

Anonymous. *Music of the Church, a Collection of Psalm, Hymn, and Chant Tunes, adapted to the Worship of the Protestant Episcopal Church in the United States*. New York: Samuel F. Bradford, stereotyped and printed by Peter C. Smith, 1828, ix-xii.

Part II
Music from 1830-1920

Frontispiece to the piano-vocal score of Amy Beach's *Mass in E-flat*,
published in Boston by Arthur C. Schmidt, 1890.

INTRODUCTION: MUSIC FROM 1830-1920

*T*he printing and distribution of tunebooks lasted until well into the middle of the nineteenth century. Both Thomas Hastings and Lowell Mason were concerned with educating Americans through their introduction and support of music education in the public schools and through their activities as publishers and compilers of music collections for use in either home or church. The Hastings essay reprinted here is a little unusual because of its specific focus on mothers singing to their young children, but it shows how far reaching was this desire to educate. Mason's essay, "Rules for the Preservation of the Voice," is similar, although more technical, than Beissel's earlier article, but it too provides an insight into vocal pedagogy in the mid-nineteenth century.

In the 1830s and the decades following, America began to look increasingly toward Germany to find examples of music as a high art. A generation or two of composers completed all or part of their formal training in composition in the conservatories of Leipzig, Berlin, and later Paris and other cities. The first important choral composer to do this and to achieve a wide audience in this country was John Knowles Paine, whose works are reminiscent of Mendelssohn, Schumann, and other mid-century German masters. His St. Peter *was the first large-scale American oratorio, taking as its models the works of Handel, Bach, and Mendelssohn. A review of its first performance contains a detailed analysis of the music and identifies its importance for this new school of American composers.*

And a school it became. Among the composers of this "second" New England School of composition (the "first" New England School included Billings and the other composers of the singing school movement) were Horatio Parker, George Chadwick, and Amy Beach. Reviews of Parker's masterpiece, the oratorio Hora novissima *and Beach's Mass in E-flat make for worthwhile reading still today. Chadwick's eloquent defense of choral singing is in many ways as apt today as it was when he delivered the speech to the American Academy of Arts and Letters in 1913.*

Dudley Buck, *a contemporary of the men in this school (Beach lived somewhat later, although she is usually associated with the Boston group for*

*stylistic reasons), was best known for his work in church music. According-
ly, his concluding essay from the manual* Illustrations in Choir Accompaniment *is reproduced in this volume, summarizing his ideas and suggestions
for the practice of church music.*

*Two other essays complete the historical grouping of writings from 1830
until the end of the first World War. The first is a thorough review of a
concert by the Fisk Jubilee Singers from* Dwight's Journal of Music, *an
important period journal published in Boston. These enterprising African-
American singers, with their contemporaries the Hampton Institute Singers,
took our country and Europe by storm, introducing audiences to and
creating a market for spirituals and early gospel music. On the other end of
the musical spectrum is an essay by Theodore Thomas, the man perhaps
most responsible for building and educating an audience for classical
symphonic music. His many tours throughout the United States, often under
distressing conditions, whetted American appetites for music as a "high art,"
a particularly Victorian concern. In the article included here, Thomas used
his bully pulpit as America's best known serious musician to preach for his
lifelong cause of educating and elevating the taste of the country's musical
public, emphasizing the importance of choral music for reaching that goal.*

Thomas Hastings
Introduction to Nursery Songs (1834)

With his contemporary Lowell Mason, Thomas Hastings (1784-1872) was a successful composer and compiler of hymn tunes. Hastings assisted in the teacher training institutes that Mason initiated and was a lifelong advocate of music education in the public schools and at home, especially in New York City, where he lived most of his life. He devoted his 50-some collections of music to various groups; the essay reproduced below comes from a book written to encourage singing in the home, in this case mother singing to child in the form of nursery songs. Hastings addresses the issues of music literacy, vocal technique and correct tone, and appropriate repertoire. His comments may be of particular interest to today's growing number of children's chorus directors.

It is a point now universally admitted among practical musicians, that all children, the deaf and dumb excepted, may be taught to sing; and that the difference of natural talent in this respect is, probably, not greater, than in reference to other departments of education. The faculty in question is never truly instinctive, but always in a great measure acquired. Nature furnishes us with organs, and with powers of perception. Cultivation must do the rest.

The fact that so large a portion of the present generation are unable to sing, is not to be attributed to physical deficiencies, but to unfortunate circumstances in the history of early education. In countries where music is continually taught in the primary schools, the children, as a matter of course, all learn to sing: and the same experiment, wherever it has been tried in our own country, has led to the same happy result. This circumstance alone shows the importance of early cultivation. If music is neglected till years of maturity, it will, in the majority of instances, continue to be disregarded through life. Infancy is undoubtedly the most favorable period for commencing the work. The foundation must be laid then if distinguished excellence is ever afterwards to be attained.

Adults, with voices of the most unpromising character imaginable, have sometimes, it is true, been taught to sing. The thing in its nature is not impracticable, but it is very difficult. It requires time and labor and perseverance, such as few, comparatively, are found to possess. But with young children, the task is neither difficult not laborious. The principle chiefly employed in forming the voice is imitation. The child, under favorable circumstances, acquires the management of its voice in singing just as it acquires in speaking the accurate pronunciation of the mother tongue. In both cases it is the imitative pupil of its mother, or nurse. Mothers should think of this, and not neglect to stir up the musical gift that is within them. Though that gift should be small, it might at least suffice to initiate the listening child in the practice of an important art which would afterwards be more successfully prosecuted.

One who wishes to acquire practical skill as a player on a musical instrument, must of necessity begin by drawing forth such tones or executing such passages, as can be mastered with the greatest facility; deferring such as are more difficult to a later period of cultivation. For all the purposes of vocal training, the mother may regard her infant child as such an instrument, not doubting but perseverance will accomplish the desired object.

There is a special season in infancy when children are full of mimicry. Then, a great portion of their daily employment, while in perfect health, is like that of the mocking-bird, to be imitating every pleasant sound that falls within their hearing. Their earliest efforts in this respect will necessarily be rude, but, by constant practice, their talent is found to improve; while, at the same time they acquire an increasing fondness for the exercise. Does not nature evidently point out this period as the precise time for making musical impressions upon the child that will be strong and indelible?

Let no one suppose that the voice is necessarily injured by early cultivation. If the little one is not induced to sing too much or too loud for its general health, there will be nothing to fear. Its voice will improve much in proportion to its practice; and when, in subsequent years, its intonation becomes for a little period broken and discordant, it will be sure to be restored in due time. Every male child, sooner or later, must pass through such a change, as the unavoidable result of physical changes in the structure or conformation of its organs. Daily, moderate practice will be the obvious and certain remedy.

Previous to the period of infantile mimicry above mentioned, the affectionate mother will often have been soothing her child with the voice of song. When that period arrives, let her continue the practice in melodies as simple as those of numbers *one* and *two*, in part first of this work. And as the child begins in the smallest degree to play the mimic, let her in turn become the imitator, so far as to seize upon every note which has resemblance to music, and thus encourage the child to repeat its efforts. The mother may thus gradually draw out and form its voice for music, just as she teaches it the articulations of the native tongue. The latter process she well understands. She begins with the simplest syllables only, and as she proceeds with those that are more difficult, the exercise is carefully adapted to the gradual progress of the child. Nothing is forced. Every thing is made pleasant and amusing to the little pupil: and the mother at every step is so amply rewarded for her assiduity, as to feel that her labor is but another name for delightful recreation.

The same course in reference to singing would be rewarded with the same success. Though the mother should be quite ignorant of the simplest principles of the science: her skill in minstrelsy would suffice for the work immediately before her. Let her also frame some simple phrases of melody, that are very similar to those she notices in the mimicry of her child, gradually heightening their character as the child improves its vocal powers. All these exercises perhaps will be inarticulate; and in some cases the child will make more rapid progress in song than in speech ....

The preceding directions may suffice for the object before us: if followed with perseverance the child will begin to sing long before it is old enough to understand the rules of the art; and this, much to its own amusement and to the gratification of its affectionate parents. Some may doubt the practicability of the course here recommended; but certainly it is an easy one. Let them be persuaded to try it faithfully and perseveringly, and the author will consent to be responsible for its success.

Thomas Hastings. *Nursery Songs*. New York: by the author, 1834, 4-6. (Excerpt)

LOWELL MASON
RULES FOR THE PRESERVATION OF THE VOICE (1852)

More than any other person, LOWELL MASON (1792-1872) is the man responsible for the inclusion of music in the public school curricula of the United States and is usually referred to as the "father" of music education in this country. Born in Medfield, Massachusetts, Mason was by trade a banker in Savannah, Georgia, for several years before returning to Boston in 1827 to earn his living as a musician. He was an outstanding organist, conductor, composer and compiler, and organizer of singing schools, in addition to his contributions to music education. He was probably best known as the compiler of The Boston Handel and Haydn Society Collection of Church Music, *which contained not only hymns and anthems by American composers, but favorite choruses from Handel, Haydn, Mozart, and others.*

In 1859, Mason, in another of his many successful attempts at educating the public, began to publish The Choral Advocate and Singing Class Journal. *Two years later, the name had changed to* The American Music Review and Choral Advocate, *from which the following essay is taken. Mason discusses diet for the singer, the changing voice, prescriptions for cold and throat ailments, and rehearsal demeanor for singers, including the importance of warming-up the vocal mechanism before rehearsal.*

"The first rule," says Austin, "for the preservation of the voice, and which is equally supported by ancient authorities and modern experience, is, that the public speaker should, if he 'strive for mastery,' be habitually temperate in all things; moderate in the use of wine, and in the indulgence of the table, and not given to any personal excess. A bloated body, and an enfeebled constitution, are not only injurious to the voice, but render a man equally incapable of any other mental or bodily exertion. The voice should not be exerted after a meal. This rule is a consequence of the first. The voice should not be urged beyond its strength, nor be strained to its utmost pitch, without intermission; such mismanagement would endanger its powers altogether, and it might break: frequent change of pitch is the best preservative. The same rule holds in music; in well-composed songs, skillful singers may sometimes, for brilliancy or effect, and to show the compass of the voice, run up and touch the highest notes, or descend to the lowest; but they should by no means, in their modulations, dwell long on the extremes. High passion disregards this wholesome rule, but the orator will not be rash in its violation; nor should the composer of what is to be spoken or sung be remiss in his attention to it."

At that period of youth when the voice begins to break and to assume the manly tone, no violent exertion should be made; but the voice should be spared until it becomes confirmed and established. Neither, according to this rule, should the voice, when hoarse, if it may be avoided, be exerted at any time.

If a boy would give himself the chance of having a contralto, establishing his constitution, and making his fortune, let him begin to think and take heed from fourteen; for a cold will break the voice before the time of nature, omissions of singing often, but not too long at a time will sink it, and vicious gratifications may ruin it and the constitution before the age of manhood. The singer may with more safety indulge at thirty, when the constitution of man is fixed, or even at forty, than at eighteen, when nature is in a state of growth and immaturity; though, indeed, many young proficients in music have made a shameful and speedy end, who have promised fair in the beginning; and might have proceeded happily, but, setting off with over much sail and too strong a tide, suffered shipwreck in the channel before they could well get out to sea.

Some things are found serviceable to the voice, and are used by modern singers; they may be equally advantageous to a public speaker. Warm mucilaginous and diluting drinks, in case of dryness of the fauces [the pillars of fauces are small ligaments that are part of the vocal mechanism], or slight hoarseness, barley-water and tea, preparations of sugar, sugar-candy, barley-sugar, and the various sorts of lozenges, which modern ingenuity prepares so elegantly; a new egg beat up is reckoned the best substance for immediately clearing the voice, and is preferred by the Italian singers. Garlic is much used, notwithstanding its offensive odor. The great means of improving the voice, as in all other improvements, is constant and daily practice. The professional exercise at the bar, the senate, and the stage, if properly attended to, with a view to improvement, may suffice for the orator of our times: but the ancients, besides this, were in the daily practice of preparatory declamation: — their rule was, after proper bodily exercise, to begin at the lowest tones of their voices, and go gradually to the highest. This was called *anaphonesis*, and sometimes the *paean* and *munio*; the former the exercise of the voice in the highest pitch, the latter in the lowest. They used to pronounce about five hundred lines in this manner, which were committed to memory, in order that the exertions of the voice might be the less embarrassed.

It is a great and general mistake among the singers at rehearsal, as the common practice is, to mutter over their parts inwardly, and keep in their voices, with a misimagined purpose of preserving them against their evening of performance; whereas the surest natural means of strengthening their delivery would be to warm, dephlegm, and clarify the thorax and windpipe, by exerting (the more frequently the better) their fullest power of utterance, thereby to open and remove all hesitation, roughness, or obstructions, and to tune their voices, by effect of such continual exercise, into habitual mellowness, and ease of compass and inflection; from the same reason that an active body is more strong and healthy than a sedentary one.

Lowell Mason. "Rules for the Preservation of the Voice." *American Musical Review and Choral Advocate*, 3, no. 4 (April 1852), 5-6.

JOHN KNOWLES PAINE
REVIEW OF ST. PETER (1873)

The first composer in the United States to achieve wide international recognition, especially from the German musical establishment, was JOHN KNOWLES PAINE (1839-1906), who was born in Portland, Maine, and received his early training there. Realizing the limits of musical education available in this country, Paine traveled to Berlin in 1858, where he studied organ and composition at the Hochschule für Musik. He returned to the United States in 1861, and a year later joined the staff of Harvard as chapel organist and choirmaster. He began teaching and lecturing at the college soon after, and in 1875 was appointed full professor of music, the first such appointment in this country. His students were some of the leading members of the next generation of composers, including John Alden Carpenter, Frederick Converse, Arthur Foote, and Daniel Gregory Mason.

His works include two symphonies, an opera, Azara *(1903), a number of occasional pieces, and several large choral works. Paine's early Mass in D Major (1867) was performed in Berlin while he was there, to generally favorable critical praise. His second large choral work,* St. Peter *(1873) was modelled after Bach's passion settings and Mendelssohn's* Elijah, *with several large, often fugal choruses combined with chorale settings and reflective solo arias and ensembles held together by narrative recitative. Both of Paine's principal choral works achieved a measure of popularity and renown in an age when music by American composers was considered to be naive or derivative of European models. That point is addressed in the following review, from* The Atlantic Monthly, *as are questions of performance practice, in addition to a description of the work and comments upon its premiere performance.*

For music lovers in America the great event of the season has been the performance of Mr. Paine's oratorio, St. Peter, at Portland, June 3. This event is important, not only as the first appearance of an American oratorio, but also as the first direct proof we have had of the existence of creative music genius in this country. For Mr. Paine's Mass in D — a work which was brought out with great success several years ago in Berlin — has for some reason or other, not particularly to the credit, one would think, of our best known choral associations, never been performed here. And, with the exception of Mr. Paine, we know of no American hitherto who has shown either the genius or the culture requisite for writing music in the grand style, although there is some of the Kapellmeister music, written by our leading organists and choristers, which deserves very honorable mention. But while such works as Mr. Dudley Buck's Forty-sixth Psalm or Mr. Whiting's Mass in C minor — admirably performed at Mount Pleasant, Boston Highlands, some two or three years ago — may bear a comparison with the best modern English music by Costa or Bennett, a higher place must be claimed for Mr. Paine. Concerning the rank likely to be assigned by posterity to St. Peter it would be foolish now to speculate; and it would be unwise to bring it into direct comparison with masterpieces like the Messiah, Elijah, and St. Paul, the greatness of which has been so long acknowledged. Longer familiarity with the work is needed before such comparisons, always of somewhat doubtful value, can be profitably undertaken. But it must at least be said, as the net result of our impressions derived from the performance at Portland, that Mr. Paine's oratorio has fairly earned for itself the right to be judged by the same high standard which we apply to these noble works of Mendelssohn and Handel.

In our limited space we can give only the briefest description of the general structure of the work. The founding of Christianity, as illustrated in four principal scenes of the life of St. Peter, supplies the material for the dramatic development of the subject. The overture, beginning with an adagio movement in B-flat minor, gives expression to the vague yearnings of that time of doubt and hesitancy when the "oracles were dumb," and the dawning of a new era of stronger and diviner faith was a matter of presentiment rather than of definite hope or expectation. Though the tonality is at first firmly established, yet as the movement becomes more agitated, the final tendency of the modulations also becomes uncertain, and for a few bars it would seem as if the key of F-sharp minor might be the point of destination. But after a short melody by the wind instruments, accompanied by a rapid upward movement of strings, the dominant chord of C major asserts itself, being repeated, with sundry inversions, through a dozen bars, and leading directly into the triumphant and majestic chorus, "The time is fulfilled, and the kingdom of heaven is at hand." The second subject, introduced by the word "repent" descending through the interval of a diminished seventh and contrasted with the florid counterpoint of the phrase, "and believe the glad tidings of God," is a masterpiece of contrapuntal writing, and, if performed by a choir of three hundred or four hundred voices, would produce an overpowering effect. The divine call of Simon Peter and his brethren is next described in a tenor recitative; and the acceptance of the glad tidings is expressed in an aria, "The spirit of the Lord is upon me," which, by an original but appropriate conception, is given to the soprano voice. In the next number the disciples are dramatically represented by twelve basses and tenors, singing in four-part harmony, and alternating or combining with the full chorus in description of the aims of the new religion. The proem ends with the choral, "How lovely shines the Morning Star!" Then follows the sublime scene from Matthew xvi 14-18, where Peter declares his master to be "the Christ, the Son of the living God," — one of the most impressive scenes, we have always thought, in the gospel history, and here not inadequately treated. The feeling of mysterious and awful grandeur awakened by Peter's bold exclamation, "Thou art the Christ," is powerfully rendered by the entrance of the trombones upon the inverted subdominant triad of C-sharp minor, and their pause upon the dominant of the same key. Throughout this scene the characteristic contrast between the ardent vigor of Peter and the sweet serenity of Jesus is well delineated in the music. After Peter's stirring aria, "My heart is glad," the dramatic climax is reached in the C-major chorus, "The Church is built upon the foundation of the apostles and prophets."

The second scene is carried out to somewhat greater length, corresponding nearly to the last half of the first part of Elijah, from the point where the challenge is given to the prophets of Baal. In the opening passages of mingled recitative and arioso, Peter is forewarned that he shall deny his Master, and his half-indignant remonstrance is sustained, with added emphasis, by the voices of the twelve disciples, pitched a fourth higher.

Then Judas comes, with a great multitude, and Jesus is carried before the high-priest. The beautiful F-minor chorus, "We hid our faces from him," furnishes the musical comment upon the statement that "the disciples all forsook him and fled." We hardly dare to give full expression to our feelings about this chorus (which during the past month has been continually singing itself over and over again in our recollection), lest it should be supposed that our enthusiasm has got the better of our sober judgment. The second theme, "He was brought as a lamb to the slaughter, yet he opened not his mouth," is quite Handel-like in the simplicity and massiveness of its magnificent harmonic progressions. With the scene of the denial, for which we are thus prepared, the dramatic movement becomes exceedingly rapid, and the rendering of the events in the high-priest's hall — Peter's bass recitative alternating its craven protestations with the clamorous agitato chorus of the servants — is stirring in the extreme. The contralto aria describing the Lord's turning and looking upon Peter is followed by the orchestra with a lament in B-flat minor, introducing the bass aria of the repentant and remorse-stricken disciple, "O God, my God, forsake me not." As the last strains of the lamentation die away, a choir of angels is heard, of sopranos and contraltos divided, singing, "Remember from whence thou art fallen," to an accompaniment of harps. The second theme, "He that overcometh shall receive a crown of life," is introduced in full chorus, in a cheering allegro movement, preparing the way for a climax higher than any yet reached in the course of the work. This climax — delayed for a few moments by an andante aria for a contralto voice, "The Lord is faithful and righteous" — at last bursts upon us with a superb crescendo of strings, and the words, "Awake, thou that sleepest, arise from the dead, and Christ shall give thee light." This chorus, which for reasons presently to be given was heard at considerable disadvantage at Portland, contains some of the best fugue-writing in the work, and is especially rich and powerful in its instrumentation.

The second part of the oratorio begins with the crucifixion and ascension of Jesus. Here we must note especially the deeply pathetic opening chorus, "The Son of Man was delivered into the hands of sinful men," the joyous allegro, "And on the third day he rose again," the choral, "Jesus, my Redeemer, lives," and the quartet, "Feed the flock of God," commenting upon the command of Jesus, "Feed my lambs." This quartet has all the heavenly sweetness of Handel's "He shall feed his flock," which it suggests by similarity of subject, though not by similarity of treatment; but in a certain quality of inwardness, or religious meditativeness, it reminds one more of Mr. Paine's favorite master, Bach. The choral, like the one in the first part and the one which follows the scene of Pentecost, is taken from the Lutheran Choral Book, and arranged with original harmony and instrumentation, in accordance with the custom of Bach, Mendelssohn, and other composers, "of introducing into their sacred compositions the old popular choral melodies which are the peculiar offspring of a religious age." Thus the noblest choral ever written, the "Sleepers, wake," in St. Paul, was composed in 1604 by Praetorius, the harmonization and accompaniment only being the work of Mendelssohn.

In St. Peter, as in Elijah, the second part, while forming the true musical climax of the oratorio, admits of a briefer description than the first part. The wave of emotion answering to the sensuously dramatic element having partly spent itself, the wave of lyric emotion gathers fresh strength, and one feels that one has reached the height of spiritual exaltation, while, nevertheless, there is not so much which one can describe to others who may not happen to have gone through with the same experience. Something of the same feeling one gets in studying Dante's *Paradiso,* after finishing the preceding divisions of his poem: there is less which can be pictured to the eye of sense, or left to be supplied by the concrete imagination. Nevertheless, in the scene of Pentecost, which follows that of the Ascension, there is no lack of dramatic vividness. Indeed, there is nothing in the work more striking than the orchestration of the introductory tenor recitative, the mysterious chorus, "The voice of the Lord divideth the flames of fire," or the amazed query which follows, "Behold, are not all these who speak Galileans" and "how is it that we every one hear them in our own tongue wherein we were born?" We have heard the opinion expressed that Mr. Paine's oratorio must be lacking in originality, since it suggests such strong reminiscences of St. Paul. Now, this suggestion, it seems to us, is due partly to the similarity of the subjects, independently of any likeness in the modes of treatment, and partly, perhaps, to the fact that Mr. Paine as well as Mendelssohn, has been a devoted student of Bach, whose characteristics are so strong that they may well have left their mark upon the works of both composers. But especially it would seem that there is some real, though very general, resemblance between this colloquial chorus, "Behold," etc., and some choruses in St. Paul, as, for example, Nos. 29 and 36-38. In the same way, the scene in the high-priest's hall might distantly suggest either of these passages, or others in Elijah. These resemblances, however, are very superficial, pertaining not to the musical but to the dramatic treatment of situations which are generically similar in so far, and only in so far, as they represent conversational passages between an apostle or prophet and an ignorant multitude, whether amazed or hostile, under the sway of violent excitement. As regards the musical elaboration of these terse and striking alternations of chorus and recitative, its originality can be questioned only after we have decided to refer all originality on such matters to Bach, or, indeed, even behind him, into the Middle Ages.

After the preaching of Peter, and the sweet contralto aria, "As for man, his days are as grass," the culmination of this scene comes in the D-major chorus, "This is the witness of God." What follows, beginning with the choral, "Praise to the Father," is to be regarded as an epilogue or peroration to the whole work. It is in accordance with a sound tradition that the grand sacred drama of an oratorio should conclude with a lyric outburst of thanksgiving, a psalm of praise to the Giver of every good and perfect gift. Thus, after Peter's labors are ended in the aria, "Now as ye were redeemed," in which the twelve disciples and the full chorus join, a duet for tenor and soprano, "Sing unto God," brings us to the grand final chorus in C major, "Great and marvellous are thy works, Lord God Almighty." The cadence of this concluding chorus reminds us that one of the noteworthy points in the oratorio is the character of its cadences. The cadence prepared by the 6-4 chord, now become so hackneyed from its perpetual and wearisome repetition in popular church music, seems to be especially disliked by Mr. Paine, as it occurs but once or twice in the course of the work. In the great choruses the cadence is usually reached either by a pedal on the tonic, as in the chorus, "Awake, thou that sleepest," or by a pedal on the dominant culmination in a chord of the major ninth, as in the final chorus; or there is a plagal cadence, as in the first chorus of the second part; or, if the 6-4 chord is introduced, as it is in the chorus, "He that overcometh," its ordinary effect is covered and obscured by the movement of the divided sopranos. We do not remember noticing anywhere such a decided use of the 6-4 chord as is made, for example, by Mendelssohn, in "Thanks be to

God," or in the final chorus of St. Paul. Perhaps if we were to confess our lingering fondness for the cadence prepared by the 6-4 chord, when not too frequently introduced, it might only show that we retain a liking for New England "psalm tunes"; but it does seem to us that a sense of final repose, of entire cessation of movement, is more effectually secured by this cadence than by any other. Yet while the 6-4 cadence most completely expresses finality and rest, it would seem that the plagal and other cadences above enumerated as preferred by Mr. Paine have a certain sort of superiority by reason of the very incompleteness with which they express finality. There is no sense of finality whatever about the Phrygian cadence; it leaves the mind occupied with the feeling of a boundless region beyond, into which one would fain penetrate; and for this reason it has, in sacred music, a great value. Something of the same feeling, too, attaches to those cadences in which an unexpected major third usurps the place of the minor which the ear was expecting as in the "Incarnatus" of Mozart's Twelfth Mass [Mass in C minor, K. 427]. In a less degree, an analogous effect was produced upon us by the cadence with a pedal on the tonic, in the choruses, "The Church is built," and "Awake, thou that sleepest." On these considerations it may become intelligible that, to some hearers, Mr. Paine's cadences have seemed unsatisfactory, their ears have missed the positive categorical assertion of finality which the 6-4 cadence alone can give. To go further into this subject would take us far beyond our limits. We must conclude with a few words as to the manner in which this great composition was first brought before the public.

The pleasant little town of Portland [Maine] has reason to congratulate itself, *first* on being the birthplace of such a composer as Mr. Paine; *secondly,* on having been the place where the first great work of America in the domain of music was brought out; and *thirdly,* on possessing what is probably the most thoroughly disciplined choral society in this country. More artistic chorus-singing it has never been our lot to hear. Our New York friends, after their recent experiences, will perhaps be slow to believe us when we say that the Portland choir sang this new work even better than the Handel and Hayden [*sic*] society sing the old and familiar Elijah; but it is true. In their command of the pianissimo and the gradual crescendo, and in the precision of their attack, the Portland singers can easily teach the Handel and Haydn a quarter's lessons. And, besides all this, they know how to preserve their equanimity under the gravest persecutions of the orchestra; keeping the even tenor of their way where a less disciplined choir, incited by the excessive blare of the trombones and the undue scraping of the second violins, would inevitably lose its presence of mind and break out into an untimely fortissimo.

No doubt it is easier to achieve perfect chorus-singing with a choir of one hundred and twenty-five voices than with a choir of six hundred. But this diminutive size, which was an advantage so far as concerned the performance of the Portland choir, was decidedly a disadvantage so far as concerned the proper rendering of the more massive choruses in St. Peter. All the greatest choruses — such as Nos. 1, 8, 19, 20, 28, 35, and 39 — were seriously impaired in the rendering by the lack of massiveness in the voices. For example, the grand chorus, "Awake, thou that sleepest," begins with a rapid crescendo of strings, introducing the full chorus on the word "Awake," upon the dominant triad of D major; and after a couple of beats the voices are reinforced by the trombones, producing the most tremendous effect possible in such a crescendo. To us this effect was very disagreeable; and it was obviously contrary to the effect intended by the composer. But with a weight of four or five hundred voices, the effect would be entirely different. Instead of entering upon the scene as intruders, the mighty trombones would only serve to swell and enrich the ponderous chord which opens this noble chorus. Given greater weight only, and the performance of the admirable Portland choir would have left nothing to be desired.

We cannot speak with so much satisfaction of the performance of the orchestra. The instrumentation of St. Peter is wonderfully excellent. But this instrumentation was rather clumsily rendered by the orchestra, whose doings constituted the least enjoyable part of the performance. There was too much blare of brass, whine of hautboy, and scraping of strings. But in condonation of this serious defect, one must admit that the requisite amount of rehearsal is out of the question when one's choir is in Portland and one's orchestra in Boston; besides which the parts had been inaccurately copied. For a moment, at the beginning of the orchestral lament, there was risk of disaster, the wind instruments failing to come in at the right time, when Mr. Paine, with fortunate presence of mind, stopped the players, and the movement was begun over again,— the whole occurring so quickly and quietly as hardly to attract attention.

The solo parts were, in the main, admirably done. Of Miss Phillips and Messrs. Osgood and Rudolphsen, it is unnecessary to speak. The soprano, Mrs. Weatherbee, of Portland, showed thorough culture and true artistic feeling; but, urged by too generous an enthusiasm, and trusting in a very powerful and flexible voice, she too frequently took part in the chorus, so that, toward the last, she showed signs of overexertion.

J. Fiske. "Music." *Atlantic Monthly*, 32 (August 1873), 248-51.

THE FISK JUBILEE AND HAMPTON SINGERS
NEGRO FOLK SONGS
FROM DWIGHT'S JOURNAL OF MUSIC (1873)

JOHN SULLIVAN DWIGHT (1813-1893) was born in Boston and became an important music critic in that city. Because Boston was in many ways the center of the classical music world in this country, Dwight was influential far beyond the boundaries of the Northeast. His Journal of Music *was published from 1852 to 1881 and included concert reports and reviews from America and Europe, in addition to articles about contemporary composers and musical events. Dwight was the self-appointed guardian of the German tradition in music and was frequently biased in his views about music outside of that tradition. Nevertheless, he was a tireless promoter of American music and worthwhile American ensembles and composers.*

The Fisk Jubilee Singers, a group of African-American students from Fisk University, began concert tours of this country and Europe in order to raise money to pay off the mortgage of their classroom building. Even after that task was accomplished, the group continued to tour as agents of goodwill for the college and for the general educational cause of the African-American student. Their many imitators included the Hampton Singers, from the Hampton Institute in Virginia, also mentioned in the essay below, reprinted from the New York Weekly Review *in an 1873 issue of Dwight's* Journal. *The writer of this article, using condescending and derogatory language and phrases common in his day but offensive in ours, talks about the genesis of these important singing groups, their style of singing, and their literature. These choirs, the Fisk singers particularly, were important in the development of the spiritual and especially in its dissemination in the North. The anonymous author quotes at great length from what were then unknown songs, but which today have become standard concert-closers, sung by school, community, church, and collegiate ensembles throughout the country.*

64

SLAVE MELODIES FROM THE SOUTH
The Jubilee and Hampton Singers.

The Editor of the New York Weekly Review, *in the article which follows, shows a just interest in the untutored religious melodies of the ex-slaves of our Southern States. The collection to which he alludes of these songs, set down in notes by Dr. Seward, may be found appended to an interesting volume just published by Lee & Shephard of this city, entitled, "The Jubilee Singers of Fisk University," presenting, in a couple of hundred pages, an account of that institution and its teachers, the personal history and portraits of the singers, a chronicle of their successful musical and missionary tour through the Union, and, as we said before, an Appendix containing the words and notes of about sixty of the songs.*

At last the American school of music has been discovered. We have had accomplished virtuosi, skillful vocalists and talented composers. They have, however, all trodden the beaten track. It has remained for the obscure and uncultured Negro race in this country to prove that there is an original style of music peculiar to America. This school is found in the songs of the Southern blacks, and they have been but lately made familiar to Northerners by the efforts of two groups of colored singers who have lately given concerts in our principal cities. Both of these bands of wandering minstrels are working in aid of meritorious educational institutions.

The Jubilee Singers who appeared here some months ago represent the interests of Fisk University, of Nashville, Tennessee. They are nine in number, including: Ella Sheppard, pianist and soprano; Jennie Jackson, soprano; Maggie Porter, soprano; Minnie Tate, contralto; Eliza Walker, contralto; Thomas Rutling, tenor; Ben M. Holmes, tenor; I.P. Dickerson, bass; and Greene Evans, bass. They have sung in most of our Eastern cities with excellent pecuniary success; and the quaint, weird melodies in which their natural talents and acquired skill have been exercised, have been further made familiar to the public, through a collection of some fifty of their favorite songs which were reduced to musical notation by Mr. Theodore F. Seward of this city. Of these songs the editor of the little book containing them, and published by Bigelow and Main of this city, says:

"The Songs — Of these neither the words, or the music have ever before been published, or even reduced to written form, at least, to the knowledge of the Jubilee Singers.

"The most of them they learned in childhood — the others, which were not common in the portion of the South in which they were raised, they have received directly from those who were accustomed to sing them. These songs, therefore, can be relied upon as the genuine songs of their race, being in words and music the same as sung by their ancestors in the cabin, on the platform, and in the religious worship.

"By the severe discipline to which the Jubilee Singers have been subjected in the school-room, they have been educated out of the peculiarities of the Negro dialect, and they do not attempt to imitate the peculiar pronunciation of their race. They have also received considerable musical instruction, and have been made familiar with much of our best sacred and classical music, and this has modified their manner of execution. They do not attempt to imitate the grotesque bodily motions or the drawling intonations that often characterize the singing of great congregations of the colored people in their excited religious meetings.

"It is true, however, both of the words and the music, that whatever modification they have undergone, has been wholly in the minds of the Singers under the influence of the training and culture they have received in the University of which they are members."

The music of these songs is generally strikingly wild. Some of them at once recall the "break-downs" made familiar to us by the negro minstrel troupes. Others suggest ordinary Sunday School hymn tunes; but the majority are unique in construction, rhythm and melody. The cultivated musician will at once perceive that they are crude and childish, but he cannot deny their originality.

The success of the Jubilee Singers seems to have inspired a number of the pupils of the Hampton, Va. Academy to "go and do likewise," and a band of nineteen members have started out on a similar mission. Being greater in force, they are more efficient in choral effects, and if less cultured than their predecessors, their performances are even more characteristic. They have given three concerts in New York (at Steinway Hall) and have, on each occasion been greeted by large and enthusiastic audiences.

The institution in whose aid their concerts are given is amply described in their programmes. It is situated in the town of Hampton, Virginia, near

Fort Monroe, and the mouth of the Chesapeake Bay, and by one of the curious coincidences of history, close to the spot where the first slaves brought to this country were landed. Here, too, the famous order declaring black fugitives to be "contraband of war," was issued, and here was established the first school for Freedmen, from which, in the providence of God, this existing institution has been developed, beginning under the auspices of the American Missionary Association and the Freedmen's Bureau, and drawing its support mainly from Northern benevolence.

The Jubilee Singers aimed to secure twenty thousand dollars with which to pay off a mortgage on their University Buildings. The needs of Hampton Normal College are much greater. The Institute wants not less than $135,000, and must raise $75,000 of this amount during the ensuing year. In their appeal to the Northern public the Hampton singers say:

"The women of the North could do no better deed than to reach out helping hands to these sisters of theirs, to whom, as yet, the nobler fields of woman's kingdom are *terra incognita*, and by wise and timely assistance, to lead them to that knowledge of better things, which they, themselves, unaided, cannot reach.

"The young men and women who sing before you to-night know their own need and the need of their race, and we ask you if there is nothing in their wild music and dusky faces which brings before you the pathos and terror of their past, nothing which reminds you how deep their ignorance has been, and how dependent their future still is upon the loving kindness and reasonable charity of their fellow-citizens?

"It does not appear to us possible that this appeal can be unheeded by the wealthy and charitable communities of the North. Every one will acknowledge the first great need of the emancipated negroes to be Education; and this can be best furnished to them through such organizations as the Hampton Normal Institute."

The words of these negro songs are as curious as the music. They are marked by an oriental gorgeousness of imagery, which sometimes approximates to poetical genius and oftener descends to mere nonsense. As originally they were only preserved orally, they are replete with repetition. In most of them the first strain is of the nature of a chorus or refrain, which is to be sung after each verse, and the return to this chorus should be made without breaking the time.

We give a few specimens of this strange religious poetry — this quaint hymnology of an ignorant, uncultivated, yet pious and devotional race. The most noticeable is "Go Down, Moses," a song which is not without historical interest, as it expresses the yearnings of the Southern slaves for freedom and their half-formed hopes of emancipation: —

When Israel was in Egypt's land,
   Let my people go;
Oppressed so hard they could not stand,
   Let my people go;
Go down, Moses, way down in Egypt's land,
Tell old Pharaoh, let my people go.

Thus saith the Lord, bold Moses said,
   Let my people go;
If not I'll smite your first-born dead,
   Let my people go;
Go down, Moses, etc.

We need not always weep and moan,
   Let my people go;
And wear these slavery chains forlorn,
   Let my people go;

This world's a wilderness of woe,
   Let my people go;
O, let us on to Canaan go,
   Let my people go.

What a beautiful morning that will be,
   Let my people go;
When time breaks up in eternity,
   Let my people go.

After a score of verses in this style, the "poem" closes with a characteristic expression of denominational preference:

The Devil he thought he had me fast,
   Let my people go;
But I thought I'd break his chains at last,
   Let my people go.

O take yer shoes from off yer feet,
   Let my people go;
And walk into the golden street,
   Let my people go;

I'll tell you what I likes de best,
   Let my people go;
It is the shouting Methodist.
   Let my people go.

I do believe without a doubt,
   Let my people go;
That a Christian has a right to shout
   Let my people go.

A spirited unison chorus is sung to these words:

I'm a travelling to the grave,
I'm a travelling to the grave, my Lord,
I'm a travelling to the grave,
For to lay this body down.
My massa died a shouting,
Singing glory, Hallelujah!
The last word he said to me
Was about Jerusalem.

The succeeding verses *ad infinitum* are simply formed by substituting the words "My Missis" or "My Brother" for "My Massa." It will be readily seen that the song can thus be prolonged till lungs and patience are both exhausted.

An odd little trifle is entitled, "Many thousand gone."

1 No more auction block for me,
   No more, no more,
   No more auction block for me,
   Many thousand gone.

2 No more peck o'corn for me, etc.
3 No more driver's lash for me, etc.
4 No more pint o'salt for me, etc.
5 No more hundred lash for me, etc.
6 No more mistress' call for me, etc.

One of the most beautiful in point of melody is "Steal Away."

Steal away, steal away,
Steal away to Jesus.
Steal away, steal away home,
   I ain't got long to stay here.
My Lord calls me,
   He calls me by the thunder;
The trumpet sounds it in my soul,
   I ain't got long to stay here.
My Lord calls me — He calls me by the lightning;
   The trumpet sounds it in my soul;
I hain't got long to stay here.
   Chorus.— Steal away, &c.

A great favorite is the following:

1 Gwine to ride up in the chariot,
   Sooner in the morning;
   Ride up in the chariot,
   Sooner in the morning;
   Ride up in the chariot,
   Sooner in the morning,

And hope I'll join the band,
O Lord have mercy on me,
And I hope I'll join the band,
And I hope I'll join the band.

2 Gwine to meet my brother there, Sooner, etc.
   Chorus.— O Lord have mercy, etc.

3 Gwine to chatter with the Angels, Sooner, etc.
   Chorus.— O Lord have mercy, etc.

The most difficult of all for any one save a Southern negro to sing —
difficult on account of its incomprehensible rhythm is this:

Didn't my Lord deliver Daniel, d'liver Daniel, d'liver Daniel.
Didn't my Lord d'liver Daniel, and why not a every man?
He deliver'd Daniel from the lion's den,
   Jonah from the belly of the whale,
   And the Hebrew children from the fiery furnace,
   And why not every man?
Didn't my Lord deliver Daniel, d'liver Daniel, d'liver Daniel,
Didn't my Lord deliver Daniel, and not a every man?

2 The moon run down in a purple stream,
   The sun forbear to shine,
   And every star disappear,
   King Jesus shall be mine.
   Chorus.— Didn't my Lord, etc.

3 The wind blows East and the wind blows West,
   It blows like the judgment day,
   And every poor soul that never did pray,
   'll [will] be glad to pray that day.
   Chorus.— Didn't my Lord, etc.

4 I set my foot on the Gospel ship,
   And the ship it begin to sail,
   It landed me over on Canaan's shore,
   And I'll never come back any more.
   Chorus.— Didn't my Lord, etc.

These dusky song writers seem to have a special enmity against "Ole Pharaoh." One song declares the intention of the writer to forward a letter to "Massa Jesus to send some valiant soldier to turn back Pharaoh's army, Hallelu!" and closes with gusto: —

When Pharaoh crossed the water,
The waters came together,
And drowned old Pharaoh's army, etc. Hallelu!

A very curious musical effect is made in "Roll, Jordan, roll," by the unexpected introduction of a flat seventh. The words begin thus:

Roll, Jordan, roll,
Roll, Jordan, roll,
I want to go to Heaven when I die,
To hear Jordan roll;
Oh brothers you ought t'have been there,
Yes, my Lord,
A sitting in the Kingdom,
To hear Jordan roll.
       Chorus.— Roll, Jordan, roll.

"Swing low, sweet chariot" tells how the singer hears a band of angels coming after him, to carry him over Jordan. Of "Sweet Canaan" it is said: — "My mother used to tell how the colored people expected to be free some day; and how, one night, a great many of them met together in a cabin, and tied little budgets on their backs as though they were going off somewhere, and prayed, and cried, and shook hands, and sung this song."
   A very odd song runs as follows: —

72

Go chain the lion down,
Go chain the lion down,
Go chain the lion down
Before the heaven doors close,
Do you see that good old sister
Come a wagging up the hill so slow?
"She wants to get to heav'n in due time
Before the heaven doors close.

Another popular song tells how "Mary and Martha just went along to ring those charming bells" — went "way over Jordan, Lord, to ring those charming bells." Another describes how "King Jesus rides on a mild white horse," with the rather inconsequential refrain: "No man can a hinder me." A version of the parable of "Ten Virgins" is sung to a very pleasing melody. We will, however, close here our extracts from these quaint rhymes with a verse of "Judgment Day."

Judgment Day is rolling around,
   Oh! how long to go;
I've a good old mother in the heaven, my Lord,
   How I long to go there too;
There's a big camp-meeting in the heaven, my Lord,
   Oh! how I long to go.
   Chorus.— Judgment Day, etc.

We have spoken of the music of these songs as American; but possibly it is of the real African origin. But whencesoever it comes it is certainly unique and entertaining, and not without its tinge of pathos. In addition to this, its hearty sincerity saves it from derision, even where it is weakest, in either sentiment or melody; for these strange religious ballads are the folksongs of some four millions of the people of the United States.

John Sullivan Dwight. *Dwight's Journal of Music* (Boston), 5 April 1873, 411-13 (reprinted from the *New York Weekly Review*).

AMY BEACH
REVIEW: MASS IN E-FLAT (1892)

By far the most important and influential woman composer to emerge during the nineteenth century in this country was AMY MARCY CHENEY BEACH *(1867-1944), known during her lifetime as Mrs. H.H.A. Beach from her marriage to a prominent physician. Although tutored in piano, Beach was mostly self-taught in composition and achieved great fame in this country and throughout Europe as both a pianist and composer. Her Mass in E-flat, composed when she was quite young, remains, with Paine's Mass in D, one of the two finest nineteenth-century American settings. Beach received a number of important commissions for choral music, including a* Festival Jubilate *for the dedication of the Women's Building for the 1893 Columbian Exposition (World's Fair) in Chicago; a* Song of Welcome *for the Omaha Trans-Mississippi Exposition in 1898; and a* Panama Hymn *for the Panama-Pacific Exposition in San Francisco.*

The first of the two selections below is a review of her Mass by the nineteenth-century critic Philip Hale, taken from the Boston Evening Transcript. *The second selection, from* Etude *magazine, is an essay in which Mrs. Beach discusses the genesis of two other works, the first choral and the second a song later arranged for choir, offering insight into her personality as well as her compositional process.*

The Handel and Haydn Society gave last evening in Music Hall the second concert of this season, under the direction of Mr. Carl Zerrahn. The Society was assisted by Mrs. Patrick-Walker, Mrs. Alves and Messrs. Campanini and Fischer. The orchestra was made up of members of the Symphony Orchestra, with Mr. Kneisel as principal. Mr. Lang was the organist. The programme included a mass in E flat, composed by Mrs. H.H.A. Beach, and Beethoven's Choral Fantasia, in which Mrs. Beach played the pianoforte part.

This mass was composed by Mrs. Beach in 1889, when she was twenty-two years old. It is a work of long breath. It shows knowledge, skill, and, above all, application, patience and industry. She has not followed closely an illustrious predecessor; she has had fixed ideas of her own, and she has not hesitated to carry them out. Her treatment of the text is modern. She has treated it subjectively and objectively; hence we find mysticism that is intended to suggest to the hearer a mood, and we also find direct dramatic appeals. There is the natural exaggeration of youth. The mysticism at times approaches obscurity, the dramatic appeals are occasionally unduly emphasized. Nor is Mrs. Beach always successful when she is most ambitious. The comparative simplicity of the "Kyrie" and the "Sanctus," the unaffected solemnity of the "Et in Spiritum Sanctum," the peaceful close of the work — these are more effective than certain passages where the composer apparently strained every nerve.

When there is so much that is creditable to the composer in this work, and when, considering her age, there is much that is remarkable, it seems almost ungenerous to speak of a few defects. The voices are at times treated as orchestral instruments. This is particularly true of certain passages given to the solo voices; and it may here be said that the solos, with the possible exception of the "Gratias agimus," are the weakest portions of the work, and they are wanting in defined and balanced melody. There is excessive modulation. Nor has the composer yet learned the fact that orchestral effects are gained by economy rather than by extravagance in handling orchestral resources. Instead of insisting upon these points, it is a pleasure to praise the sincerity of the composer's purpose, to admit gladly the many excellences of the work, and to welcome it as an interesting contribution to the musical literature of the United States, presented by a woman of this town.

The performance was, as a whole, eminently satisfactory. The chorus-work was excellent throughout, in attack, in volume, and in appreciation of the desired expression. The trio that opens the "Laudamus te" was poorly sung, but the task was not an easy one, and with this exception the solo singers were more than adequate. When Mrs. Beach came upon the stage she was greeted with long-continued and enthusiastic applause; and the applause did not cease until she struck the opening chords of the Beethoven

Fantasia. When this Fantasia was first given in Vienna, with Beethoven at the pianoforte, the concert lasted from 6.30 until 10.30; the cold was intense and the theatre was not heated; the orchestra played so badly that Beethoven left the pianoforte, complained bitterly, and then insisted upon a fresh start from the very beginning. There was no such combination of circumstances last evening to annoy Mrs. Beach; and the work, which is now chiefly interesting as a species of sketch for the Ninth Symphony, brought the concert to a close.

Philip Hale. "Causerie. First Performance of Mrs. Beach's Mass. The Second Concert of the Handel and Haydn." Boston *Evening Transcript*, 8 February 1892, 5.

AMY BEACH
THE "HOW" OF CREATIVE COMPOSITION (1943)

The process of musical composition cannot be reduced to any single formula, because each type of music sets its own creative pattern, according to its own demands. Critics tell us that the creation of poetry follows a number of given steps: first, the poet becomes stirred by a vigorous emotional impulse which, a pure, abstract emotion, would be unable to reach the understanding of others; in second place, he reflects more calmly upon this emotion and seeks to find a graphic thought symbol with which to convey it; and in third place, then, he seeks to clothe the combination of emotions plus thought with the most beautiful and suitable words, meters, and rhymes. That, in the most general way, approximates the stages in musical creation, as well. In other words, the composer must have emotional and spiritual feeling to put into his work; he must achieve a comprehensible translation of his feeling through form; and he must have at his disposal a tremendous background of technical, musical craftsmanship in order to express his feelings and his thoughts. Thus, the craftsmanship, vital though it is, serves chiefly as the means toward the end of personal expression.

So much for the generalities of the process of composition. In actual practice, each form brings requisites of its own. Purely contrapuntal composition, for example, demands less emotional inspiration and more mathematical skill. In vocal writing, the initial impulse grows out of the poem to be set; it is the poem which gives the song its shape, its mood, its rhythm, its very being. Spiritual, or sacred music requires an even deeper emotional impulse. (To me, all music is *sacred*; in using the term in its limited sense, I am merely accepting the convention of language.) The steps the composer follows in developing any of these types depend, naturally, upon his own inborn abilities, the force of his creative urge, the way his mind and soul "work," his background, and his training. No one can tell you exactly how you must set about creating a musical composition — indeed, one of the chief charms of composing is the sense of wonder and mystery surrounding its sources. What causes one person to seek to express himself tonally? What causes the form and color of his utterance to differ from those of anyone else? Simply, we do not know!

How New Works Are Born

Let me tell you a story to illustrate my own creative process. When I first returned from Europe, back in 1915, a friend, the late Dr. Howard Duffield, then pastor of the First Presbyterian Church in New York, asked me if I had ever thought of making a setting of Saint Francis of Assisi's *Canticle of the Sun*. I never had thought of it, and Dr. Duffield kindly gave me the text, together with vigorous assurances that I *must* try to set it. I was very busy then, playing piano concerts all over the country, and I forgot all about the matter.

Ten years later, in 1925, I went to the wonderful MacDowell Colony, in Peterboro, New Hampshire, to write a suite for two pianos (subsequently published by the John Church Company). I had no thought of working at anything on the day of my arrival; I simply rejoiced in being there. However, I did get out my manuscript paper and tumbled it upon my worktable, to be ready for writing the next day. In moving the paper, I saw something fall from between the sheets. To my surprise, I found it to be the text that Dr. Duffield had given me so long before. I took it up and read it over — and the only way I can describe what happened is that it jumped at me and struck me, most forcibly! The text called melodies to my mind. I went out at once under a tree, and the text took possession of me. As if from dictation, I jotted down the notes of my "Canticle." In less than five days, the entire work was done. I put it aside, to let it "cool," and the demands of the work I had planned to do crowded it from my mind a second time.

Then, some years later, I was asked for a sacred work the requirements of which, as to length and fitness, exactly suited the work I had dashed off and forgotten. I got out my "Canticle," did no more work on it than copy it out in neat and legible fashion (my rough notes are intelligible only to myself!), and there was the work, as it is known to-day.

1830-1920: Beach

It happened more than once that a composition comes to me, ready made as it were, between the demands of other work. *The Year's At The Spring* was "born" the same way. The Boston Browning Society had asked me to set that poem, for their annual celebration of Browning's birthday. I agreed to do it, but put it off because of pressing work. Shortly before the celebration, I went to New York, for the premiere of my "Violin Sonata." On the train going back, it occurred to me that the time was getting short for my Browning song. I did nothing whatever in a conscious way; I simply sat still in the train, thinking of Browning's poem, and allowing it and the rhythm of the wheels to take possession of me. By the time I reached Boston, the song was ready ....

Benjamin Brooks "The 'How' of Creative Composition: A Conversation with Mrs. H. H. A. Beach." *Etude*, 61, no. 3 (March 1943), 151, 208-9. ©1943 Etude Music Magazine. Reprinted by Permission of the Publisher, Theodore Presser Company. (Excerpt)

DUDLEY BUCK

CONCLUDING REMARKS FROM
ILLUSTRATIONS IN CHOIR ACCOMPANIMENT (1877)

Primarily a church musician and teacher, DUDLEY BUCK (1839-1909) was also a pioneer in the composition of large-scale choral works, including the Forty-Sixth Psalm, The Light of Asia, The Story of the Cross, The Legend of Don Munio, *and other works. He also wrote dozens of shorter anthems and a great deal of service music. Buck's music is well-crafted, but with an ear toward what would please the popular taste of his day. His* Illustrations in Choir Accompaniment, *from which these "Concluding Remarks" were taken, was intended as a manual for church organists and covers such topics as registration, the playing of hymns, the accompaniment of chant and solo quartets (prominent in even the larger churches, these four paid soloists took the place of bigger, volunteer choirs), the accompanying of solo voices, the playing of "thorough bass," and playing accompaniments with orchestra. These remarks provide insight into some of a nineteenth-century choral director's rehearsal procedures.*

In the preceding pages, it has been the author's endeavor to make clear some of the modes of treating the organ as an accompanying instrument.

He has striven to show that, while the pianist may confine himself to the notes of an accompaniment as he finds them, the organist must modify the same in many cases, or order to adapt them to his instrument.

If this has been understood, it must have been perceived that such deviations from the exact notion have not been idly made, but were advocated for the purpose of conforming to the spirit, rather than to the letter, of a given composition; also to afford the voices unimpeded support.

He has further endeavored to make evident that an accompaniment must not be considered by itself, but in its compound relation to the voice or voices accompanied; the two elements together forming the complete whole.

Although no better support for voices can be found than that afforded by the organ, it nevertheless frequently proves a poor instrument *to rehearse* with. Both its merits and defects as an instrument contribute to this result.

In the first place, the distinctness with which it sustains every tone of the harmony, causes it to render *too much* support to the voices for purposes of rehearsal. Besides this, it measurably prevents the organist (supposing him to be the director of the choir, which he always should be) from accurately hearing the mistakes and faults of the singers, especially if the choir is a large one.

In securing promptness of accentuation and rhythm, in the first practice of a new composition, the piano is far preferable to the organ.

When a choir has once made itself fairly familiar with a piece, the organ will then furnish all the rhythmic accent necessary, if properly handled. The piano, beyond securing intonation and accent, does not support the voices in the sense that the organ accomplishes this. With the piano, the singers are forced to rely upon themselves to a far greater extent, and defects in performance are far more readily detected.

For these reasons, every choir should hold their rehearsals, of new compositions at least, with piano. Afterwards the piece may be rehearsed with the organ, if, in the judgment of the director, it is necessary. This will sometimes be the case, more especially in pieces provided with an obbligato accompaniment for the organ.

The young organist taking charge of a choir will likewise find the frequent rehearsal *without accompaniment* (or such portions of pieces as seem to present peculiar difficulties) to be of the greatest value. In this way, even timid singers learn to be independent, while the director can give his entire attention to the true balance of the voices. This is the more important, as even in choirs (quartet or chorus) where the parts may be termed well balanced, it is frequently necessary for one part to sing louder or softer than another. This occurs not merely in case of a melodic design, which is intended to be "brought out" in some particular part; it may also be necessary to the proper blending of a single chord. Here it becomes the director's duty to see that the voices which have such intervals as fourths and fifths do not unduly assert themselves, and that the thirds and sixths are so sustained that the harmony may seem complete to the ear.

Glancing back over the various chapters of this work, the author is fully sensible of many shortcomings in the presentation of the different subjects. He has been encouraged to proceed, however, by the fact that no previous attempt has been made (so far as he is aware) to put in print a certain amount of what may be termed "traditional matter" bearing upon accompaniment. The various organ "methods" have but little or nothing to say on this subject, nor does it strictly come within their province. Our better organists become familiar with various modes and expedients in organ accompaniment, partly from some good teacher's example, and partly through their own natural talent. In the latter case, such knowledge comes to them after long experience, and as a result of familiarity with the nature of voices, as well as with that of their instrument.

It furthermore comes to them in the light of an original discovery in this direction.

To hasten such discoveries has been the principal purpose of the preceding pages.

It may possibly seem discouraging to some readers of this work that they are called upon to familiarize themselves with *so many* points of treatment, often trifling in themselves, in order to accompany well.

To such faint-hearted ones, the author would fain say a word or two in conclusion.

He has not pretended to treat his subject exhaustively, and therefore fully believes that any church-player (to be thoroughly worthy of the name of a good choir-accompanist) must be familiar with the majority of the ideas herein advanced; even if he apply the principles they involve in a practically unconscious manner.

As regards counsel and advice towards accomplishing this end, no language of his own could here prove so applicable as the following golden lines of encouragement:

"The more an artist faithful toils,
The more unto his work gives heed,
So much the more doth he succeed.
Therefore each day thy task renew,
And thou shalt see what *that* will do;
Thereby each purpose is attained,

Thereby what seemed so hard is gained,
And, step by step, thou shalt discern
The knowledge which thy hand must learn."
GOETHE (*Artists' Apotheosis*)

Dudley Buck. *Illustrations in Choir Accompaniment, with Hints on Registration*. New York: G. Schirmer, 1877, 172-73.

HORATIO PARKER
REVIEW: HORA NOVISSIMA (1893)

HORATIO WILLIAM PARKER (1863-1919) was born in Massachusetts and made his career in both Boston and New York, after studying for a time in Europe. This pattern was also followed by many of his contemporaries, such as John Knowles Paine, Dudley Buck, and George Chadwick. Parker was an influential teacher at Yale, and his students included both Charles Ives and Douglas Moore. His reputation as a composer rests primarily on his vocal works, including about 50 choral works and a number of anthems and other service music, some hymns, and the operas Mona *and* Fairyland, *the first of which was commissioned by the Metropolitan Opera House in New York. His largest choral work, one which continues to receive occasional performances today, is* Hora novissima. *Considered to be Parker's masterpiece, it was accorded high praise not only in this country but in England as well, where it was performed at the Three Choirs Festival in Worcester in 1899, as the first American composition of any kind to be heard in that venue. Taking his cue from Handel and Mendelssohn, Parker crafted a magnificent oratorio with eleven movements in two parts, including a massive double choir movement. In this review of the first performance from the New York* Times, *the anonymous author talks about the significance of the work and briefly comments on the lackluster first performance.*

AMUSEMENTS
The Church Choral Society

The Church Choral Society has made good history in the course of its short career. Although it has just completed its fifth season, it has enabled the lovers of sound ecclesiastical music to hear some of the most admirable of the new works in this field, notably Dr. Dvorak's noble "Requiem." Last night in the Church of the Holy Trinity, at Madison Avenue and Forty-Second Street, the society performed for the first time anywhere, Mr. Horatio W. Parker's "Hora Novissima," a modern church cantata. Mr. Parker is an American, a New Yorker, who recently won a prize for a cantata in the National Conservatory contest. The present work has already been complimented by publication in London at the hands of the notable old house of Novello, Ewer & Co.

Of course there was no little curiosity among those who are informed as to the progress of music in this city about the new work, and as Mr. Parker's other compositions had given promise, it was earnestly hoped that this one would establish his reputation as one of the most gifted of the rising American school. It may be said at the outset that the issue of last evening's performance was happy. Though inadequately performed, the "Hora Novissima" made a deep impression and at once took rank among the best works written on this side of the Atlantic. It will bear comparison with the productions of foreign composers, and we have no doubt whatever that it will be received with praise in England.

The text is one of the many medieval Latin poems of the Church, and while in sentiment it provides the composer with all the emotional food necessary for a rich ecclesiastical composition, its angular and unyielding rhythm presents difficulties that only a musician can rightly appreciate. These difficulties have been overcome by Mr. Parker with surprising ease. His musical rhythms are so numerous and graceful, and at times so finely original, that the hearer wholly loses sight of the monotonous prosody of the poem. This in itself is a demonstration of Mr. Parker's mastery of the technic of composition, but it is, perhaps, the least striking part of his achievement.

What will impress itself most forcibly upon the general hearer is the young composer's splendid fund of melody. His melodic ideas are not only plentiful, but they are beautiful in themselves and fruitful in their suggestiveness. Many a man who could not fairly be called a composer has written good themes; no one but a composer can produce themes which lend themselves easily to the various processes of musical development. Mr. Parker's themes are all thoroughly in keeping with the subject matter of his text, and are always graceful, sometimes splendidly vigorous.

The prevailing characteristics of the music of the "Hora Novissima" are fluent and refined melody, ecclesiastical spirit, and a noble dignity of treatment. In addition to these things there is displayed a remarkable command of variety in style. The young composer, without even leaving the atmosphere of the Church and without once ceasing to preserve his own individuality, reminds the hearer at different times of Verdi, Gounod, Mendelssohn, and the Netherlands masters. There is a bass solo of fine proportions which is not unlike Verdi in the best moments of his "Manzoni Requiem," and there is a soprano solo which has all the poetic sweetness of Gounod without a trace of effeminacy. And there is an a cappella chorus which is one of the finest specimens of pure church polyphony that has been produced in recent years. It might have been written by Hobrecht [Obrecht], Brumel, or even Josquin des Pres. It is impossible to write higher praise than this.

The choral writing throughout is superb in its treatment of parts, and the composer's mastery of climax is quite uncommon. The instrumentation is extremely — at times excessively — rich, and the accompaniment is always ingenious in its alternation between complete independence and polyphonic use of the melodies allotted to the voices. The final chorus, while it is perhaps somewhat overloaded with instrumental device, is a stirring and broad piece of writing which brings the work to a most effective close. As a whole the composition will impress every hearer by its revelation of the writer's mastery of the formal material of his art. It sounds not like the work of a young man, but like that of one of years of experience. It may safely be set down as one of the finest achievements of the present day, a work which opens up a rich and brilliant future for Mr. Parker, and which does honor to the United States.

The performance suffered from the inadequate size of the chorus. The work was sung smoothly, but it ought to be given by a chorus of 300 or 400 voices to get full justice. The solo singers were Mrs. Theodore J. Toedt, soprano; Miss Ruth Thompson, contralto; S. Fischer Miller, tenor, and Ericson[?] Bushnell, bass. Mr. Parker conducted the performance.

"Amusements," New York *Times*, 4 May 1893, 12.

THEODORE THOMAS
MUSICAL POSSIBILITIES IN AMERICA (1881)

The classical music scene in the United States was drastically altered in the late nineteenth century by the work of the German-born THEODORE THOMAS (1835-1905), who immigrated to this country when he was ten. He began his career as a violinist, traveling throughout the South for a year playing solo programs in taverns and saloons, before returning to New York, where he played in theatre orchestras. His leadership abilities and musical talents soon led to engagements to play as a soloist and in chamber music, and eventually he took up conducting. In 1862 he formed the Theodore Thomas Orchestra, and for nearly thirty years it appeared on tour throughout the United States and at home in New York, as the premiere symphonic ensemble in this country. Thomas almost single handedly forged a high standard of orchestral playing, at the same time tirelessly building audiences for serious music from coast to coast. In 1891 he moved to Chicago, where he was engaged by prominent businessmen to form and conduct the Chicago Symphony, and it was there that he also realized his life-long dream of erecting a building designed solely for the performance of orchestral music, the Theodore Thomas Orchestra Hall.

Thomas was also a strong advocate of good choral singing throughout his career, and established and conducted choirs in Cincinnati (where he began the series of spring concert series known now as the May Festival) and in New York and Brooklyn, in association with both Philharmonic orchestras, which he conducted in addition to his own ensemble. The following essay (slightly shortened from the original for Scribner's Magazine) *presents Thomas's thoughts on choral singing, its contemporary state of practice in this country, and his enthusiastic hopes for the future of music in America.*

The Americans are certainly a music-loving people. They are peculiarly susceptible to the sensuous charm of tone, they are enthusiastic and learn easily, and with the growth in general culture of recent years, there has sprung up a desire for something serious in its purpose in music, as in the other arts. The voices of the women although inclined to be sharp and nasal in speaking, are good in singing. Their small volume reveals the lack of proper training, but they are good in quality, extended in compass, and brilliant in color. The larger number are sopranos, but there are many altos, and there would be more and they would be better were it not for ruinous attempts to make sopranos of them. The men's voices do not compare favorable with those of the women. They lack strength and character, and a well-balanced chorus is hardly possible as yet without a mixture of English or German voices to give body to the tone. Of late years, probably because of the growing attention to physical training, there has been a marked improvement, and many good and beautiful voices have been developed, chiefly barytones [*sic*] or high basses. The incessant pressure of work which every American feels, prevents the men from paying much attention to music, but as the country advances in age and begins to acquire some of the repose which age brings, there will come possibilities of development which cannot now be estimated.

In considering, therefore, the present condition of musical development in this country, I am led naturally to speak first of vocal music. Although the contrary has been asserted, I think it is in the vocal direction, and not in the instrumental, that the present development of the art tends. We have no public instrumental performers of American birth who can rank with our singers in public estimation, nor is there at present more than a very limited demand for instrumentalists. New York is the only city in the country in which an orchestral player can make a living, and even here he must give lessons or play at balls and parties, thereby losing or injuring the finer qualities of an orchestral player. Boston, in spite of many efforts, cannot support a large, well-balanced orchestra. Philadelphia has no standing orchestra, and in Cincinnati and Chicago the orchestral musician must eke out a living by playing in beer-gardens and saloons. The only demand for piano players, except of the highest order, is as teachers, and of those we have many and good ones, who do what may be called missionary work. Singing, on the other hand, appeals to almost every one, and there is a certain demand, even if limited, for singers in the churches.

When we consider that music is taught in the public schools throughout the country, we might expect some evidence or result of this teaching among the people. Much money is spent in our schools for instruction in this branch, and what does it amount to? Many of the children learn like parrots, and soon forget the little which they have learned. Those who retain this knowledge find it a drawback when wishing to go in the study of music. The fault is not in them, but in the system taught. So faulty is that system that it would be better to abolish singing entirely from the schools than to retain it under the present method. It does more harm than good. I consider the system at present followed in this elementary instruction, called the "moveable *do* system," fundamentally wrong, and experience has confirmed me in this opinion. It is a make-shift, invented by amateurs. Pupils should learn something about absolute pitch of tones, instead of merely their relative pitch. The "moveable *do* system" shuts the door against this knowledge. The first tone of the scale in every key is *do*, and that term *do* never suggests to one who has thus studied music any fixed, absolute conception of pitch; for example, *do* is sometimes C and sometimes D, while to the musician C and D are as distinct sounds as the vowels a and e. The system will enable a pupil to sing a simple hymn tune which has no accidental sharps or flats, but it is wrong thus to limit pupils to so restricted a capacity. In my experience, those who have learned to read music according to this method never free themselves altogether from it. It should be considered as necessary to be thorough in the study of music as in that of mathematics. I do not say that it should be carried to the same extent, but that, so far as it is carried, it should be taught understandingly and well — taught so as to pave the way for future study, when desirable, and not so as to block it up. I attach a great deal of importance to this matter of correct musical instruction. If we start right in the schools, the public taste will soon advance to a higher standard. It is from the young that the church choirs and singing societies must be recruited, and if a correct foundation is laid when the rudiments are learned, the progress to a more advanced position is natural and easy.

While singing under proper direction is a healthy exercise, great injury can be done to the throat and vocal organs by allowing the children to sing, or rather scream, at the top of their voices. Most of the school singing which I have heard in this country is screaming, not singing, while in

England and Germany I heard nothing of the kind. On the principle that no person can teach another what he cannot do himself (a principle which I believe in to a great extent), I hold to the opinion that the teachers of singing should themselves be singers, with a good method. Singing ought also to be taught without the aid of an instrument, unless it be occasionally to support the pitch.

At present, the musical standard of the American public, taken as a whole, must be pronounced a low one. If we should judge of what has been done in music by the programmes of concerts given in the larger cities, we might rightly claim for this country a high rank in cultivation. Those concerts, however, appeal not to the general public, but to one class only, and that a limited one, as any one who observes the audiences can easily see. This class is growing in numbers as well as in cultivation, but it is still far too small to support more than a limited number of concerts, as at present those of the New York and Brooklyn Philharmonic societies. The general public does not advance in music, partly from want of opportunity, partly from the habits of the people. The average American is so entirely absorbed in his work that when he goes out in the evening he looks for relaxation in some kind of amusement which makes little or no demand upon his intellect, and he has no difficulty in finding it.

As regards general musical culture, the public may be divided into two classes — those who go to the theatres, and those for whom the church is the social centre. In both church and theatre, the standard of music is a low one. In the church, where first of all sincerity should prevail, and where nothing but healthy food should be given, the music is looked upon as an attraction and given as an amusement. It is largely operatic, it appeals to the senses only, and is too often of the sickly sentimental order. In those churches only which have congregational singing is the sense of what is suitable and decorous not offended. In this criticism I do not include some of the Roman Catholic churches. The priest estimates at its full value the power of music over the masses, and cooperates with the organist to produce a good musical service. Why cannot this be done in the Protestant churches? Pleasing music need not be trifling or sentimental; there are many beautiful works, not suited for the concert-room, which are intended for devotional use. But the greater part of the church music is a sort of patchwork — a little piece from this composer and another piece from that, put together by an amateur. A higher aim ought to be set, if not in the first place because of the art itself (though why this is not a praiseworthy purpose I do not see), at least for the sake of truth and propriety. The most exalted and artistic church service is the most proper one. The music that will inspire those feelings which ought to fill the soul of every worshipper is noble, good music — not sentimental, not secular, but lofty and devotional. That this low standard of church music exists is not owing to the want of competent organists, for we have many of ability, but rather to the fact that they are hampered in their attempts to introduce better music by the solo singers, as well as by the want of interest on the part of the minister, and, in many cases, by the desire of the business committee to "draw" and please the congregation. Recent years have also given us composers of undoubted merit ....

I have mentioned thus hastily some of the defects of our methods of musical instruction, and pointed out some of the obstacles to our advancement to a higher musical standard. What are the remedies? I was once asked by a gentleman what he ought to do to make his children musical. He perhaps expected me to advise him to send the girls to Italy to study vocalization, and to set the boys to practising the violin so many hours a day and studying harmony. I told him to form for them a singing class under the care of a good teacher, that they might learn to use their vocal organs, to form a good tone, and to read music; after they became old enough, to let them join a choral society, where, for two hours once a week, they could assist in singing good music; and, above all, to afford them every opportunity of hearing good music of every kind. This gentleman knew nothing of music, but thought the advice "sounded like common sense."

If we arrived at that point where it is considered necessary to give music a place in the common-school education, it is time that something like organized work should be done for the general cultivation of taste. The formation of singing societies would reach the people, and the knowledge which the children are supposed to gain in the schools would be sufficient for participation in such societies. So far as the singers themselves are concerned, everybody who has ever sung in a chorus knows that nothing so awakens an interest in music as helping to make it. The sympathies of hundreds are enlisted through their personal relations with the singers, and gradually a correct taste is formed and developed. If the proper means be put in use, and those who are willing to do something for music will organize for work with a purpose in it, such is the power of music that the growth will be steady until the general state is one of worth and dignity. In European countries, while the highest mark attained by the advanced class is no higher than here, the love for and understanding of music is more widely diffused. The Philharmonic concerts do not appeal to the general public; they are for this advanced class, and are well supported. But this class does not grow in numbers as rapidly as it ought. The steps by which the people can be led up to the plane of these concerts are lacking. They were once partly supplied by the Central Park garden concerts, which were managed in a way that gave no offence to the social ideas of the people, and hence had their support. It is of great importance at present to give the people the right kind of food. Their taste has been awakened and they are willing to be led. The way in which music is often taught is an insult to any person of common intellect. The intelligence is not appealed to, but the pupil is treated like a child, and often remains, musically speaking, a child his life long.

The value of a visit to Europe, at the proper time, is of course great for those studying music; but pupils should not be sent there for technical instruction, but for the knowledge of other schools and methods — in short, for the experience. A great many singers are sent to Italy; and what results have we? If they devote themselves to vocalization and really learn to vocalize — and many do not — they come back without a repertory of practical value. They display their acquirements in some show pieces of operatic airs to which they have given all their attention, and for which there is no demand. Many singers are excluded from opportunities of appearing in good concerts, because they have no pieces in keeping with the character of the programmes. Why send them so far to acquire that which is of no use to them? What a waste of money and, more serious still, what a dreadful ruin of moral character often results! No teacher in a foreign country can rightly understand how to prepare pupils for practical work here. Though the taste for singing was awakened by Italian opera, and though the Italian method of using the voice commends itself to us, the educated American is not satisfied with the Italian repertory, and soon outgrows it. I am satisfied that we shall never have a standard opera, that will take hold of the people, until we educate our own singers for the stage, and choose our repertory from the best Italian, French, and German works ....

It will be seen, therefore, that we have in this country the possibilities of a great musical future. We have the natural taste of the people for music, their strong desire to have only the best, and their readiness to recognize what is the best when it is presented to them. We have exceptional natural resources for the making of musical instruments. Nature has done her part of the work generously; it remains for us to do ours.

Theodore Thomas. "Musical Possibilities in America." *Scribner's Magazine* (March 1881); reprinted in *Theodore Thomas: A Musical Autobiography*, ed. George P. Upton, Vol. 1. Chicago: A.C. McClurg and Co., 1905, 265-75. (Excerpted)

GEORGE WHITEFIELD CHADWICK
A PLEA FOR CHORAL SINGING (1913)

GEORGE CHADWICK (1854-1931) was one of a number of composers during the latter portion of the nineteenth century known collectively as the Boston Classicists or the Second New England School.

Chadwick settled in Boston after studying in Germany and France and for most of his career was associated with the New England Conservatory of Music. He began to release the hold that the German conservative style had on American music, incorporating in his own music elements of French Impressionism as well as suggestions of American Indian music. His style was intellectual and sophisticated, with a tendency to favor dramatically-inspired themes in his overtures and symphonic poems. He also wrote several important choral works and three operas. The lecture below was given by Chadwick in 1913 to the American Academy of Arts and Letters and the National Institute of Arts and Letters at their annual meeting in Chicago. In it, Chadwick pleads not only the cause of choral music, but also the cause of music for the common man.

About the year 1836, a musical society was organized in the little town of Boscawen, N.H. The town records state that it had a membership of singers, and of players on the flute, clarinet, bugle, violin, and bass viol, and that it was in existence for more than forty years. This society was the successor of an earlier one which was organized before the beginning of the eighteenth century, called the Martin Luther Society, of which Daniel Webster and his brother Ezekiel were members, and to which they contributed a bass viol and a bassoon.

Such musical activities were not exceptional or peculiar to that little town; on the contrary they were typical of the interest in music all over rural New England, for in those days every village had its church and every church its choir, and in that church and choir the social as well as the religious interests of the place were largely concentrated. There were very few organs in the churches, so they brought their bass viols, large and small, and sometimes their clarinets and flute. To this day these old instruments, mostly of American manufacture, are to be found in the garrets of old New England houses.

This musical interest was not confined to the rural districts; it invaded the towns and cities, and from these choirs was eventually developed the Musical Convention, a kind of periodical singing-school, of which the Worcester Festival, in Massachusetts, is a direct descendant. Also, great choral societies were formed, like the Handel and Haydn Society of Boston, which has been one of the most powerful factors in the creation and preservation of musical taste in that city. Besides this, some of these country players of the viol, the bugle, and the clarinet strayed into Harvard College (it was easier then than at present), and, to the consternation of the Faculty, formed a Musical Club called the Pierian Sodality. From that small and much disparaged association descended in the third generation, through the generosity and public spirit of one who had himself quaffed the Pierian spring, the Boston Symphony Orchestra. For the Harvard Musical Association sprang from the Pierian Sodality, and through its efforts orchestral music was nurtured and kept alive in Boston amid a period of storm and stress until the Symphony Orchestra was organized; and largely owing to the influence of the Harvard Musical Association, the chair of music at Harvard University was established. Such was musical New England in the early part of the last century.

And how is it now? In the country, beyond the reach of the trolley, a musical desert, a barren waste broken only by the occasional squeak of a wheezy cabinet organ drooling out a ragtime gospel hymn, or a vulgar scrap of vaudeville music issuing from the strident horn of a talking-machine. The village blacksmith no longer rejoices to hear his daughter's voice singing in the choir. He listens to a paid — and usually overpaid — quartet choir simpering and snickering behind their curtain and to an organist who regales the congregation with selections from the operas, or thinly disguised imitations of them. And in the cities, grand opera, so-called musical comedy, symphony concerts, chamber concerts, artists' recitals, great schools of music, pianolas and talking-machines — everything to amuse and entertain the public, but not much which includes it in active musical life. All these things are very well, very amusing, sometimes even educating; but they can never take the place of that music which is made in the home and by the family,— made by the people, for the people, and through which the people may achieve a part of that spiritual uplift which is the highest and best element of the musical art. For without the interest of the people themselves in choral singing and in home music, the support of the general public is not to be expected.

Why is Germany considered to be the most music-loving nation? Not because opera and concerts are cheap and good; that is the effect, not the cause. It is because everybody, from the Emperor down, is expected to sing, and does sing. Students sing in their corps-meetings, and soldiers on the march. Every workman in a factory belongs to his little Gesang-Verein. In Leipsic alone there are sixty or seventy of these societies. The English have the reputation of being an unmusical nation, which, in my opinion, is not at all deserved. They may be somewhat lacking in discrimination, but their appetite for music is simply omnivorous, and there is no town of a thousand inhabitants in England without its choral society. Very often it has an amateur orchestral society also. The great choral festivals of England, in Birmingham, Worcester, Gloucester, Hereford, Sheffield, and London would not be possible except for this wide-spread interest in choral singing among the people. It is their joy and delight, and they even have a musical notation of their own which is a direct result of it.

To be sure, there are many choral societies in the large cities of the United States, and in many places musical festivals are annually given, with performances of choral works of greater or less importance, at which the choral forces study during a portion of the year. These festivals are usually assisted and sometimes arranged by the symphony orchestras of large cities, which happen to be on tour. In such cases, as for example at Worcester and Cincinnati, at the University at Evanston, at the University of Michigan at Ann Arbor, and above all, at Toronto, where the unrivaled Mendelssohn choir holds an annual festival assisted by the splendid Chicago Orchestra, the results — both artistic and financial — are so decided that the struggling choral societies of larger cities may well envy them their success.

In the larger cities the choral societies, particularly those which have been longest established, are meeting with little support from the public, and with a lack of interest on the part of singers which makes it difficult for them to keep their ranks full. The young people who are trying to study singing with a teacher, but who would learn much more by singing in a chorus, usually regard their voices as too precious for that purpose, and the others would much rather play bridge-whist, or dance, or go to a moving-picture show. They dislike to bind themselves to attend rehearsals of serious music which may possibly interfere with these diversions.

And this is not altogether, as some have supposed, because our American public has lost interest in the older forms of classic choral music,— the oratorios of Handel and Mendelssohn and the great works of Bach; rather it is because our young people have not been brought up to sing, and thus have never experienced the keen delight of self expression through the singing voice and the inspiration that comes through participation in a choral performance.

But there *is* a class of our people who have discovered these pleasures, for themselves. They are the wage-earners, the artisans, the domestics, even the day-laborers, who have been organized into People's Choral Unions in several places. This movement, originally started by Mr. Frank Damrosch in New York, has spread to other cities, large and small, with excellent results to the community, both socially and artistically. These choral societies in a certain way have taken the place of the old-fashioned singing-school. The conductor is usually an enthusiast who gives his services gratis. The members pay a small sum at each rehearsal for the running expenses and the organization is self-supporting.

Beginning with elementary instruction in sight-singing and voice-production, these people are eventually trained to take part in the performance of oratorios and choral works. A large proportion of the members in large cities is of foreign birth, and they are setting a good example to our native-born citizens who are idling away their Sunday afternoons or dozing over lurid Sunday papers.

If we hope ever to become a really musical nation, this interest in choral singing must extend to all classes of society. The great choruses of England are recruited from families of the well-to-do, and even from the nobility, as well as from the working-classes. In Germany, the Gesang-Verein includes people of every station in life, banded together by their common love of music. And so it must be in this country, if we are to realize the vision of Walt Whitman, and "hear America singing."

But before this millennium can arrive there is much work to be done. The soil must be fertilized and made ready to receive this seed from which a musical nation is to grow. To do this we must begin at the very beginning. And the beginning is in the *school*; not only in the public but in the private school. For in the boy's preparatory schools, with the exception of those which have a daily church service and choir, the teaching of singing is almost wholly neglected; and one direct result of this is that college choral singing, with the exception of the glee clubs, is almost entirely confined to the football-field, or to convivial occasions.

In the public schools good work is being done and much has already been accomplished. In some of the Eastern schools works like Haydn's Creation have been performed by high-school choruses. When their students can accomplish so much it would seem money well spent for the school authorities to provide competent solo singers and an orchestral accompaniment,— but unfortunately they are not always so liberal. There is room for improvement not only in methods but in administration, and especially in the adjustment of the study of music to the rest of the curriculum of the school. Above all, the question of politics should be absolutely eliminated. The training of youthful voices should never be intrusted to unqualified persons — be they ever so useful Republicans, Democrats, or Progressives.

One thing more! The women's musical clubs have become a potent musical influence all over the country. They are ceaselessly working, studying, and organizing, and to them more than to any other one factor is due the growing appreciation of good music in this country. To them the American composer owes much, for they have insisted that he shall be heard, and respected. These clubs usually include a chorus, — necessarily of sopranos and altos only; but could the "mere men" be annexed, in a strictly ex-officio capacity of course, what glorious choral results would soon follow! No longer would choral music languish in this country. In one generation, or before, choral singing would become universal, as it is in England and Germany, to the great advantage of the community socially, morally, and vocally; for it is no longer a subject of controversy that music does exert a salutary influence. It is conceded, even by those who are oblivious of its delight and deaf to its appeal; even its therapeutic value has been demonstrated.

So, let these devoted women use all those arts of persuasion for which their sex is so justly renowned, and, even by force if necessary, bring their husbands, brothers, sons, and lovers into the musical hive; and there compel them to serve their queens loyally and faithfully in the cause of song. It would add the brightest jewel to their already glittering diadem.

George Whitefield Chadwick. "A Plea for Choral Singing." *Proceedings* of the Public Meetings of the American Academy of Arts and Letters and of The National Institute of Arts and Letters, second session, 15 November 1913, 56-59.

Part III
Music Since 1920

Manuscript page from Kirke Mechem's "Kind Miss," one of five
American Madrigals, © 1976, Carl Fischer, Inc. Used by permission of the composer.

INTRODUCTION: MUSIC SINCE 1920

*T*he great serious music (choral music included) of the nineteenth century, with its broad Germanic shoulders, gave way after World War I to a decided French influence, exemplified in the works of composers like Charles Martin Loeffler and later Virgil Thomson and others. About the same time, composers began to search out "American" influences, looking for inspiration and melodic material in the music of the former slaves, in Native American melodies, and in the popular music of the twenties and thirties, particularly jazz.

Another prominent issue, particularly in the thirties, was the idea of music for the working class, or as Daniel Gregory Mason calls it in his essay, "Music and the Plain Man." William Grant Still, the dean of African-American composers in this country, deals with the influence of his heritage in a short essay, and Ernest Bloch addresses some of the same concerns in regards to his Jewish faith in the essay on his principal choral work, "My Sacred Service."

The performance of church music continued in the twentieth century to command the attention of choral composers. One of the leading church musicians of this century, Leo Sowerby, discusses his concerns in an article taken from the pamphlet Ideals in Church Music, written for the Episcopal Church, but applicable to most other Protestant denominations. Ned Rorem, an acknowledged atheist, also contributes to this on-going discussion in his "Notes on Sacred Music."

By mid-century, American composers, like practitioners of all the arts in this country and elsewhere, had splintered into so many factions influenced by so many different elements, that easy categorization becomes difficult if not impossible. Several prominent composers from this era are represented here by lengthy interviews. William Schuman, long a force in higher education as well as in composition, gave a lengthy and fascinating interview in 1973 to readers of The Choral Journal, as did Vincent Persichetti a few months later. Similar "conversations" with Kirke Mechem *and Undine Smith Moore complete this group of composer interviews. Finally, reviews of significant works by Bernstein and Sessions, and a lecture, "Writing for the Amateur Chorus," from the master of that craft, Randall Thompson, conclude this compilation.*

DANIEL GREGORY MASON
MUSIC AND THE PLAIN MAN (1928)

DANIEL GREGORY MASON (1873-1953) was born into a family of musicians. His grandfather, Lowell, had been an important leader in the musical and educational life of Boston in the early part of the nineteenth century. Daniel's father, Henry, was a piano manufacturer, the founder of the Mason and Hamlin Piano Company. So it was not surprising that Daniel Gregory Mason took up a career in music. He studied with Paine in Harvard, then with Chadwick at the New England Conservatory and with Arthur Whiting in New York, and taught for many years as the MacDowell professor of music at Columbia University. Mason was a rather conservative composer. Among his best works are those for chamber ensembles, particularly the string quartet.

In addition to his many compositions, Mason wrote widely on music. The essay following is taken from his book The Dilemma of American Music. *In it he makes a case for the importance of making music, arguing that there is no substitute for the joy and effort of participation, especially in a choir. His rather quaint reactions to the "dangers" of relying on player pianos and other such mechanical music-makers nonetheless buttress his argument that music is best as a participatory art, not a passive one.*

I

Only observers deluded by the systematic optimism, the "hurrah-boys" attitude of so much of our American opinion, can believe that all is for the best with our music, in the best of possible worlds. It may be true, as we are so constantly reminded, that we spend more millions of dollars on music than any other nation, but the question still remains: Do we get good value for our money? In other words, is our musical life satisfactory not only to our financial pride but to our emotional and aesthetic sense? Is it wide and deep and pervasive, free of fads on the one hand and crudity on the other? Does it solace as well as divert us? The answer must be, one fears, either a negative one or a highly qualified affirmative. The lack of breadth, solidarity, pervasiveness in our music life is only too apparent to any candid observer. It does not range freely up and down through our whole society, but separates into layers, a thin froth at the top, dregs at the bottom, and, to let the metaphor have its way, very little that is either nourishing or refreshing where the beer ought to be. In other words, the "high-brows" and the "low brows" divide our music between them; the plain man has no use for it, and leaves it severely alone, much to his own loss, and to that of music. What are the reasons for this neglect, either contemptuous or bashful, of music by the plain man, and what hopeful signs are there that it may be modified?

In the widest, most general terms it may be said that in all periods it has been the amateur spirit, the personal love for music and personal effort to participate in making it, with whatever technical limitations, that has brought the plain man and music together; and that, on the other hand, it has been the professional spirit, the regard for high technical finish above aesthetic emotion, the contempt for limitations and imperfections, that have separated them. It was the love of singing among plain people that sustained Bach, it was the violin- and violoncello-playing gentlemen of the Esterhazy and other courts who inspired Hadyn's musical quartets; it was the wide diffusion of musical feeling among Austrians who themselves sang and played that made Beethoven possible. We Americans, on the other hand, live in an age and country that rank science far above art, we take the efficiency expert as our model of the god-like, we are distrustful and impatient of all limitations, all imperfections, all individual irregularities, and tirelessly seek to "standard-ise" or "organise" them out of existence. Hence, among us the life-giving amateur spirit has largely succumbed to large-scale productions under professional expert direction. The dangers of such a course, it is true, have begun to arouse our critics. Such books as "Babbitt" and "Main Street," such plays as "R.U.R.," "The World We Live In," and "The Adding Machine," have begun to show us the horrors of a world in which individualism and the amateur spirit have been crushed by machinery and the herd. Movements toward a more free, individual, and joyous creative activity have spontaneously arisen in several fields, notably in the theater. They begin to appear, somewhat uncertainly, in music.

One can easily imagine how one of the most significant of such movements, that towards more and better choral singing, both in college glee clubs and in more adult groups, might be regarded by a typical efficiency-expert. Why on earth, he might ask us pityingly, should we try to revive so primitive an instrument as the human voice, an instrument of a miserable octave or two of range, which trembles, which quavers, which most precariously even holds the pitch, in a scientific age that has given us such perfect and powerful engines as the mechanical piano, the phonograph (with megaphone attachment), and radio? We might as well exchange our high-powered cars for ox-carts, our incandescent bulbs for guttering candles. We live in an age compared with which that of Beethoven is barbarous, primitive, childish. We can produce music in quantity, accurately standard-ized, overwhelmingly sonorous, and distributable to a thousand centers at once. We can do all this, and yet we are not satisfied. We want to sing!

Yes, we want to sing; there can be no doubt about that. Although it is not long since the Harvard Glee Club, bravely pioneering under the guidance of Dr. Archibald T. Davison, showed us that college men can sing good music and sing it stirringly well, already these sounds, so novel to a generation accustomed to being serenaded only by "Bullfrogs on the Back," are being re-echoed in swelling chorus from California, Columbia, Leland Stanford, Princeton, and other colleges the country over. We have seen the extraordinary spectacle of the Harvard Glee Club making a concert tour in France, and at home joining well-known symphony orchestras in producing classic masterpieces. We have seen ten college glee clubs of thirty men each participating in intercollegiate singing competitions in Carnegie Hall, New York. We have even seen the movement spread from the colleges to the preparatory schools, so that our boys are by way of being trained from early years to participate actively in the production of good music by the oldest and most fundamental of all instruments, the voice.

Similarly, we want to play; convincing proof of that is the growth of school, settlement, and college orchestras. Pioneers like Glenn H. Woods of Oakland, California, have done wonders in developing the possibilities of instrumental music in educational institutions, both practically and theoretically. Harvard, Yale, and Columbia have long had their student orchestras, of which the Pierian Sodality at Harvard is the prototype; and now their example is being followed by most colleges, and even high schools, in large cities, and indeed by many even of the grade schools. Mrs. Satis N. Coleman, in her book, "Creative Music for Children," tells how she has set the smallest children to ensemble playing, on instruments of their own manufacture. At the same time the settlements are doing invaluable work in giving lessons on instruments to those who will be the future members of the high school and college groups. A striking instance of the educative value of all this activity may be cited from Columbia. The college Glee Club, dissatisfied with the trivial music rendered by the Mandolin Club, its associate in concert tours, separated from it by a process denominated by Dean Hawkes as "divorce without alimony." At the same time, undergraduate sentiment expressed itself clearly in favor of an orchestra of less primitive instruments than mandolins, to play better music. In all such cases, the initiative comes, to a surprising degree, from the undergraduates themselves.

Now if the efficiency expert is right in regard to the technical superiority of professional and machine-made music, what justification have we for welcoming this singing and playing of amateurs as a good omen? This is a question to be answered only by calling attention to a distinction that we have sadly neglected in America during the last twenty or thirty years. We must distinguish between our capacity as consumers, in which we want the best music that money can buy, and our activity as producers, which is primarily educative or taste-formative, in which the quality of the product is of secondary importance, but the intimateness of the process is capital. We rightly judge professional music from the point of view of the consumer; but amateur music must be judged from that of the producer. Psychological-ly, the act of doing the thing oneself, however crudely and stumblingly, gives one an insight into it that one can never get by hiring someone else to do it. To one who does not feel his own way into it, it will never become alive. Our national timidity in artistic matters, our fear of making fools of ourselves by individual activity before the herd, our superstitious reverence for great names and reputations, and above all for great prices, have cheated us out of countless humble activities that would have given us untold joy. As an Englishman once put it: "You Americans hire singers from the Metropolitan Opera House to entertain you of an evening, instead of singing, dancing, or playing, according to your talents, as we do in England, to amuse yourselves."

II

Particularly fatal to our amateur activities has been the inhuman technical superiority of the mechanical instrument, a sort of super-professional. The credit side of our account with the "musical Ford" or "horseless pianoforte," as Mr. Arthur Whiting calls it, is so easily discernible, and has been so tirelessly set forth by the writers of advertisements, that it needs no mention here. It is the debit side, particularly as it affects the amateur and his taste-forming activities, that has been neglected. Mr. Whiting, the most convincing as well as by far the most amusing devil's advocate who has presented a brief in the matter, begins by describing an average musical family, in which "Sister has a sweet touch, and Father shares, sympathetically, her struggle to round out a phrase, for although he does not know it, their combined effort is part of the emotional experience." To this humble paradise, enter a serpent in the shape of a pianola. Mr. Whiting describes it in unforgettable sentences:

> They all stand before the just-arrived mechanical player, which, being entirely self-possessed, has even more platform imperturbability than the applauded virtuoso, even a larger number of decorations on its chest from the hands of grateful sovereigns, is as well set up and as shiny, exhaling a delicate odor of the varnish of its native ware-rooms. After a few introductory sounds which have nothing to do with the music, and without relaxing the lines of its inscrutable face, the insensate artist proceeds to show its power. Its security puts all hand-playing to shame; it never hesitates, it surmounts the highest difficulties without changing a clutch. Always masterful and headlong, it can, if required, utter notes faster than the human ear can follow. Bouquets of adjectives, thrown by the excited audience towards the unperspiring, unexhausted performer,

fall unnoticed at its feet. Since that memorable first performance, poor Sister has hardly touched the keys.

In this tragical though expected and common *dénouement* — "poor Sister has scarcely touched the keys" — we have the clue to the disastrous effect, which we see all about us, of too much mechanical and professional music on musical taste. The loss of personal participation means the loss of the intimate sense of the soul of musical expression — melody. For this is substituted either some comparatively superficial interest, such as the curiosity of the habitual opera-goer or recital-enthusiast about personalities or mere brilliance of technique, or the purely sensuous enjoyment of the stimulus of crude rhythm of the "jazz-fan," or else complete indifference such as often alienates the plain man from music entirely. In other words, aesthetic sensibility, the love of beauty, which is the indispensable basis for love of the great classic music of the world, becomes paralysed or atrophied when there is no personal activity to sustain it. It may even never be awakened at all in children who hear nothing but popular music produced by whole-sale. In such unfortunates there will be either complete indifference to music, or at most a response to the crude nerve-stimulant of "jazz." Such people are the robots of a mechanized and dehumanised musical world.

Fortunately, however, music, like hope, springs eternal in the human breast. The most complete scientific mechanisation, the most admirable modern organisation, cannot wholly discourage it. It sprouts as a weed in spring from under a steam roller. Thus Father, in Mr. Whiting's sketch, "discovers, after many trials, that the brazen readiness of the mechanical genius does not attract him; that while all the notes that Sister missed are sounded with authority, yet when he anxiously pushes the button marked 'expression' something is lacking which before gave him satisfaction. He longs to hear again that bashful, hesitating sounds which once charmed him, that human touch which said something to him, although imperfectly."

It is because the college glee clubs and orchestras have, consciously or unconsciously, made a discovery akin to Father's that they are so cheerfully singing and scraping and blowing, all over the country, at this moment. They hardly expect to rival the precision of intonation of a victrola record, the note-per-minute utterance of a pianola, or the beauty of tone and perfection of phrase of the Philadelphia Orchestra or the Flonzaley Quartet.

But by actually struggling with a quartet by Haydn, let us say, they are fitting themselves to appreciate it when they hear the Flonzaleys play it far better than they could by buying any number of records of it. What is more, they are bringing the plain man back to music, back from indifference, and also back from jazz. They are changing some of the dregs in the glass into good beer. What they may eventually do to the froth is another matter, and one of fascinating interest, since the sterility of mere professionalism is as evident in this day of Schönberg, Scriabine [*sic*], and Stravinsky, as the crudity of the merely popular, and music obviously needs the plain man as sorely as he needs music. The glee clubs and college orchestras and students in the settlements, then, deserve all the support we can give them; their activities are of far more promise for our musical future than many that make much more noise in a Babbitt-ridden world. If we spent as many hundreds of dollars yearly on forming ourselves into amateur groups to produce music for the creative joy of it as we do thousands on hiring professionals and manufacturing machines to amuse us, we should become a music-enjoying and perhaps even a music-producing instead of a musically exploited people.

Daniel Gregory Mason. "Music and the Plain Man," in *The Dilemma of American Music and Other Essays*. New York: MacMillan, 1928, 28-39.

WILLIAM GRANT STILL
AN AFRO-AMERICAN COMPOSER'S POINT OF VIEW (1933)

*Long considered the dean of African-American composers, WILLIAM
GRANT STILL (1895-1978) left a large body of music, much of which
continues to receive performances today. Born in Mississippi, Still
grew up in Little Rock, Arkansas, and attended Wilberforce College
as a pre-med major. Still's stepfather was an opera lover and
encouraged the composer as a boy to study music, and eventually
Still learned to play the violin, cello, and oboe. While working with
W.C. Handy for a brief period in 1916, Still decided to take up the
study of music as a profession and subsequently enrolled in the
Oberlin Conservatory, attending before and after a stint in the U.S.
Navy during World War I. He also studied composition briefly with
Chadwick in Boston and with Edgard Varèse in New York.*

*Still made arrangements and orchestrations both for radio shows
and popular orchestras and worked for a time in Hollywood. He
also devoted time to composing serious music, and his reputation
rests on these compositions, most of which have African-American
themes. Among his best known works are the* Afro-American
Symphony *(1931) and the orchestral pieces* Ebon Chronicle, The
Colored Soldiers Who Died for Democracy, *and* The Peaceful
Land. *His important choral works include the oratorio* And They
Lynched Him on a Tree *(1940) for contralto, narrator, chorus, and
orchestra and* Song of a City *(1939). He also left a large number
of chamber works and seven operas.*

*As influential as he was, Still wrote little compared to many of
his contemporaries. The short essay below is taken from a compilation of writings by various authors collected in the book* American
Composers on American Music. *Still gives some general thoughts
on music and talks briefly about his compositional process.*

Melody, in my opinion, is the most important musical element. After melody comes harmony; then form, rhythm, and dynamics. I prefer music that suggests a program to either pure or program music in the strict sense. I find mechanically produced music valuable as a means of study; but even at its best it fails to satisfy me completely. My greatest enjoyment in a musical performance comes through seeing as well as hearing the artist.

The exotic in music is certainly desirable. But if one loses sight of the conventional in seeking for strange effects, the results are almost certain to be so extreme as to confound the faculties of the listeners. Still, composers should never confine themselves to materials already invented, and I do not believe that any one tonality is of itself more significant than another.

I am unable to understand how one can rely solely on feeling when composing. The tongue can utter the letters of the alphabet, but it is the intellect alone that makes it possible to combine them so as to form words. Likewise a fragment of a musical composition may be conceived through inspiration or feeling, but its development lies altogether within the realm of intellect.

Colored people in America have natural and deep-rooted feeling for music, for melody, harmony, and rhythm. Our music possesses exoticism without straining for strangeness. The natural practices in this music open up a new field which can be of value in larger musical works when constructed into organized form by a composer who, having the underlying feeling, develops it through his intellect.

William Grant Still. "An Afro-American Composer's Point of View," in *American Composers on American Music*, ed. Henry Cowell. Stanford, Calif.: Stanford University Press, 1933, 182-3. Reprinted with the permission of the publishers. © 1933 by the Board of Trustees of the Leland Stanford Junior University.

ERNEST BLOCH
MY SACRED SERVICE (1933)

Although born in Switzerland, where he first established himself as
a composer, ERNEST BLOCH (1880-1959) immigrated to the United
States in 1916 and is usually considered an American composer. He
crafted a large body of compositions and was an influential teacher
besides, counting among his students Frederick Jacobi, who like
Bloch demonstrated a Jewish influence in his music; Quincy Porter;
and Roger Sessions. He taught at the Mannes School of Music in
New York, the Cleveland Institute of Music (where he was director
from 1920 to 1925), and later the San Francisco Conservatory of
Music and the University of California at Berkeley.

His opera Macbeth *(1910) is considered one of his finest works,*
as are both the Israel *and the rhapsodic* America *symphonies.*
Avodath Hakodesh, a Sabbath Morning Service, more commonly
known as Sacred Service *(1934), is one of only three choral works*
that Bloch penned, but it has achieved a permanent place in
twentieth-century American choral repertoire. Scored for baritone
solo, organ, and orchestra, the Sacred Service *is a moving,*
eloquent work that transcends mere liturgical purposes. The
composer's essay below touches on the genesis of the work, his
compositional process, and his attitudes towards church and choral
music in general.

I am afraid this lecture is going to be very long, for in order to present my
work properly, I should be a good singer, a pianist (which I am not), have
an orchestra, a cantor, four voices of the chorus, all at the same time —
together with the Hebrew text, which you can see makes it difficult.

In about one and a half hours I must try to explain my conception of this
service, which has taken three years of hard work, a whole lifetime of

experience, thought, living, human sufferings, contacts with men, and the suffering all around the world which I have absorbed.

My whole work is made up of this contact with the world and its people. Had I been born on a desert island I could not have written it. It contains life with its joys, sufferings around me and within me, the plants, rocks, clouds, the birds, the animals; all of Nature have contributed to it. I have been only the humble worker, trying to do his best.

This work of mine is dear to me because it has caused me so much trouble. I shall give my conception of it to you, for as the mentality of people differ, their interpretation of it will be different. Take the word "music" for instance. It may mean merely radio, or phonograph record, the operas of Wagner, or modern music. The difference[s] of race, people and education give a different conception.

This work has been composed from the text of the Prayer Book of the Reform Synagogue of America, and while it is named the *Sacred Service*, or *Sabbath Morning Service*, it embraces the whole of humanity, rather than a creed or sect.

I have made a few slight modification[s] from the prayer text, put in certain parts that were not usually sung and ended with an English text. The work is written for baritone-cantor, mixed chorus, four voices SATB (eight singers can do it), a piano part, or organ.

I knew from the text there was a great message to be given to the world. I did not write that only first-class artists could interpret it; but, that any modest musicians, providing they could sing the notes and felt the text could carry the message. For my own pleasure I wrote it for full orchestra and chorus. For its first presentation, I would prefer a first-class orchestra, chorus and baritone, and I conducting, for the message of it I have lived and wish to deliver.

This work instead of being made up of fragments is written in five parts, which have to be played without interruption, as a unity. The text as a liturgy is very beautiful. It is a whole drama in itself, and like the mass of the Catholics it must go on without interruption. It requires fifty minutes and will be used to end the Service for the Reform Synagogue. For fifty minutes I hope it will bring to the souls, minds and hearts of the people, a little more confidence, make them a little more kind and indulgent than they were and bring them peace. I have not written to astonish the world with a spectacular achievement. I have a message to deliver — that is all.

When I was approached to write from the text, I was given the Union Prayer Book; but, I could not write this work before knowing exactly the meaning, significance, depth of each word in the Hebrew language. I made my Hebrew "communion" when I was 13; but, I was not educated religiously and my life was lived among the Gentiles. Just as a plant has to go to its roots for nourishment, I, too, had to go back to my own soil for growth. I did not know the language, and I could not put sounds in music without knowing the meaning of the words, so I was compelled to learn Hebrew.

Providence acted here, as I was to learn the Hebrew language from Cantor Reuben Rinder, who suddenly met with an accident and so I was forced to learn it by myself. Just as a lady who goes to a doctor and pays a high price for a prescription which in itself does not cure her, as she must do that job herself, so I, too, had to learn the Hebrew grammar and with what patience.

I had kept for many years a little Hebrew dictionary, from which I had to learn the letters and sometimes it took an infinite time for every word. Instead of merely translating, I had to go to the roots and imagine my feeling when I found the word *olom*, for instance, meaning the universe, space, eternity of time. When you are in the business of "moving and expressing," have imagination and go deeply into things, and find something enormous, it makes you actually suffer.

From my early youth I have asked questions of my mother, "Who is God?" "Where is God?" "Has God a shape?" To which she answered, "Yes, but God has no shape, no form. We cannot see Him just as we do not see air." She told me He was in everything, everywhere, in the stars, in the trees, within me and I would dream and wonder. You can imagine how I got along with my comrades in school!

When I received this text, it was the thing I had been waiting for my whole life, with my own ideas, conceptions and beliefs. Yet, even in its pure simplicity, the problem was hard, the thing was so clear and yet so remote and mysterious. Its deep, cosmic significance came to me.

My conception of God and religion has been put into this work. I am not a religious man, outside at least. I have been in all kinds of churches, and been moved and bored in them. I have been deeply impressed with the little synagogue of Lengnau in Switzerland. My father told me that the old people and poor would come at four or five o'clock in the morning, praying for help and guidance to bear their poverty and misfortune. My father always said that we cannot take religion from the people, as they need to hold to something.

My religion is a living religion. Oppressing humanity is not a living religion. I have prayed without words — it is something organic. I have trusted my heart and soul to an Unknown Mind. I am too small to know whether there is life after death. "Wisdom is not the meditation of death, but of life." (Spinoza)

I grow humble when I look into words. Take the word "God" when it comes in the text. God is so immense that one cannot define it. In this Jewish Service, it takes shape according to a certain Liturgy and my conception of the word "God" that had no form and shape, must take on a certain form, in spite of the limitation of my own soul and within the limitation of the Liturgy.

The whole Service is a kind of history of all of mankind, of the family life and the cosmic. In the Reform Synagogue Service there are certain fragments, like "Lift up your heads," and I was puzzled and distressed when I tried to interpret the meaning.

The first part is a Meditation, a simple Prelude, principally musical, written in tonality, and for unity I used the old modes, as musically I had to make the work compact. Music enters first the external ear, then the inner ear, the heart and finally the mind or soul. The motive is very simple.

After the Meditation, the Cantor and chorus come. With my own limitation I can not only give you a general idea of the work; but, if you can feel a little of the spirit in which it was written I will be satisfied.

The whole text is Hebrew, translated into Italian and English. I have been asked by four different organizations to conduct it in Europe, among them the Catholic, which is very gratifying, as it is a message not alone to be given to the Jews, but to humanity in general.

It contains the old Jewish message of faith and hope in life. It is a human thing. When I used the word "Israel," I thought of it in a symbolic way. I wrote from my heart, with my roots in Jewish soil, for the whole outside world. The entrance of this Jewish element is dramatic.

117

You must first imagine a Temple of Service, with good in everything that is made, and beautiful. Then comes a motif, a cosmic thing, with the force of the Universe. Then comes the Proclamation of Faith. Then a more human thing, a chorus of exaltation, then the misery of humanity, thus forming the exposition.

The second part is like the Sanctus of the Catholic Church which was originally taken from the Hebrew.

The third part is liturgic, woven around the Torah and the Laws of Moses, with its organization, discipline, symbolism. When I read, "Lift up your heads, oh ye gates and be ye lifted up ye everlasting doors and the King of Glory shall come in," I could not understand what this was about. It mystified, puzzled and worried me. I was in the Switzerland mountains at the time, the day was foggy, the fir trees drooped, the landscape was covered with sadness, I could not see the light. Suddenly a wind came up, the clouds in the sky parted and the sun was over everything. I had understood. I felt God was within me at that time in lifting up the clouds. They were simply doors painted with the varnish of communism, technocracy, the cults, sects, fetishisms of today, which we cannot understand, all our ideas in a Babel. We were in a fog, we could not see the Truth, nor understand God and Life. But, when the clouds lift from out of our mind and life, and our hearts become as a little child, then the Truth will come in as a King of Glory.

I did not imagine a God with a beard and crown; but a God of Force, Truth and Good for the happiness of humanity, speaking of Him in a fine, human way. Like a physician trying to understand the law and the truth of the body, curing so many people and yet in all humility saying: "I never cured anyone," I too grow humble before Life. Here again you must understand the accepted discipline of life, the man who will deprive himself that others might benefit.

The third part of the Service then ends with the *Exaltation*.

The fourth part says, "Then put the Law away in the Ark now that you have understood it. It must be a Living Thing, rejoicing, happiness, the exaltation of all mankind, ending with the Tree of Life and that all those who are supporters of it are happy."

The fifth part is that man has to accept the Law as unlimited. There is a[n] *Adoration*, a short Epilogue, the Cantor or Rabbi talks to you, giving a personal message, in English, Italian, Hebrew, in all languages. My difficulty here was not to regulate the rhythm, to combine the talking and singing, bringing the whole philosophical message of humanity, brotherhood, and lamentations of mankind, asking what this is all about. Then in the distance, outside of space, time, everything, you hear the chorus, as a solution of the laws of the universe and eternity, the smallness of this space, of life and death, and in what spirit you are to accept it. The work ends with a *Benediction*.

As I play and sing each part now, I will again give a sort of description. *Meditation*, the first part[,] gives motifs from which the whole thing is written, very simply. It comes in many forms. Different harmonization and then against a cosmic motif, chorus, Cantor, the chorus takes it again. It comes in a liturgical manner and again with a cosmic meaning, mysteriously. Then there is the unity of nature, the unity of man, a beautiful human element, through it all you will find the cosmic element. It is chanted in a family life. Here one feels God Himself knows how beautiful life can be made with joy inside, not through external possessions.

From the precept comes the emotional part, against the secular life, symbols of laws, of organization, which change according to the sense of the words. Then the symbol of the Rock, "my helper, shelter," is symbolic of the whole misunderstanding of the world, the lamentation of the rich because they are poor and the poor because they are; all asking for the help of God, thus, with the *Amen* ending the first part.

In the second part we are in another world, more earthly. This is the *Sanctification*, a dialogue between God and Man, the chorus discovering the law of the atom, the stars, the whole universe, the One. He. Our God. Then the crowd on earth taking up the chorus, our King, our Lord, our Liberation, then the Exaltation, and Allelujah. This is a shorter part, more compact and very different.

In the third part, Man has to put himself into a state of mind of humility and within his limitation accept the order of the whole. First, there is a *Silent Meditation* which comes in before you take your soul out and look at what it contains. Then a chorus, orchestra, the Cantor-priest with the symbols of head and door; then the chorus, "Who is this King of Glory?" and the answer, "He is the King," then the symphonic music.

After the House of Jacob is a chorus of the people, "Let us walk in the Light of the Lord." The Cantor-priest says then that Humanity is one, we are a simple children; then the exaltation, which the chorus repeats. Then the unity of mankind, the immensity of everything, the greatness of the world, everything in Heaven and earth, nothing omitted. Then follows a motif in the lydian mode, taken from the counterpoint which I studied at the Conservatory five years ago.

The fourth part — calling upon the people to praise the Lord, in the style of the French. After the *Allelujah*, the cantor-priest sings, "The Law of the Lord is perfect, the text of the Lord is truthful, the Precepts of the Lord are enduring." Then the fear of the Lord enters in the softest way, like a little wind, not as a mighty earthquake. "Thus a good Doctrine was given to you, do not forsake the precepts, the Tree of Life, the Supporter of health, for those who follow this pathway are sure of happiness."

The last part is like an Epilogue. Here is the whole realization of humanity, the love of God, when all men will recognize that they are brothers, a fellowship in spirit and united, and on that day the world shall be one. Then there is a terrible crash, as if suddenly poor, fleshy man thinks of himself, his fears — death.

I was moved by the text. When I wrote this part I was in terrible distress, hopeless, something within myself was breaking my life and heart. Then appeared a philosophy of the whole of life and death, that in the fullness of time we shall know why we are brought sorrow as well as happiness, to wait patiently and be of good courage, then surely our souls would be satisfied. Not to question, but to have faith and not judge people's actions.

Then in the enormous silence, outside of space, comes an impersonal Voice, with the Law of Eternity, that everything was and will be; that He is, He Shall Be, without beginning, without end. "He is my God, my Living Liberator." Then the motif of the third part when the man is purified of heart.

When I saw the last small violet in the field, dead, after giving everything it could, I, too, thought I was never going to finish the work. The last twenty-five measures took me two years to write. I wanted something lyrical, a joy for the people. Two years of groping in the darkness it took to deliver the message to the people, the conquering of death, life, suffering with the highest sense and in the highest proportion. "Judge not that ye be not judged." If I were a judge and had to condemn a man, I would ask his forgiveness for condemning him, as the social law has commanded me to condemn him.

Then after the orchestra and chorus give this message of faith, hope and courage, we must send people back to their routine of living, cooking, laundry and so on. Thus, the Cantor-priest gives a *Benediction*, the chorus answers, "Amen," and they leave.

Ernest Bloch, "My Sacred Service," in *Ernest Bloch: Creative Spirit, A Program Source Book*, ed. Suzanne Bloch and Irene Heskes. New York: Jewish Music Council of the National Jewish Welfare Board, 1976, 11-16.

VIRGIL THOMSON
CHORAL EFFECTIVES (1945)

VIRGIL THOMSON (1896-1991) has long been known by the moniker "Dean of American Composers." Born and raised in Kansas City, Thomson received his training at Harvard, studying with Archibald T. Davison and Edward Burlingame Hill (both pupils of Paine) and later in Paris with Nadia Boulanger (1921-22). After a brief stint teaching at Harvard, he returned to Paris to live and compose (1925-40). There he established his reputation with several notable compositions, particularly the opera Four Saints in Three Acts *(1928) to a text by his friend and mentor Gertrude Stein.*

Thomson achieved wide notice and influence when he returned to the United States and accepted an appointment as chief music critic for the New York Herald Tribune *(1940-54). He also wrote a number of best-selling books, including a collection of reviews from his years at the New York paper. The rather acerbic essay below is remarkable for its stand against the artistic merits of choral singing, more remarkable given the composer's oeuvre of about 40 choral works, some extended. His important choral music includes a two-part Mass (1934),* Seven Choruses from Medea *(1934), and the* Missa pro defunctis *(1960) for two choruses and orchestra.*

Choral music almost never sounds well in performance. Chamber music, orchestral music, even the opera can be produced efficiently and satisfactorily, given experienced workmen and enough rehearsal. That is because everybody involved knows the purpose of the enterprise, which is to produce the music in hand efficiently and satisfactorily. In choruses this purpose is only a part of the business, the other part, probably the more exigent one, being to provide musical exercise for the participants.

Amateurism, in other words, is inherent to the present setup. There are professional choruses, of course, though not many. And they perform less well, for the most part, than the amateur ones. In the instrumental field, in recital repertory, in the theatre, though there is much good amateur music making, the standards of execution that prevail are those established by professionals. And by professionals I mean exactly what is meant by professionals in any activity; I mean they receive money. But in choral singing, and this is true all over the world, the highest standards of efficiency are those set by amateurs, by societies in which the members pay for the privilege of participating.

The advantages of amateurism in the choral field are well known. Nothing is so lifeless as a professional chorus. Amateurs put passion into their work; they will rehearse indefinitely; they adore their conductor. They love the whole business. Indeed, there are few greater sources of lasting satisfaction than the practice of communal singing. It is the very richness of the experience that produces both the virtues and the defects of our great choral organizations.

The chief trouble with these is that they have no standard size. The modern world has never arrived at any agreement about what number of choral executants makes for maximum musical efficiency, for the very simple reason that in our best choral societies, all of which are amateur, the privilege of participation is recognized as of such great value, culturally and humanly, that it is not considered loyal to refuse it to anyone who can meet the technical requirements. Since these do not need, for the best execution, to be very high, all our societies tend toward hypertrophy; they get too big for efficiency. They begin small; and as long as they have only fifty or sixty members, they do beautiful work. Then they start growing, overflowing on every stage; and nothing stops that growth but the architecture of Carnegie Hall, the limits of how many can be crowded on the platform behind a symphony orchestra.

By this time they have lost their flexibility and most of the effective repertory. They look very impressive in their robes as they sit there waiting through three movements of Beethoven's Ninth Symphony just to stand up in the last and force their voices. Gone by now are the days when they could sing the great choral literature of pre-Baroque and modern times. They go through a certain amount of it, even reducing their number for an occasional work that just won't let itself be sung by 250 people. But once they have become 250 people, their chief work is serving as an adjunct to symphony orchestras. They cannot deflate. And since at that size nothing sounds well but shouting and whispering, they lose first their beauty of tone, next their variety of tone, next their diction, with which goes all rhythm and preciseness of attack, and finally their ability to sing on pitch, leaving to the orchestral musicians the responsibility of making clear to the audience the harmony of any piece. They just shout and whisper and stand there looking impressive in cassocks or gowns or in dark suits and maidenly white dresses.

These thoughts occurred to me the other evening at a concert in Carnegie Hall of the Collegiate Chorale. This excellent organization is just beginning its downward path. All it has lost so far is tonal beauty. Our next best outfit, the Westminster Choir, a semiprofessional organization made up from students of the Westminster Choir School in Princeton, has gone one step farther; it has had no diction for five years. The New York Oratorio Society, once, I am told, musically high class, has nothing left but a medium pitch average. The Harvard Glee Club, twenty-five years ago a virtuoso group in its own right, is now, so far as musical values are concerned, only an occasional tail to the Boston Symphony Orchestra's kite. The Dessoff Choirs have gone symphonic too. They have not much tone left; but their pitch, rhythm, and diction are still good.

The truth is that almost none of the great choral literature, ancient or modern, will stand blowing up. It is chamber music of personalized expression and high coloristic refinement. This applies to all liturgical music and also to the choral works of J.S. Bach, though we have become so accustomed to hearing these sung by depersonalized armies, like the Schola Cantorum and the Bach Choir of Bethlehem, Pennsylvania, that few living musicians know the brilliance and real power they can have when produced with limited effectives. The only part of great choral literature, as something over and beyond orchestral works with choral interpolations, that can stand numbers is the oratorio. Handel can be blown up both chorally and orchestrally and still sound well. It doesn't have to be, but it can. That is because it is broadly dramatic in conception. It is theater music, the theater's only first-class contribution to choral art.

If music were the only aim in choral singing, we could standardize the procedures and improve the sound of it. Unfortunately the social, the religious, the cultural purposes served are no less valuable. And so we have a whole literature of the most sensitive music in the world shouted at us by a football cheering section. There is nothing to be done about it. One cannot argue with a social custom. Nor would one wish to hamper the functioning of one so rich. But as a reviewer attending concerts regularly and listening, as George Antheil used to say, not so much *to* music as *for* it, I am more often than not, at choral ceremonies, reminded of one of the season's classical sentiments. I salute you with it, choral devotees, even as I wish that we critics might perhaps, just for Christmas, occasionally be greeted so. "God rest you merry, gentlemen! Let nothing you dismay."

Virgil Thomson "Respective Composers: Choral Effectives," in *The Art of Judging Music*, New York: Alfred A. Knopf, 1948, 133-5. © 1948 by the Estate of Virgil Thomson. Used by permission.

LEO SOWERBY
WHAT CHURCH MUSIC CAN BE (1956)

Organist, teacher, and composer, LEO SOWERBY (1895-1968) is best remembered for his church music. Written in an eclectic, though predominantly conservative mode, his music includes a large number of pieces for organ and nearly 200 choral works, most of the latter anthems or service music. He was born in Michigan, but went to college in Chicago and spent the greater part of his life there at the American Conservatory of Music, before moving in 1962 to Washington, D.C. to found the National College of Church Musicians. The thoughts he expresses in the essay below summarize his feelings about music in worship — both what is appropriate for worship and what the future holds. The essay is taken from a pamphlet entitled Ideals in Church Music *(1956), prepared for the Joint Commission on Church Music for the Protestant Episcopal Church in America.*

Certainly, a good deal of what is written today is of doubtful value; it may not live. But just as it is right and natural that the composer of today should express himself in the idiom of today, so is it right and natural that his work, if it measure up to the proper standards, should be performed today — not tomorrow — for only by trial and error will that which is most worthy be discovered. The great musical literature of the Church [in] general is the fruit of centuries of the same trial and error. The living composer cannot be true to himself if he does not express himself in terms of his own experience. If he be sincere and wise, he will be guided by tradition, without being a slave to it, and he will not despise the lessons of the past. To quote David McK. Williams, one of the outstanding American composers of church music, "The composer who 'plays safe,' and who thinks and works only in terms of his predecessors, no matter how great his craftsmanship, has no claim whatso[e]ver to creative artistry and never will have." He calls upon the modernist to be a seer, and a prophet, and says, most pertinently, that "if he were in need of authority to encourage him, other than his inner urge, he might well take as a slogan the first verse of the 98th Psalm — 'O sing unto the Lord a *new* song'." Dr. Williams further says: "The Church owes the artist her protection, understanding, and encouragement. There should never be a service of importance without the touch of today in it. There should never be a church building erected without the signature of today on its walls. There is no danger of losing the priceless inheritance of the past. The Church will always cherish and use it."

On the part of many, both of those who are churchgoers and of those who are not, except on Easter Day or for an occasional duty call made necessary by a wedding or funeral, a misconception exists as to what proper church music should be. Many people stay away from church, not only because they fear to risk a "hell-fire and damnation" sermon, but because they dread being bored by dull or lugubrious music, which too often, alas, is thought to be appropriate "sacred music." The music used in the church need not be, and should not be, dull; it need rarely be mournful, and need not frequently be slow-moving. It certainly may be joyous, brilliant on occasion, ecstatic even; it can be the perfect expression of spiritual power, majesty, and glory. It may interpret all moods that have as their basis the *dignity* requisite to all church art, which means that all that is insignificant, shoddy, and cheap, or that which has its genesis in purely worldly experience, must be excluded. The wife of my former rector, the Rev. Duncan Hodge Browne, used to say that it was a fact that very frequently the music of a service carried with it deeper religious conviction, and actually brought the worshipper into closer communion with his Maker, than did much of the theorizing vouchsafed to him from the pulpit.

Hindrances to the Development of Good Church Music

When I speak of church music, I include all the music, not least of which is that played upon the organ. How often one hears a desecration of the sanctuary by the performance of transcriptions from opera or light intermezzos in place of something truly fitting the nature of the instrument and the service that it should help to beautify. It is depressing to be obliged to record that far too many churches have installed electronic inventions, which short-sighted people, whose eyes are fixed on the money bags rather than toward the Fount of all art, have caused to be used as substitutes for the king of instruments; these electronic devices are definitely more suitable for the theatre or the beer-hall. The use of such an instrument does not represent progress in the Church, for it is too obviously an inferior substitute.

The music sung by the people — the hymns and chants — we cannot consider in a paper of this length. But mention and consider we must the music sung by the choir, and sung by it, it must be remembered, as the deputy of the people. The basic idea underlying all the music of the Church is that it is performed as an act of praise, worship, prayer, or thanksgiving directly to God. How wrong, then, is the thought that the people who come to worship must expect that they shall be entertained by the music. The choir does not sing to the people, but the people come to take part in a corporate act of worship and praise. Too frequently, people do come to church with the idea of getting rather than of giving — giving themselves to their Maker and in service to their fellow men, as an act of dedication. True, the people should understand that of which they are a part, and the service in which they join, and even the music that is sung should not be altogether of a type which they cannot comprehend. But so many people have the idea that what they hear must definitely please them! They forget that part of their reason for being in the Church is to be instructed. If, as time goes on, they are not led on to a higher appreciation and understanding of finer and greater things, music included, the Church's mission has not been fully realized, and these same people have progressed not one whit. What, then, has the music of the Church meant to them? Why, either a headache, or an entertainment, pure and simple. An entertainment cannot, surely, be the ideal of the house of God!

A few churches appear to admit that they believe in such diversions, for how else can one understand the degradation of the holy place by so-called "sacred concerts" for which opera stars are imported, as well as their operatic music. This sort of thing is not common, and it can be seen by all that those churches which maintain a high standard of music have no need to indulge in such extravaganzas.

128

Reflections on Our Repertoire of Church Music

One might ask why a choir at all? Can the people not praise God in a manner fitting and acceptable to Him, without the help of a special group of singers, paid or unpaid as the case may be, which arrogates to itself functions that should be the responsibility of the worshippers themselves? Some churches, following the old puritanical ideals, seek to do without a choir. We saw the devastating effects of the Puritans on the liturgy and music of the Church when we spoke of the Puritan ascendancy in seventeenth century England. Choirs were done away with, music was outlawed. The ancient fathers of the Church, in their great wisdom, found that the singing of the people was too imperfect a thing to offer to God, and so they determined that a specially selected group of musicians should be trained to do as perfectly as might be what the mass of the people could only do indifferently or badly, feeling rightly that only the finest and purest that could be offered was worthy to be given to the service of the Almighty. Let it be insisted that the choir is also a group of worshippers, and more than this, that they are ministers; in the early days of the Church the choristers were actually drawn from the priestly caste. Some churches have only a solo singer to do this service; the unavoidable stressing of personality in such a situation must always be repugnant to any one who believes in a liturgical service of worship and understands the function of music in that liturgy.

The literature of church music is the oldest, and perhaps the richest, literature in all the branches of music. Your attention has been called to the outstanding schools of composition which have contributed to it — the early plainsong, the unsurpassed contrapuntal music of the sixteenth century, the music of the Reformation or that inspired by it, the highly mystical music of the Russian liturgy, and the music of the nineteenth century and of our own time. How tremendously rich we are in the possession of this wealth of great music written for the church and conforming to its highest ideals of usefulness! Is all of this in general use? Certainly in some of the great city churches, but it is also certain that in many of our parishes there is no realization of even the existence of much of the music just mentioned. Let us attempt to discover the reason. In actuality, there are many reasons, but they may be boiled down to two. The first seems to be that too few church musicians have the broad background and knowledge necessary to the understanding of the entire body of music of all periods at their disposal; and further, many of them are not well enough trained in their own profession to interpret it properly. So they follow the path of least resistance by performing music that makes no demands on them or on their choristers, and which is sure to be "safe," forgetting that there is much great music that is perfectly simple to perform if only one be acquainted with it and understand its idiom. The second reason lies in the fact that many individuals in our congregations, either because of their ignorance, or their selfishness, or their desire to flaunt their own authority and importance, continually say, "Let us have the music we want to hear, the familiar hymns, the old music we loved when we were children in the Church," etc. So far as this indicates a real desire to participate, it is all to the good. One might observe, however, that such an attitude indicates a complacency and a willingness to carry on indefinitely in the old rutted ways, rather than a real desire to participate in a constructive sense. The unfortunate factor is that such people have, apparently, few ideals and no knowledge on which to base the primary principles of good taste, so far as music is concerned. This lack of ideals is our principal cause for concern as we examine the situation.

God forbid that the children of today should be brought up on the emotional stuff, in the form of hymns and anthems, that many of us were fed when we were children. One associated with a church, in whatever capacity, scarcely expects to dictate to the parson what he wants preached by him (though I cannot deny that this, too, has been known of), so why should he expect to be able to make demands on the person in charge of the music? What basis has he for believing that he has a right to obtain what amounts to a sensuous pleasure from the music he hears performed? He should expect that the choirmaster shall have as full knowledge of what is suitable and fitting to be sung as the priest will have of what shall be preached or prayed. If either the one or the other is a competent practitioner of his own profession, he should be trusted; and if either is incompetent, he should be replaced; but neither one should be dictated to by people who know nothing of the task these men have to perform.

Since 1920: Sowerby

A Minimal Program

I wish to make it clear that the situation I have just outlined does not obtain universality — not by any means! — but the abuse is so widespread that it must be stressed in very plain terms. It is heartening to know, from actual experience, that the younger generation, when left to its own devices, will have none of the pseudo-romantic music which their elders took to their hearts a generation or two ago. They accept and seem to appreciate music of greater strength and austerity, largely because they are better equipped by present-day methods of education to make it their own.

All concerned, clergy, musicians, and people, should do what they best can in ordering the service of worship for the greater glory of God. Can He be pleased, can He be cheated, with trivial, trite, or sensuous bits of music? To put it another way, can the best instincts of man, can his conscience, be satisfied with anything less than that he knows to be the highest form of artistic expression, even though he may not fully comprehend it? The true Churchman will have faith even in that which he cannot completely understand, if he but dimly sense it to be the thing which he should endeavor to know. God will be pleased with the best we have to offer (witness the Parable of the Widow's Mite!), but with nothing less than the best. He must surely expect us to give to the limit of our capacity in all things. So in the field of church music, we must ever strive to offer Him the best we have and know. By the best, I do not mean the music of one certain period, ancient or modern, or of one certain style, but the great music of all periods, that which has most fully described the longings and aspirations of all those great composers who knew that their genius and abilities were vouchsafed to them as a sacred trust by their Divine Creator and who so nobly have striven to return to Him, in praise and thanksgiving, the best that lay in them to create.

Leo Sowerby. "What Church Music Can Be," in *Ideals in Church Music*. Greenwich, Ct.,: Seabury Press, 1956, 15-21.

LEONARD BERNSTEIN
REVIEWS: Mass (1971)

Few works have entered the twentieth-century American choral repertoire as controversially as Mass, fittingly written by the sometimes controversial LEONARD BERNSTEIN (1918-1990). Conductor, composer, pianist, author, teacher, mentor — Bernstein left behind legacies of greatness across a wide spectrum of musical endeavors. His career was launched by a notable debut on the podium in 1943, when he substituted for an ailing Bruno Walter with little notice. West Side Story, *the* Kaddish *and* Jeremiah *symphonies,* Candide, *the Chichester Psalms, and many more of his numerous compositions have entered the permanent repertories of orchestras, opera companies, and choruses in this country and abroad.*

Mass *was written in 1971 for the opening ceremonies of the Kennedy Center in Washington, D.C. The eclectic, "popular" music; the unconventional text, which combines the traditional Mass text and elements of a Jewish service, with additional lyrics by Stephen Schwartz and Bernstein; and the seemingly anti-religious nature of the drama, all resulted in a nearly universal chorus of condemnation for the work. Reviewers commented that the work was stylistically too diverse, often superficial, and unworthy of a composer of Bernstein's stature. Time and distance from the premiere have modified these concerns to a point, and scholars and critics have since found much to commend, concluding that the music and text reflected the inability of people to struggle successfully with the Vietnam war, the fractured nature of society in this country during the late sixties and early seventies, and the failure of societal and religious institutions to successfully grapple with these and other modern problems.*

The following articles were written by the chief music critics of two influential East Coast newspapers, reviewing the first perfor-

mance in Washington. While the critics share some common observations, their bottom-line views contrast in significant ways.

From the Washington Post

New Theater En 'Mass'
by Richard L. Coe

"A Theater Piece for Singers, Players, and Dancers" is Leonard Bernstein's subtitle for his "Mass" and his definition of the work as "theater" is precise.

Mass is one of the new theater, less a story in the traditional sense than it is a mood and a statement. The mood is of today and the statement is of hope.

A melange of music, dance, and drama, "Mass" goes back to one of the oldest dramas of man, the sacrifice of the individual for the catharsis of all as expressed in the classic Greek works, as it was in the early Christian Church, which turned the Last Supper into a ritual which has stirred and comforted centuries of mankind, a rite into which Bernstein has poured the stresses of modern complexities.

It is a creative, even daring idea, taking the ritual from the sanctuary in which we are accustomed to viewing it and, as it were, rethinking it in terms of the medieval church which virtually restored theater as an artistic form after the Dark Ages. So numerous and allusive are the "Mass" symbols that this is one of the few recent works for theater one could see profitably again and again. To the practicing Catholic these symbols will be more evident and searing than to those unfamiliar with the mass and its meanings.

But — and here is where the word "theater" comes into play — Bernstein has seen the mass as an emotionally moved observer, using the form to express in a general sense what he personally has discovered within himself about our times.

Oliver Smith's multi-colored, starkly simple setting is a sanctuary surrounded by a city's bustle and variety. A young leader expresses the compassion of God for all his flock as the mass progresses from the Kyrie to the Gloria to the Credo to the Sanctus. He speaks, sings, that is, in terms of his people and as the climax to the ritual, the Holy Communion, is reached, the sacrifice itself, the leader, now become the Celebrant, envisions the futility, or the seeming futility, of the sacrifice. The people are not living up to the ideal. There is a roar of Old Testament anger, then dissolution and silence, silence, silence. The mass is over and will be repeated again, again, and again.

Theatrically this is as far from Bernstein's last work, "West Side Story," as that Shakespearean adaptation was from "Wonderful Town" and "On the Town." An artist has expanded his consciousness to draw present meaning from the traditions of the past.

Staged with marvelous imagination by Gordon Davidson, the Kennedy Center's complex production is magnificent. Those who've said the new center has no thoughts for creative innovation will have to eat their words for a couple of years at least. For the christening of the Opera House, Roger L. Stevens (a co-producer of "West Side Story") has stirred up the lately stagnant waters of the American musical stage.

Undoubtedly, "Mass" can be performed in simpler fashion and as a work still "in progress" can be further pointed and refined, but in giving an innovative work a definitive creation, the Kennedy Center already has enriched the American performing arts.

* * *

From the New York Times

Bernstein's New Work Reflects
His Background on Broadway
by Harold C. Schonberg

There were heated arguments about the John F. Kennedy Center for the Performing Arts even before it opened. Tonight, the big palace on the Potomac was officially inaugurated, with a performance of Leonard Bernstein's Mass in the Opera House. Because of the nature of the music, still one more element about the center will be controversial. Indeed, the arguments had started with the first public rehearsal last Sunday.

There were those who dismissed the Mass out of hand as vulgar trash, saying derisively that it was worthy of the building. There were those who were distressed about the treatment of the Catholic liturgy, especially the moment when the Cross is destroyed. There were those who said that Bernstein had put his finger exactly on what ails the Church today, and that his Mass was a relevant commentary on religious problems.

And there were those, especially among the youthful members of the audiences, who screamed and applauded and cheered and cried and said it was the most beautiful thing that they had ever heard.

The text of the Bernstein Mass follows the Catholic liturgy, from the Kyrie through to the Agnus Dei. But that is only the framework. Additional texts have been supplied by Bernstein and Stephen Schwartz. In some of the orthodox sections of the Mass, Bernstein has created a stylized, chantlike settings [*sic*], on the order of what Stravinsky did in his "Symphony of Psalms."

Elsewhere, there is a wild mélange of everything. One can hear rock, Broadway tunes that echo "West Side Story" and "Fancy Free," rags, Beatles, ballads, Copland, chorales, revival-meeting-tunes, hymns, and marching bands.

The work employs huge forces — more than 200 participants — and the list of credits reads like an honor roll of show business. Settings by Oliver Smith. Choreography by Alvin Ailey. Costumes by Frank Thompson. Lighting by Gilbert Hemsley, Jr. Produced by Roger L. Stevens.

The conductor was the talented Maurice Peress, who had been selected by Bernstein as an assistant conductor of the New York Philharmonic about 10 years ago. Mr. Peress is conductor of the Austin and Corpus Christi Symphonies, both in Texas.

In this Mass, which the composer describes as a theater piece for singers, dancers, and players, there is a story line and a set of premises. The Priest-celebrant, a Christ figure, comes from youth and eventually returns to youth. He has symbolized orthodox religion, but orthodox religion no longer works.

Orthodox religion, implies the text of the Bernstein Mass, certainly has not stopped the butchery in Vietnam. Nor has it supported the pacifistic endeavors of the Berrigan brothers: the "Dona Nobis Pacem" — "Give Us Peace" — of the Mass is a strong antiwar statement. It is at this point that the Celebrant goes mad. He breaks the Cross, despoils the altar, rids himself

135

of his vestments. (Mad scenes for men are rare. One previous attempt was Peter Maxwell Davies's "Eight Songs for a Mad King," composed a few years ago.)

What the world needs, says the Mass, along with Ludwig van Beethoven, about 150 years ago, is the brotherhood of man. To emphasize the point, there is a great laying-on of hands when choir boys descend into the audience and press the flesh of everybody in sight. "Pass it on," they whisper. The audience is suffused with peace and love.

Leonard Bernstein's Mass, almost two hours long without an intermission, is a very chic affair. It offers a sentimental response to great problems of our time. Musically, it is a stylistic phantasmagoria that uses the fashionable techniques. Amplification, for instance. Everything is amplified, as at a rock concert — the singers, the orchestra, and there also is lavish use of four-track pre-recorded tape. The result can be ear-splitting.

With this kind of score, it was, of course, impossible to gauge the acoustics of the Opera House. That will have to wait for the performance of the Ginastera opera, "Beatrix Cenci," Friday night.

The fashionable elements include orchestrations by Hershy Kay and Jonathan Tunic. The musical ideas all are Bernstein, but as is customary in Broadway musicals, other hands have helped dress them up. By far, the best sections of the Mass are the Broadway-like numbers — the jazzy, super-rhythmic sections. Bernstein at his best always has been a sophisticate, a composer of skillful lightweight music who can turn out a snappy tune or a sweet-flowing ballad. That is what has made his work on Broadway so superior. And, fortunately, about two-thirds of the Mass is gay and lighthearted.

But in his more serious music, Bernstein has tended to sound derivative. When Bernstein struggles with the infinite, he has generally been thrown for a loss, as in his "Jeremiah" or "Kaddish" symphonies. And so it is in the Mass. The serious musical content is pretentious and thin, as thin as the watery liberalism that dominates the message of the work. At the end, both music and text descend into a slick kind of bathos.

For love and the brotherhood of man will not solve our problems. Better housing, jobs for everybody, and adherence to the Bill of Rights will do a lot more. Anyway, the ones who talk loudest about universal love are generally the ones who are the greatest haters. At times the Mass is little more than fashionable kitsch. It is a pseudo-serious effort at re-thinking the Mass that basically is, I think, cheap and vulgar. It is a show-biz Mass, the work of a musician who desperately wants to be with it.

So this Mass is with it — this week. But what about next year?

Richard L Coe. "New Theater En 'Mass'," The Washington *Post*, 9 September 1971, C15. © 1971 The Washington Post. Used by Permission.

Harold C. Schonberg. "Bernstein's New Work Reflects His Background on Broadway," The New York *Times*, 9 September 1971, D1. © 1971, The New York Times Company. Used by Permission.

NED ROREM
NOTES ON SACRED MUSIC (1972)

Composer, author, and teacher NED ROREM (b. 1923) began composing songs and writing the poetry for them as a young boy growing up in Chicago. Both pastimes pointed directly toward his future, and he has come to be regarded as one of the pre-eminent American song composers. He has also written widely on music, both in the form of diaries and reminiscences, as well as compilations of short essays and other ruminations on the nature of art and music. Rorem studied with Sowerby at the American Conservatory in Chicago and later with Aaron Copland and Virgil Thomson in New York. He lived much of his early life abroad, particularly in Paris where he studied with Arthur Honegger.

Rorem's principal choral works include The Poet's Requiem *(1955),* A Whitman Cantata *(1983) for men's voices and brass, and* An American Oratorio *(1984), in addition to a large catalog of part songs and anthems. His "Notes on Sacred Music" was originally published in the* AGO Music Magazine *(January, 1973). In these remarks, Rorem discusses not only the nature of this music, but the uses to which it has been put in worship both in the past and in the present.*

I do not believe in God. I do believe in poetry, which isn't the same thing although people compare them. God explains the unexplainable and, however cruelly, he soothes. Poets reflect; they do not explain nor do they soothe. At least they don't soothe me. But the fact of them is more intelligent and thus rarer than the fact of God, and sometimes for moments they take me out of myself.

If poetry were synonymous with religion, poets in middle age would not so frequently turn toward God. Yet neither they nor God can finally stop wars, nor even change our life in smaller ways. During periods of strife when we need them most, both God and the poets disappear.

Alec Wyton, choir director of St. John the Divine writes (*Choral Music*, January 1972), "Ned Rorem is a typical example of a splendid musician who devotes some of his time to the church .... [He] is also the author of one of the more pornographic books in our bookstores today .... God is not fussy about the channels of His grace, and the truth may come from the most unexpected source, and I would rather have the music of Ned Rorem with all the integrity and greatness of it than the pious, awful platitudes of [an] Ithamar Conkey, who I am sure never broke one of the ten commandments ...."

Now, God did not give me a talent for church music, he gave me a talent for music. Nor does his voice necessarily speak through any text I've chosen to musicalize. When I write music on so-called sacred texts it is for the same reason I write music on profane texts: not to make people believe in God but to make them believe in music. Music is not a shortcut from heaven, it is an end in itself. For some, that end is hell. What I seek in the Bible is poetry, not sanctity; my best songs are on the verse of sinners.

Integrity? Ulterior motives propel me around every corner. Fortunately, fruits born of bad motives aren't always rotten. Still, some can be unpalatable.

"The Lord's Prayer" is my shame. Years ago I fell in with a publisher's proposal, that if Malotte could hit the jackpot I could hit it harder. So I set the prayer to music, it was widely distributed and publicized by the publisher, and then we awaited glory. But not only did my version not displace Malotte's, it never even made money. And that was divine retribution.

My taste in poetry surely has much to do with whatever reputation I may enjoy as a "vocal" composer. Yet commissioners of songs usually have their own favorite poets. These commissioners might concur with my taste (the handful of recitalists interested in American songs are not, as a rule, illiterate), in which case I fulfill the commission without compromise. For example, when Alice Esty and Caroline Reyer, respectively, asked that I set the poetry of Theodore Roethke and Kenneth Koch, I was delighted; the poets had both been on my own list anyway, just waiting for the right moment .... But when I agreed, as I once did, to set the verse of Mary Baker Eddy, the result was terrible. Not because her verse was bad poetry, but because it was not my kind of bad poetry.

Then why is my "Lord's Prayer" terrible, since it is good poetry? Because it is not necessarily *my* good poetry. (We can concede to the greatness of certain works which nevertheless leave us cold.) And then, I wrote the piece more for gain than from conviction. It was not the setting but the *kind* of setting which is contemptible, for it panders to a sentimental public. I've often composed, without embarrassment, for the needs of a performer, but the needs of a performer and the tastes of an audience are separate considerations. From its contrived height on the word *Glory* down to the footnote advertising an alternative version for organ, the piece drips opportunism, and to this day when congratulated on it I turn over in my grave. Not that gain and conviction can't go hand in hand. Beethoven did write the "Hammerklavier" to pay a laundry bill. But no one told him *what* to write.

Heaven forbid that I preach integrity. I am not a particularly honest person, I don't even know how to fake it. But to be a successful whore is not easy either, and to sell oneself for what one doesn't believe is to despise the buyer, and finally oneself.

Then can composers write as "good" a piece when on commission as when on their own? They will conform to specifics of dimension so long as specifics of language are left to them. They'll all tell you that hard cash and guaranteed performance are their truest inspiration.

"I do not write experimental music," said Varèse, "My experimenting is done before I write the music."

To experiment with music in the church is to fight a losing battle. If the battle could be won, the church would no longer be the church but a socio-political ground. The reason for experiment is to bring action. The church was never a scene of action but of reaction, making rules, not following them. Great classical works sprang from the quite reactionary promotion of the Gaetanis, the papal lines, the Medicis and Borgias, the Esterházys. Even today the capitalist families, the Rockefellers and Fords, are those who make of art an issue which, being a non-essential, is generally absent from more liberal parties.

Insofar as the church becomes action it dispenses with ritual. Catholics react, Quakers act. Quakers never use music and are the most socially progressive of church groups. By underplaying the motionless symbol of the trinity, Quakers emphasize the need for political movement. When they reinforce that need politically, they do so in silence.

Brought up a Quaker, meaning in silence, I needed noise. So I became a composer. As a composer I am apolitical. As a Quaker I am superpolitical. There is no halfway point. To give a church concert for war orphans is commendable, but no more intrinsically so than any other benefit that is an admixture of oil and water, like a society ball for cancer.

Belief in God once provided nourishing soil for art. To believe in God today is to be removed, to be impotent before more urgent problems. To reanimate belief by experimenting with, say, rock in church, is to underestimate both musical rock and the holy rock.

So much pop expresses extramusical concern, points of view more than points of heart. When it succeeds it succeeds autonomously; luring youth to church via rock concerts is asking them to accept a diluted version of what they can get better at home.

Bernstein's *Mass* or *J. C. Superstar* are absolutely swell, so long as they aren't sold as apocalyptic breakthroughs but as spectator sport. Their foolproof scenarios are from the same book that has provided the stuff of good theater since the medieval passion plays, and the stuff of good fiction from Saint John of the Cross through Anatole France to Gladys Schmitt. But theater and fiction the stuff remains, not revelation.

The difference between a church mass and a stage mass is that one is for participants and the other for spectators. To persuade spectators that they are in fact participants is to insult true believers, although the persuasion is itself show biz and, on its terms, legitimate. Less legitimate is the next turn of the screw: the introduction into the church of the rock mass. Now if a rock mass on stage is entertainment masquerading as revelation, introduced into the church it remains entertainment and thus retains its integrity, while the church sells itself cheap. If Bach's *B-minor Mass* in concert is more impacting as art than as revelation, is a rock mass in church more impacting as revelation than as art?

(What about the frenzy of a Baptist revival meeting? That's quite pop! It's also quite real, emerging as it does from the service. Pop is quite unreal, also quite real, emerging as it does from the service. Pop is quite unreal, being superimposed onto the service.)

Although Quakers, our parents used to send Rosemary and me to other denominational Sunday schools from time to time. That was squelched when we came home and confectioned crucifixes. Nonetheless, on holidays our family attended Catholic or High Episcopal services, "for the pageantry." One Christmas, arriving late at the Church of the Redeemer on 56th and Blackstone, father asked the usher: "What time did the show start?" "We don't refer to it as a show," was the chilly reply.

Imagine such a reply today. *The* mass may not be a show, but *Mass* sure as hell is.

Must the compulsion for originality equate invention of new languages? Aren't new accents, new pronunciations, enough? Must we be Polyglot or Babel? Is rock in church a new accent, or an old accent in a new context? Is the context so new?

A pleasure not to be underestimated is a composer's knowledge that his dalliance with King James involves no infringement of rights. Woe ye who touch the New English Bible! No living or recently dead poet, no Yeats or Plath or Auden is guarded by a tougher dog in the manger. This Bible is no longer everyman's property, and permissions are hard come by: the publishers, holding out for a killing on cassettes, make even God serve Mammon. Were this the sole source of sacred texts, a composer would stop composing for the church altogether. Technically a preacher quoting from the N.E.B. should pay a copyright fee too. Let him meanwhile expose the legal eccentricity which keeps this book out of public domain.

Music's meaning, like the language of dolphins, is not translatable into human prose. If music were translatable it would not have to exist. What we call musical messages actually come through words which have been set to music. Those words used to be of a complex poetic order and highly symbolic, being Latin.

Non-vocal music has no meaning literarily, or even physically. It cannot say happiness, or hot and cold, or death — except by association. It says

To assume a need for "message" music is to assume a need for vocal over non-vocal music. The need is not recent. Most of our century's best music has been for voice, and so has most of the worst.

Commerce, which dictates our needs now, knows we want more than a message: we want an easy message. Commerce decrees the greatest good for the greatest number, hence Jesus freaks, the bromidic English litanies of *Superstar*. The same message was always there, but in the Latin masses of Stravinsky, Britten, Penderecki, Poulenc. Today, since it is not music but music's message that is popular, that message must be in the vernacular. By definition the vernacular is not symbolic. To understand a language is, in a sense, to hear it no longer. Because we know what it is saying, we do not listen to our native tongue as to a foreign tongue.

Emerging from the cerebral into the simpleminded, rococo into barbarity, we realize that though neither genre is inherently "bad," both are decadent because they engender nothing first-rate.

Why have I, an atheist, composed so extensively for the church?

I was not composing for the church but for anyone who wanted to listen, using texts I believed in. I did not believe in them for their subject but for their quality.

That the glory of God is its chief sentiment does not qualify verse, or any Sunday School primer would be on a par with the Psalms of David.

The glory of God is expressed in, not through, the verse.

I can't prove it, but probably no composer creating for the church today believes in God. If he does, that belief does not of itself make his music persuasive, if it is persuasive.

As for the church as seat of experiment, that is to let the composer — the non-believer — dictate the rules of service.

Ned Rorem. "Notes on Sacred Music," *AGO Music Magazine* (January 1973). © 1973 by the American Guild of Organists. Reprinted by permission of The American Organist Magazine.

WILLIAM SCHUMAN

IN QUEST OF ANSWERS:
AN INTERVIEW WITH WILLIAM SCHUMAN (1973)

One of the most influential choral composers in the mid twentieth century was WILLIAM SCHUMAN (1910-1992). Long associated with both the Juilliard School of Music and Lincoln Center for the Performing Arts in New York, Schuman was a prolific composer in all genres, particularly compositions for orchestra. His body of twenty-five choral works may seem small, but a great many have been standard choral repertoire in this country since first published. Among the most popular are the Mail Order Madrigals *(1971); the* Carols of Death *(1958),* Pioneers! *(1937), and* A Free Song *(1942) all set to Whitman texts; and the oratorio* On Freedom's Ground *(1985). The interview below, first published in* The Choral Journal, *needs little introduction. It offers a fascinating portrait of Schuman discussing a wide range of topics — his work, his ideas and attitudes about music, and his life — in a thoughtful, articulate, engaging manner.*

Interview Panel:
  Frank Pooler [then Director of Choral Activities at California State University-Long Beach]
  Paul Salamunovich [then Director of Choral Activities at Loyola Marymount University]
  Michael Zearott [then Director of the 1972 Ojai Festival]
  Ray Moremen [then Chair of the Editorial Board of *The Choral Journal*; Moderator]
  Walter Rubsamen [then Chair, Department of Music, University of California-Los Angeles]

Moderator: There is an enormous "churning of the arts" and what appears to be needed is the finding of some overall pattern, a meaning that can tie the diverse activities of many musicians together so that some figure in the design or mosaic that's in the process of forming may be discovered. Should the ACDA be so presumptive as to think it should and could be the primary instrument to help channel the music energies of composers and performers into imaginative and innovative directions? If so, such artists as you can lead us. Because of your pre-eminence and experience in the music scene of America, you have gained a perspective that permits you to correlate and synthesize what is presently taking place and to give direction to the future of musical America. But first, may I read a paragraph from your letter in anticipation of this interview?

Dr. William Schuman: It's your property.

Ray: "It seems to me that our interview should probably relate most specifically to why, known primarily as a composer of symphonic music, I have composed and continue to compose choral music? What are the reasons for this? What are the problems in selecting text? You and any colleagues that you may select to join you will, I know, have many questions streaming from such a general topic. I would hope that you will have had an opportunity of looking at two of my most recent choral compositions: *Declaration Chorales* and *Mail Order Madrigals*, both within the last year. In any case, I think that a good interview depends on the preparation of the questions. It's easy to answer questions. It's harder to ask them, that's why I'm trying to push this responsibility on you."

As a prelude to the questions we are eager to ask you, would you be willing to give us a brief chronological sketch of some of the high points of your life? Hearing about these things, first hand, and bringing us up to date about yourself will be a refreshing experience. So please go ahead.

W.S.: Well you're asking me for an autobiographical statement. To answer it briefly I think I'll start with "now" rather than "I was born in." I retired from Lincoln Center at the beginning of 1969 and a year later an interviewer for the [New York] *Times* came to see me and I told him that for the first time in 35 years I was not under an institutional umbrella and he said: "How do you find it?" And I said, "I can report total sunshine," and that was the headline in the *Times*: "Schuman reports total sunshine." Well, all my professional life I've carried on very heavy administrative responsibilities. Now I am living as a composer and have been doing so for several years and I find that one of the things I'm doing increasingly is turning again to choral music — and I think I have a fairly sizeable catalog of choral music — and in the last year since I retired from Lincoln Center, since you asked me (it's always a little embarrassing to talk about one's self, but I mustn't be coy), in addition to composition I serve on a number of boards because I find that I have to have some foot in the outside world. I can't stay home 24 hours of the day and write music. My wife would go crazy and my publisher would go broke. So I have to do other things and I find great pleasure in serving on the Koussevitsky Foundation and the Naumberg Board and two of the groups I started at Lincoln Center. One in film, incidentally, because I'm a film buff and the other in chamber music about which I am equally enthusiastic; and a number of other organizations. I've been chairman of the BMI Student Composer Awards for over 20 years since it started and I still continue with that. So I have a very active outside life. I've also become very much interested in the new technology of the video cassette because I believe, even though it sounds far-fetched, I believe it's going to revolutionize one form of learning. I consider it a learning device and not a teaching device. There's a great difference and I also do not think it'll put print out of business; I don't go along with those who say that.

I want to say that while I emphasize choral music I believe deeply in the symphony orchestra, and just before I came here I was in Rochester where they did a new symphonic work of mine. I believe the symphony orchestra is here to stay and the fact that many young composers don't write for the symphony because they feel that they won't get performances is only half the truth. I think that many of the present day techniques, without evaluating them but describing them, many of them do not give the orchestral players a *line* to play. They'll give them a point here and a point there, but I think a player must feel that his instrument is being exploited and to exploit an instrument you have to give it a juicy part. So I feel that part of the problem of the symphony orchestra is that young composers are not writing, not because they don't think they have opportunities but because, in my judgment, the music that's written often is not germane to a symphony; and I want to make it clear that I'm not legislating what symphony orchestras can be. It's very different today than it was before Stravinsky and before Stravinsky it was very different from, say, Monteverdi and I have no doubt that it will continue to evolve.

Now comes a question before it's asked, "What about electronic music?" Electronic music I think can be explained very simply. Electronic music is the invention of an instrument. If a cello had never existed before, someone would have invented a cello. Someone, or many people, have now invented electronic music, electronic technologies. Now whether these technologies can be used for an artistic end remains to be seen. I think in the hands of composers of genius, undoubtedly, they can be, and the advantage, to put it in the singular, is that it can do things that human beings can't do. It can play faster, slower, lower, higher, skip; it can do all these things. Now that's the technology. That in itself is the means and has nothing to do with music any more than taking a picture. Photography is not an art in itself; it's the photographer who is an artist. Painting is not an art; it's the painter who is an artist, and the same thing is true about writing music. The mere writing of music is not an art. Anybody who has the techniques manages to write music; it's the composer who makes an art of writing music. So I'm going far afield in these remarks and I hope you don't mind that I'm doing so.

But to continue, when I left the Center I took out a folder marked Commissions Pending; all the commissions I couldn't execute over the years. I decided that instead of just writing for the big Eastern orchestras: my ninth was for Philadelphia, my eighth the Philharmonic and my seventh for the Boston and so on down the line.

I thought I would accept commissions from other sections of the country. So I accepted a commission to do some choral music for the University of Iowa [should read: Iowa State University] at Ames and began searching for a text. We'll come back to the problem of the text. My wife had given me a copy of the 1897 edition of the Sears Roebuck catalogue which fascinated me. I started reading through it and I arranged texts for my *Mail Order Madrigals* and as the music came out they are sort of vignettes with an American base. I think they sound like quite serious music, especially the fugue at the end, "Women Can Be Beautiful."

I did the *Declaration Chorale* which was commissioned by Lincoln Center for its International University Choral Festival and am now planning more choral music. My next big commission is a work in which I plan to use a solo viola. My present idea is solo viola, orchestral winds, pitched percussion and women's voices [*Concerto on Old English Rounds*]. The sound in my ear of a solo viola against women's voices is quite stunning. My next big work for 1976 — will also have chorus.

Frank: It is quite evident to me in looking at the text of the *Declaration Chorale* that you had in mind the participation of choruses from the countries in that International Festival. After you have received a commission; say from the University of Iowa [Iowa State]; quite apart from finding a text, what else do you take into consideration?

W.S.: I had extended talks with Mr. [Douglas] Pritchard [Director of Choral Activities at Iowa State], who I know has done some articles for the *Choral Journal*, and he just said, "Write anything that you want to write" and so I had no special feeling. From my view as a composer Iowa is no different to me than any other place. I would approach the commission with the same seriousness, naturally, that I would for a major orchestra. I have to tell you one, I think, amusing thing. The program on which the *Mail Order Madrigals* were first performed was perhaps the strangest ever given. It was a program of the Boston Symphony Orchestra under the direction of William Steinberg. The first half, conducted by Pritchard, consisted of a cappella music of mine, opening with the *Prelude for Voices*, followed by *Carols of Death*, then *Mail Order Madrigals*. Then Steinberg performed the Brahms *Requiem* — I think in penance for the first half. You must agree that it was a strange program. When this Boston Symphony program was broadcast I heard it in New York. There was no explanation, nothing about the first half.

No, I had no special feeling about Iowa being different. I was told that it was a good chorus; and it turned out to be a good chorus; and it would be carefully prepared. I knew they wanted a major effort and I felt a great sense of responsibility because this was the first of a series of commissions that they were planning.

So just to finish the question you asked: I was for seven or eight years at Lincoln Center, I was president of Juilliard for 17 or 18 years and I taught at Sarah Lawrence for 10. That adds up to more than I should like, but in any case that's about it.

And my early, early life was basically baseball. That was my real passion in the world.

Ray: Yes, we sense that mighty passion in your opera *The Mighty Casey* which was performed here by Jan Popper.

W.S.: Well, I have given you a biographical summary and if you have any questions to ask me that I have left out, I will be happy to fill in.

Frank: I know Doug Pritchard and his fine work very well, but I think what I was getting at was when you receive a commission from — say — an academic chorus or an academic orchestra and have not been told to "write anything you want," do you have to acquaint yourself with the technical facility of such groups?

W.S.: There are many choruses that we don't have to talk about, but in institutions of higher learning if there's a good conductor, they're always good choruses. Some may be better than others, of course. You see when I think of choral music I rarely write what you would term esoteric choral music. To me choral music is a way of reaching people in larger numbers and I have a great passion for the chorus. It goes back (and this much should be autobiographical), it goes back to my days at Sarah Lawrence College when at 25 or 26 I was a teacher there. One day the choral director was sick and so a call came from the administration to ask if there were someone in the Music Department who could conduct the chorus that afternoon, since they were giving a concert at the Scarsdale High School. Nobody else was around and I said I would love to try it and it turned out to be one of the most exciting things I have ever done. I had conducted orchestras (not well) but had never conducted a chorus though I had written a few choral pieces. I remember they were singing Mendelssohn's *Lift Thine Eyes*. I couldn't believe it, it was so exciting you know and such a beautiful piece. It was so wonderful, well prepared and the concert went very well and the administration asked me if I would take it on, and then I was astonished because I know nothing about the voice and I've always been of two opinions. I think sometimes if a choral director knows too much about the voice, he's terribly careful. I know nothing about the voice so my conducting of a chorus is always visceral. I believe in the whole visceral thing of a chorus. Just to hear a chorus sing C major; man, I'm in heaven! I mean I love the sound of a chorus. I consider the chorus a much more personal instrument than an orchestra and also the whole business of the words, e.g. that *Declaration Chorale*. I challenge anybody to find those words in Walt Whitman. It's a pure fabrication of mine. I took three words here from one page, six words from another page, and put them together to make sense for my purposes. In fact, I've done so much of the adaptation of Whitman that someone did a Master's thesis on my treatment of Whitman because I changed all his "I's" to "We's" which makes it better for choral music. Whitman is a poet of big ideas and emotions. He's not a poet of tight form. If you set a Shakespearean sonnet, which I would never have the temerity to do, you couldn't change anything, or if you set a sonnet of Edna St. Vincent Millay or most poets, you can't make changes. But Whitman is a great, grandiose thinker. He's a Singer of Democracy which, of course, has always appealed to me and I can adjust the order of his words to make them right for my purpose. I always feel that he would have approved. Now this is a very romantic notion, I realize, but I just know in my bones that he would have approved. Now if I'm wrong, he's just turned over.

Paul: I was astounded when I read the text. How could you have found anything more perfect for an International Festival?

W.S.: I didn't. To find the word "peace" in Whitman is very difficult. You have to read hundred of pages and maybe one place I found the word "peace"; so I put it in. The whole thing ends with peace. But Whitman was not one who sang of peace *per se* except by depicting the horrors of war. He sang of the glories and also of the defects of America. He has always appealed to me and I've set a great deal of Whitman and I intend to set a lot more. I believe in him because he believed in America as I do and in the sense of, "My country right or wrong," meaning, if my country is right, I want to try to keep it that way and if it's wrong, I want to try to change it.

You see the problem of text for choral music is terribly, terribly difficult. The *Prelude for Voices*, a text of Thomas Wolf, was composed many years ago when I was studying with Roy Harris. He thought the work too arty to use as a text. I never did. We didn't agree on that but I was always grateful because his comments were always wonderful and penetrating. I just think that some poets and some words hold up for you and others don't. It's a purely personal evaluation.

To answer what I'm planning, I've accepted a major commission for the bicentennial and I can't tell you what it is, for I'm not free to. My big problem is how to find the right text. This is going to be a big work for chorus and orchestra. How to find the text? This is the most difficult thing because nobody, but nobody, even Walt Whitman, can capture the spirit of America in a single work. You can't possibly do that. You can't give a history lesson and you are not going to write a chronological piece, so what I hope to do is to take certain things out of the American experience that have been meaningful to me and to try to find words from American authors, not necessarily well known authors. The sources might be newspaper articles or letters or, certainly, well-known authors. I am devoting major time to this for the next year because it will take me two years to compose the work and have it ready and at least a year to find a text. Finding the text is the most difficult thing. I spend more time finding a text than I do writing the music. I would never use a text unless I thought that music could enhance it; and that, in itself, for me, rules out great poetry, that is poetry so complete in its original form that you can't possibly enhance it by treating it in another way. So I try to find words that can be given a different emphasis, that can be given a different dimension and that's what I look for and with the Whitman, of course, I have the greatest time. No one will ever find where *The Declaration Choral[e]* words came from, not even the scholar who did the master's thesis because this was really a paste job. I read and read until I found all the words that I wanted and strung them together. So it reads as though it was written just for that occasion, to be sung by a chorus representing 16 or 18 countries.

Ray: You were speaking a moment ago about colleges. From your experience as a teacher and as one acquainted with the demands of the concert world, do you think college programs for training choral conductors valid for today's students?

W.S.: I am not in a position to answer that because I've been out of the academic world for so long I really don't know.

Ray: In hearing so much rock and roll on the radio and T.V., does the choir person have a valid image of sound suitable for classic pieces?

Paul: It has been stated that the efforts of the choral director has [*sic*] now been doubled to correct the bad qualities of tone; and that I know myself for, I believe, so vividly in a certain quality, e.g., in Renaissance there would be a head tone so to speak. The quality we get so much from the jamming music of today is a very hard sound. I find my work doubled; harder to get the tone that I like.

Mike: I notice in Mr. Schuman's works that which we would expect from a very mature composer, the meticulous voice leading which musicians can understand even in the most chromatic moments. But some of the music that is now expected to be sung, e.g., Nono and others; it requires almost perfect pitch even to come near it and so I, too, wonder if we're training singers to sing newer music? Do you think the young composers make much of an attempt one way or the other to concern themselves about such details? It would seem to me that music so complex needs to be tailored to be really performed. Do you think about these things when you write?

W.S.: Well, I'm going to answer your question but I want first to go back to the other one about the sounds. I think the sounds of popular music in whatever form have always been omni-present. If you go back to the early '30's or early '20's or whenever it was — say when Frank Sinatra was in his glory or the crooners were in their glory, there was as much difference from that world of crooners to the kind of choral music we are talking about as there is today from the world of rock and roll, with the exception, of course, that rock and roll delivers in amplified high decibels which is part of its "aesthetic." My experience is that in the classroom, if you have a good conductor there isn't any problem. A famous Greek teacher said, "My fee is X" and the student replied, "Well, I've studied before with so and so and his fee was so and so." Then the famous teacher said, "It's doubled." So if you just had virginal voices that haven't been exposed to earlier influences it's an easier problem.

Getting back to the other question, I'm unpretentious about what I would say about writing choral music. I love the sound of the chorus. I have a feeling that certain things don't work in a chorus, e.g., if you sing a minor ninth in a chorus, an open minor ninth, it simply sounds as though it's an octave out of tune. I'm sorry, I happen to believe this.

Mike: Especially with a choir with a large vibrato.

W.S.: I just believe it. I've tried it by experimentation, so I would, therefore, not do it again because I don't think it works. Now if you have lots of sounds in between; that's a different point. Similarly, you learn in elementary harmony that if you have a major chord in the first inversion you don't double the E of C major; you just don't do it. But in a chorus, a double E in the first inversion, especially in a closed octave, is a gift from Heaven and so there are certain things that are just right for a chorus. To me the problem is that people do not view the chorus or the madrigal group or the large chorus or the small chorus as separate media. But each is just as special as the string quartet or orchestra or band. Each has qualities that are germane to the special quality of the group. I spoke before about writing for the symphony orchestra; I think the same thing applies to the chorus. I think a choral work is only interesting to the participants when each line has some interest. It's not interesting to go from block harmony to block harmony. I mean, you don't need a chorus for that. It can be effective, I don't deny that, but I think you must pay attention to the line. I also pay attention to spelling. I'm very careful about spelling because, even now, if I write something for the orchestra with chorus, say in G sharp minor; I write it in A flat for the singers because it's easier to read. It's just easier and if I make inharmonic [*sic*] changes, I always put the pitch in parenthesis. I put the wrong spelling down so they see what the note is. Maybe it's because I have been a practitioner that I am not interested in getting brownie points for fancy notations. I'm interested in making the notation as clear as I can possibly make it. I'm interested in making sound. I'm interested in making an emotionally valid experience, not just for the listener but for the performer.

Mike: That is something that should concern the new generation of composers. Why is it that many contemporary composers put out badly notated manuscripts, manuscripts that take too much time for the conductor, let alone the singers, to figure out. With limited rehearsal time how can they expect a performance — a good performance by a large orchestra?

W.S.: The professionals, the real professionals, are professionals because they're perfectionists, the real ones; the others try to make some impression through being original and, of course, trying to be original is an absurdity. You're either original or you're not original. You can't make up your mind to be original, point number one. Point number two: originality has very little to do with merit. I think that in the history of music you can think of many examples of composers who were original but who really didn't impress as great and others who weren't particularly original but who made great contributions. I mean that, when you come to think about it, Bizet really wasn't that original; he was just that good. I don't think that he opened up any new paths; he was a brilliant orchestrator and a marvelous composer and I have great respect for him. On the other hand, someone like Moussorgsky was brilliantly original, and if he had also been a great technician I think his music would have greater impact. Or to bring it more to home (and this is very dangerous for me to say but I don't hesitate to say it), I'm an admirer of Ives as a great original. But in my judgment Ives will never have a truly exalted place in the history of music because technically he was an amateur. Now I know that this is an unpopular view to express. It happens to be my view. It doesn't take away from the genius of his ideas; they were glorious. Nobody thought of these things before and you know we doff our hat to Charles Ives because he was an original spirit. God bless him and music needs him. But he was not, in my judgment, a professional in terms of technical finesse. In the long run, these lacks will cause his music to diminish as its originality is no longer novel.

Is there any great composer who did not have a solid technique? I mean they speak about the gaucheries of the orchestration of Schumann; it didn't interfere with his music. I once thought for fun I would like, anonymously, to rescore the Rhenish symphony. It would be great fun; but it would sound much worse because what he did, with all its imperfections of orchestration, was to give the music the quality that it has. Part of the genius of any composer is to know what he is, and the best example of that that I can think of, is that of Chopin. He knew that he was a piano writer. He knew it! He tried a couple of forays elsewhere, but to the benefit of the world, he knew that he was a piano writer. I think a composer has to understand what kind of composer he is and part of his gift is to understand. No composer can be better than he can be. I mean he can knock himself out trying to be something else. He has two things to be: to be honest and not to try to be a faddist. If you try to be fashionable, that's the way to be out of fashion. If you are honest and write the only music you can write, and the best way you can write it, now I am sounding quite moralistic about this so I don't eschew it — if you do that, then you've done the only thing in your life as a composer that you can do. To the degree that you deviate from that — you're false.

Ray: Although your later music has characteristics of your earlier compositions, you have kept abreast of the times, and in certain respects, ahead of the times. How would you say that your mind, through experience, has changed over the last 15 years?

W.S.: I've just gotten older and it is absolutely not a conscious effort on my part at all; nature takes over. It's just that one's palate changes as one's appetite changes. I mean, I could not have written the *Carols of Death* which came in the '50's in the '30's. You change because you develop. But it's as you say, "it's all of a piece." I do not believe there's such a thing as progress in music (just to make another little speech). There is no such thing as progress. There's change. If there were progress you would have to say that Beethoven was a better composer than Pope Gregory.

Ray: Are values enhanced by change? Are they being eroded in this new era, or are they just being changed?

W.S.: Well, I think every generation worries about the erosion of values. In my experience, and I try my best to keep up with the younger composers;

I go to listen to their music. I haven't been moved by a new piece of music that I've heard in the last 10 or 15 years employing so-called avant garde techniques. But I've heard a lot of music that I respect and the composers, some of them, a handful, are wonderful. They're serious people; they're trying to do a job. They have my complete allegiance. I've worked through various institutions to support them. I support them because I love them, but I don't have to like them. I love them as a biological fact of being a composer. I love composers and I want to succeed and I work whenever and wherever I can with younger composers. I just want to make this one more point: The most terrible thing is for a man who gets older to decry the younger generation. I don't do that at all. I find the same number of gifted people now that I have always found; the same number of charlatans who were always there. People talk about the generation gap; I say, thank God there's a generation gap! Life would be terrible without one! The younger generation could not take over unless it tried to upset the values of the former generation. When I worked with Roy Harris, if you wrote a dominant seventh chord, that was the equivalent of blasphemy from the mouth of a bishop, you know.

Mike: You said, "The values change."

W.S.: I did not say that values change.

Mike: I mean to say, do you not think that there is definitely a feeling, and perhaps there hasn't been so much of this in previous music history, of people not wanting to follow a strict type of training and discipline. Certainly this trend has been observed by faculties in various schools. Older composers really feel that the younger ones are going off the deep end. Experimentation is valid; this has to happen. Thank God for it, as you say. On the other hand, why do you feel that you haven't been moved by a new work in 15 years? Is it on that basis?

W.S.: I agree with what you say because I've heard this on all sides. On the other hand, I think that in the good schools and good departments of this country composers are getting thoroughly trained. Now if they aren't trained, they're not going to succeed because there is no substitute for technique. It must be there to serve the ends of the composer.

Mike: Doesn't 15 years seem like a long period?

W.S.: Yes, but mind you, when I say that I haven't heard a piece that moved me, I would be the last to say that that was the composer's fault. I would never say he doesn't speak my language. I would always say I don't speak *his*. I should learn to speak his. In other words, I'm not indicting these pieces, I'm simply reporting my personal evaluation because I'm an honest person.

Mike: But it's not only your personal feeling about what you like, necessarily; you are speaking from the standpoint, I presume, of one who has heard a tremendous amount of music, as an expert in music. This implies more than just your own likes and dislikes.

W.S.: But it's not technique.

Mike: It's beyond that?

W.S.: For example: the piece I heard that came the closest to it was a piece of George Crumb, called *Ancient Voices* [*of Children*]. I respect him. He's a very serious man and original thinker, but the piece turns out to be exotic and I have nothing against the exotic but the exotic has one characteristic: it begins to pall. You know a drinker after a second martini will add a drip of pernod. I don't know what he does to the third and fourth but exoticism must be nourished every time, otherwise it ceases to be exotic. And so when you hear a piece (and I don't mean to characterize Crumb as purely that; I am only talking about this particular piece), I was disappointed to find that it was exotic because exotic music does not hold up. Now, you can argue why should music hold up? This is another argument. They say why should music be immortal? Is immortality a test of value? Well, I would say it's one test. I suppose you could write a piece as a great experience for once only. There's nothing wrong with that. That's like popular music; you write for this moment.

Ray: What is the mission of music?

W.S.: You've asked me a very, very difficult question and I wish you could answer it for me.

Ray: Maybe, it's the wrong question.

W.S.: No, it's a wonderful question because when you say, "What is the mission of music," I think that the mission is personally interpreted by every thinking artist. I don't think it is a mass mission. I am talking about the kind of music we're discussing and, incidentally, I think we all have to have the courage of making a differentiation between entertainment music, which is certainly valid, and the kind of music that transcends entertainment. We're talking about music that we feel engages the mind and touches the heart in a deeper, more spiritual way than popular music. But to somebody that's turned on to popular music nothing could be a higher musical experience and so it would be the height of snobbery and presumption to say that our kind of music is better. That's the reason I spoke about progress. When you say, "What is the mission?", music certainly has a mission for a man who can't make a living at it. Let us start with that: composers can't make a living at writing music. Therefore you use the word, "calling." It's a "calling" and what makes it a calling is something that I can't explain and I doubt that anybody can really explain. It's just that I've never known anyone to leave the art of music because he didn't make a living at it. He might have to drive a taxi cab or sell insurance but he doesn't leave it and success has nothing to do with it. Yet, I hesitate to ascribe to music higher motives, higher moral motives or ethical values than I do to other pursuits. After all, remember that Wagner was the favorite music of Hitler Germany and Germany was as musical a nation as existed. That didn't preclude their amoral society. I don't want to give music powers that I don't think it necessarily has. To me it is a profession. You write music because you want to write it. In my own life, I took one vow when I was a young man. I said, "You are going to be your own patron. You're not going to have to go to society women for support. You're going to be your own patron." I've always been my own patron and, therefore, I can write anything I want, and every piece of music I've written is because I wanted to write it. That to me has been of extraordinary importance. Now I have had to pay a dear price for that, but to have been my own patron was worth it. Every day of every year of every decade.

Ray: You were speaking about long-term values, I think, when you said something about spiritual significance. It was Ingmar Bergman who said that art had lost its basic drive when it was separated from worship. What is the relationship between great art and music, or religion and spirituality in context with the life and work of some of the musicians of the past?

W.S.: That's all in the history books. We all know, the augmented 4th, for example, was forbidden at one time by the edicts of religious doctrine. At one time the 3rd was even frowned upon. Yet during those periods some great art was created and so I would hesitate to say that an oppressive society, whether it be the dictates of religious sect or totalitarian dictatorship, necessarily, would affect art. It can affect it. I always come back to the individual composer.

After all, choral music is one of the great tools of religion and people of religion are terribly bright because they know how moving choral music is; and it's the same thing in the world of dance. The dancers, mostly, have no idea what's going on in the pit but if you took the pit away, you'd lose 80% of the emotional validity of the dance as far as I am concerned. I've worked with the dance. I've done a number of works: four major works for Martha Graham and one for Antony Tudor. I've worked in that field and like it, but the dancers have no idea of how much emotion comes from the music. I think, similarly, that the formal religionists often have very insufficient ideas of how much the emotional force of their service comes from the music.

Getting back to choral music; I think it is an over-simplification to say it's a people's art: the reason I find choral music so exciting for amateurs is that you can achieve the highest level of music making; you can't do it with an amateur orchestra but you can with choral music.

Paul: Going back to this idea of sound or tone, do you have a preconceived idea of the sound you would expect from a chorus? In hearing differing performances of your compositions, have you been able to accept the differing interpretations; do you view some with criticism and surprise because they were not in the framework of your imagination?

W.S.: You have to accept them because it's after the fact. But it's absolutely true what you say, because, for example, this *Declaration Chorale*; I hear a great **umh**, like that, to begin with.

Paul: Hard sound?

W.S. Not hard, but forceful with everything. It's got to be a "gutty" sound. Just as some orchestral conductors who'll round everything out, there are choral directors who will sacrifice everything for a beautiful sound and they drive me up the wall. A choral sound should no more be an abstract sound of beauty than an orchestral sound should be. A choral sound has to vary with the pieces being performed. One of the comments I liked was made by my friend, Leonard Bernstein, who said, "My orchestra should sound like the Debussy orchestra one day and the Beethoven orchestra another and the Mahler orchestra," and that's right. That's what I think a choral director has to strive for. If you do *April is in my Mistress Face*, this is a certain kind of thing; if you're doing a piece for massed choir, then that's another kind of thing. I think that too many choral conductors have only an abstract sense of beauty, of "beauty of tone" (and I put "beauty of tone" in quotes) that's false. The chorus is the instrument. The reason a chorus exists is to present the choral literature that composers have written. That's its basic reason for existing, because if it didn't have the literature, it could only sing folk songs. Since choral literature is the reason for its existence, the choir's obligation is to perform the music in a manner germane to the aesthetic and technical directions of the composer as he has recorded them in the hieroglyphics of his manuscripts and publications.

Mike: I don't think there are too many composers who have written with so many different styles throughout, yet the strength and simplicity of your writing are not obscured by artificial complexities.

W.S.: I especially appreciate your speaking of simplicity because I, also, think that the choral medium is getting too complex. I don't think such

160

developments are germane to the nature of the chorus. If you hear too many voices going on at once, you don't really hear anything except a mass effect and, technically, if it's too difficult it gets lost. I can tell you that *The Carols of Death* are considered quite difficult by choruses, especially the first one. I never found them difficult when I wrote them. I also find if the text is published, if the audience has the text, the impact is increased 50%. That's 50%, not 10, but 50%. I don't think that's necessarily true of all works but I'm a great believer in it for some. I know that not all choral conductors agree with this view. My feeling is that if the audience sees the words it can relate more immediately to the music.

But to go back to the composer vis a vis the conductor. The conductor is in charge of your music and if he is a sensitive conductor, will know the style. He'll have the means to investigate and realize the entire composition — the whole. Well, I mean that's what I would call a CONDUCTOR if I wanted to use the word in capitals; and God knows when you send out your music into the ether as a composer it's up to luck sometimes.

Conductors and composers are the two categories of musicians who are trained completely in the techniques of composition; I mean that's their training. They are the only two. The instrumentalist is trained, necessarily, in the techniques of his instrument but choral conductors, orchestral conductors and composers, these are the people who should know literature because that's been their training. The specialists tend to know only their own musical needs.

Paul: Mr. Schuman knows that Frank Pooler has made quite a reputation around this country with what I will loosely call avant-garde music — I don't know what else to call it — speech type of music in sounds. What is your opinion of such music?

W.S.: I'm all for it as I said before, because I think it extends the possibilities of the choral medium and there may be some composers who will write for it. You see to me there's no such thing as a bad kind of music. There is no such thing. I don't care what kind of music you are talking about; there are only better or poorer examples within a kind. There's no such thing as a bad category of music. I am an enemy of people who have blinders, who say music can be only this. Even if it's music I agree with,

I would disapprove of dogmatic narrowness because the exciting thing about music is that it's never ending and the avenues of expression and techniques are always open. Having said that, I emphasize what I said earlier, "Support that thesis but never be false in terms of evaluating what you hear." If you always support the effort then you are always in good shape and I think you're being a responsible citizen. I don't think you are being a responsible citizen if you say you like something that you don't like in order to be fashionable. You know Stravinsky! Someone was complaining to me the other day about Robert Craft's book, in that he put all those big words in Stravinsky's mouth. He said, "I heard Stravinsky talk and it was plain talk."

Mike: His television appearance revealed him as a man of erudition and simplicity, too.

W.S.: Well, he was. When I visited him in Hollywood the first thing he made me do was to take off my shoes to measure my height against the wall to see whether I was taller than Auden. I found him very easy; you know, I once worked for him. This story was told me by a friend at lunch a couple of weeks ago who was decrying Craft — and I'm not taking a position on that for I don't know enough about it — but he said that Stravinsky was such a simple man that when someone asked, "What do you think of Richard Strauss?" He is said to have replied: "Well, you know, fine! He's a good conductor, well trained musician; you know he has done a lot of things. I just don't like his music."

Frank: One of the things that interests me most about talking to a composer of choral music is that I want to tell him that I'm always a little intimidated when presenting his music to him for the first time, and again it has to do with notation. Now it would seem to me if you would just write a couple of sentences, like: "The hell with tonal beauty. Let's have some real conviction here; this is what I'm really concerned about," I would be able were my personal bent toward beauty of tone to combat it in this instance.

Paul: I want to get a little more specific in defense of choral conductors who are careful about sound. Being an adjudicator and festival director, I travel a great deal around the country. When I walk into a situation and am supposed to perform pieces of music that I have picked maybe a year ahead and I find out that I don't have the Steinway but a bad upright piano pulled out of the local bar. Well, before I want to perform that music I'm going to reconstruct that piano (or chorus, in this instance). I have to with all my heart. I think that when Rubenstein [*sic*] comes to Los Angeles there's a big Steinway sitting in some basement music store that's left only for him when he comes to town. He knows that piano and what it's going to sound like. He might, if they gave him another piano, refuse to perform and choral directors, in defense of them, have this same prerogative. If they are well trained they want, first of all (and their job is doubly difficult these days), to construct an instrument and then hope they can also develop versatility in the imagination of that instrument after refining the sound. I, too, am terribly frightened of performing a composer's music in front of him; in fact, at one festival I dropped the piece because the composer was the adjudicator. If I could sit with him and find out his conceptions of the sounds I would be more at ease. It is a frightening thing to perform for composers.

W.S.: I'm sorry to hear you say that. I've worked with so many conductors and I've never had problems. The reason I wouldn't want to put in too many specifics in the score, e.g., should you have a descending line, say over 20 bars, and you say, "Don't ritard"; it's rather insulting, you know. Why should you say that to the man? I have another reason. I believe very much in the interpretive artist. I think the composer should put down as much as he can in notation and in reasonable words and then — one of the interesting things is that there is such a thing as the interpretative artist — there's not just one way of doing a piece even being faithful!

Paul: This is the question I was trying to ask about 15 minutes ago. When have you ever gone into a presentation of one of your pieces, and although finding it somewhat different, soundwise, from your conception and imagination, yet have found it acceptable?

W.S. I've done more than that. I've often changed notation to make an improvement.

163

Ray: I am particularly pleased to hear you remark that there's not one way of doing a piece. Robert Commanday, in a recent article about Furtwaengler said: "No two interpretations of the same work are alike. This is the clue to the character that made his performances such vivid, immediate experiences." Is this not one of the marks of a masterwork: one that cannot be fully comprehended by any single individual in any one performance? Isn't the reason we come back to it, time after time, to discover some new dimension? The plays of Shakespeare are masterworks, precisely, because their riches seem never to become static or exhausted.

Mike: It seems to me that we know very few composer-conductor combinations where the composer has been really able to put an absolute definitive version, even in the case of a pianist like Rachmaninoff. Well, the only one I can think of, right off hand, is Stravinsky. A lot of people still think his own conducting of his pieces is in some ways definitive. It was so funny to read his own comments about the recordings of Boulez and of Leonard Bernstein (I believe) where he said: "Don't worry; you know at that bar, maybe, it should be a little faster." I mean, after all, it's a special feeling; that's the whole feeling, is it not?

W.S.: The thing to me is, conductors bring an interpretation to a piece of music. They must. No matter what you put down. If you put down the descriptive sentences you've suggested, to me, you are denying the whole idea of an interpretative artist. Being faithful to the text still gives an enormous latitude. I just had a new work done last Friday, a big orchestral work that I did for the 50th anniversary of the Eastman School and I made some changes because of the rehearsal, some things that I heard that I liked very much but didn't have in the score, and I discussed them with the conductor afterwards and this is not infrequent. These are editorial changes. When I was a kid, you know, I was so cocky I published the *Symphony for Strings*; I just published it before I ever heard it. It's not because I'm more conservative, but the older I get the more I like to hear and see what a couple of conductors do with my scores before publishing them. I think this is absolutely right that the conductor has an enormous role within the purview of the given text. Bartok liked my 3rd Symphony very much and he wanted to discuss it with me. He said he had one criticism and I said,

"What is it, Maestro?" And he said: "You don't give an exact metronome mark; you say circa 60'. Why don't you give an exact mark? Why do you always say circa?" And I said, "because I think of the tempo in that general area." I said, "but I can't be exact. I'll sing the music several times differently, so I want to indicate to the conductor the general area and also (and he didn't agree with this) a good conductor makes all sorts of tempo changes within a performance of the piece that are really not tempo changes. You can't write this into the score."

Frank: You indicated a little earlier that you were fairly well acquainted with some of the newer "new notation" choral works. Are you acquainted, specifically, with any of them?

W.S.: I've seen some but I can't say that I have any real knowledge of them. One of the things that I've been doing since I left Lincoln Center is trying to catch up on all this, and one of the points I made earlier is that I do think, by virtue of the date of your birth, you have a certain body of music that you relate to. I'm 62 years old, so *Mathis der Mahler* was a new work to me because I was around in 1932 or '33, or whenever it was introduced in New York, when I was a very young composer. So it has to do with the music you grow up with and it will be the same for all young people who today are interested in avant garde music.

Ray: You've established your trademark and it's strong and original, too; but music, in the nature of itself, has to move. For example, I witnessed a spectacular performance by a pianist who invited themes from the audience, then proceeded to improvise in the style of Handel, Scarlatti, Bach, and whoever. Brilliant and enjoyable as it was, it was a heritage imitation. If imitation cannot be taken seriously, what course is open to the contemporary composer other than that of the avant garde? Are we at the end of the road, musically, or will new people, new personalities open up a glorious future?

W.S.: Well, my impression is that it's never been a better time. My impression of the new effort is that it's opening up all sorts of things, more so in recent years and I'm very optimistic. I think the composer is always going to be on the scene and presenting new ways of doing things. The new movements to me, whether I respond or not, I'm not blinded to the fact that they're opening up all sorts of horizons. I'm very optimistic about this period.

Ray: But we need a synthesis ...

W.S.: I know that you use that word frequently and I know that everybody says that Bach was a great synthesizer, and so forth and so on. But I never feel that way. I just feel that composers of genius come along rarely but every decade or so, or two decades, and they help point the way and people spring from that. After all, in my time all the young went to Aaron Copland. They no longer go to Aaron Copland, which I think is their loss, but they will go to others who have techniques that are more of today; and that's the way it should be. The other would be hopeless, you know, really, the other would be "sticking to daddy" and that's no good. What we have here and now is very healthy and, incidentally, quite predictable and traditional.

Mike: But are we up to the point of training people to play and sing this music? Nobody writes anything easy anymore. It's getting too far ahead of us. Should there not be more specific classes in the new techniques?

W.S.: A lot of this has to do with, I think, ineptness of notation. I'm all for the need of new kinds of notations that you speak of and the increased study; obviously, there's a need there but when it comes to conventional metric notation so many things can be stated in 3/4 and 4/4.

Mike: They did a work of George Crumb here. Well, it has circles and it's very beautiful to look at. It would make magnificent wall papery (not to be facetious) but it is full of the most incredible things that a conductor must figure out and say: "Oh, that's what he means."

W.S.: Well, maybe he couldn't find another way of saying it ... I don't know. The only other point I want to make is if I have any criticism — and this is not in the choral field because it doesn't apply to the choral field to my knowledge — but it applies to symphony orchestras, major symphony orchestras. There's a whole repertoire (now I don't speak personally, because my music is performed) but I am speaking for others whose music is not performed. There's a whole existing repertoire that has grown up in the '30's, '40's, and '50's and '60's that is ignored; and this is ridiculous because these pieces are repertory pieces, pieces that would make it easier for the avant garde pieces. One of the problems is that when Elliot Carter, for example, was first played in New York, the audience was bewildered. Had they been played liberal doses of all the new music that was acceptable then I think they would have been better prepared. The orchestras should exploit standard modern pieces of Americans.

Ray: Is the general public indifferent to artistic values and will music of serious or difficult nature, of necessity, be limited to an elite few?

W.S.: Well, naturally, no one can answer that question. This country, I guess, is the prime example where the attempt is made to make music available on a democratic basis. I think, sometimes, democracy is misunderstood because to me democracy in music doesn't mean reaching the least common denominator. It means making music available to all without lowering standards and, obviously, if you look at statistics you know that music has barely held its own. It's only held its own in numbers because of the population growth and you know all of us believe in it so much we think it has to be for everybody. But it doesn't. It doesn't have to be for everybody.

Ray: Then we aren't succumbing to the least common denominator in taste?

W.S.: No, I don't think so. I think the standards remain just as high as they ever were.

Paul: An interesting point I'd like to bring in here. My first love is church music — Catholic church music — and you know from history at one time the church was the fostering and preserving patron of greatness, and now the [C]atholic churches have fallen away from this position and it's an abyss. Do you have any comments to make about this area?

167

W.S.: Well, one has to say that music in religion is used as a tool and it's used by people as a tool — not musical values qua musical values — and we may as well face it because this is what it is. There are individual ministers in the various faiths who believe in music and love music and want to have music of high content, perhaps, even if it doesn't serve but, basically, it's "gebrauchsmusik" — music to make a point. It's that way today and I think it mostly always was that way. We look back to the past. What made music so exceptional? What made the Gregorian chant? Why was there so much conjunct motion? Why was the skip so frowned upon? Because these intervals, it was believed, were secular in effect and took away from the religious element. I think music was used as a tool even then. Now you know much more about it than I do. I'm far from a specialist but this is my belief.

Mike: Let's face it. The questions that Paul raised are the questions that face all of us as musicians. You say that you feel good about the non-demise of the symphony orchestra — you feel that it's still quite viable. How can that be when we not only hear about music in the church is going down hill but that in places like Chicago, music in the schools is being given up and in Los Angeles we don't have teaching in the elementary schools? Where are we going to have audiences to keep any orchestra or any choir ...?

W.S.: Okay. What did 80 or 90 years of the MENC prove to music? Is the American public more aware of aesthetic values? I would say, "No!" Did tooting the clarinet help develop a generation of music lovers? The answer is, "No! It hasn't." I deplore the decline of it because some wonderful work was taking place and I wasn't aware of this mass decline but I felt — I've always felt — that public school music wasn't very effective. I think there is a whole new look that has to come into art's education [sic] and I also add that we don't know how to do it. And let me add that I love bands and hope their place in the schools is secure.

Mike: You don't think it will happen in the schools? Does that mean more private teaching?

W.S.: I think something can happen in the schools to develop aesthetic awareness, but it hasn't happened yet.

Mike: Well, even in high schools — aside from good choral training — one doesn't find too much emphasis on harmony and things like that. Isn't the question: "How can we develop approaches that will add to the aesthetic sensibilities of the American public through the educational system in the United States?" How can we be other than apprehensive when our students hear rock music almost continually; when the FM music stations are going out — the one FM station in this city of 10 million is dying to the point of ridiculousness? I don't know what's happening in New York but we hear that two stations that were impressive there are gone.

W.S.: Well, the answer is, you can't make any progress by wringing your hands. You have to make whatever efforts you can. For example, I've worked very hard in the field of public television and I'm a great advocate (I don't even speak of commercial television because that's self evident), but the people in public television don't trust music. They don't trust the material of music. They think it has to be visual; everything has to be a Mickey Mouse treatment. There's no music on public television that amounts to anything anymore than on commercial TV. Now I can just tell you that I'm working on it and I know a number of other people who are and I am hopeful that, eventually, something will happen, but you cannot bemoan the fact that we are in a minority pursuit and let's not kid ourselves. Now the only part of school music (aside from bands) that's still a major pursuit is choral music. If choral music goes by the boards, we're sunk, because to me the whole thing, the only avenue for good music in a mass way is choral music: high school and college choral music. Band music in the schools is fine; it's a good activity and certainly doesn't do any harm and when bands are good, they're great but it hasn't developed any great lasting thing. I happen to love the band; I write for the band. I think they're great, especially in the mid-west — I don't know about the coast — the east is mostly terrible, but the mid-west is certainly great and choral music is all over the country and if you tell me it's dying, then I'm really going to be depressed and I'm not easily depressed.

Ray: Now we're about to come to the end, but ...

W.S.: I came to the end of my knowledge two hours ago.

Ray: Oh no! But just one more question. Are there many young people throughout the country who are going to carry the torch? I recall that I was present years ago when you introduced Leonard Bernstein to a Town Hall audience. You told of his meeting you on the Harvard campus to be your student host on your visit there. You said that if anyone had told you then that this young man would be conducting the New York Philharmonic 10 years later, you wouldn't have been the least bit surprised. My question: Are there young people that come to mind today who hold this promise of unusual achievement?

W.S.: Well, I think, Michael Tilson Thomas is an obvious example and I'm sure there are others that I don't know, but I would like to conclude my part in this discussion by telling you that I got a call the other day illustrating the most wonderful nerve that Americans have that I love. I got several telephone messages from somebody who was calling from some mid-west university I never heard of, so I didn't return the call immediately. When the phone rang again I picked it up. The voice said: "My name is so and so and I have a term paper due tomorrow on your music. Do you mind if I ask you a few questions?" I said: "Well, I'm delighted you're doing a paper, I do indeed, but because I have some guests here I can't talk to you very long." He said, "Well, what will I say about American music?" And I said: "Believe in it!" And this is what I say about choral music.

Frank Pooler, et al., "In Quest of Answers: An Interview with William Schuman." *Choral Journal* 13 (February 1973), 5-15. © 1973 The American Choral Directors Association, P.O. Box 6310, Lawton, Oklahoma 73506-0310. Used by permission.

VINCENT PERSICHETTI

IN QUEST OF ANSWERS: AN INTERVIEW
WITH VINCENT PERSICHETTI by Robert E. Page (1973)

Another composer whose choral works made up a large portion of his creative output, like Rorem and Schuman, was VINCENT PERSICHETTI (1915-1987). Born in Philadelphia and educated at the Curtis Institute and the Philadelphia Conservatory, Persichetti taught for nearly forty years at the Juilliard School of Music in New York. He wrote an important biography of William Schuman, as well as an influential textbook Twentieth-Century Harmony *(1961), in addition to a lengthy catalog of music. Besides being a prolific composer of symphonies, Persichetti wrote a large number of chamber compositions, pieces for band, solo songs, and nearly twenty-five choral works. Among the most important of the latter are the* Mass *(1960), the* Spring Cantata, Te Deum, *and* Stabat Mater *(all composed in 1963); a* Winter Cantata *(1965) for women's voices; and, perhaps his most important choral work,* Celebrations *(1966) for mixed chorus and band, to poetry by Walt Whitman.*

The interview below, from the November, 1973 issue of The Choral Journal, *offers keen insight into the composer and his compositional methods, as well aspects of style in several of his more important works.*

R.P.: Can you recall the time and perhaps the initial stimulus for your considering of the vocal/choral idiom as a significant vehicle for your musical expression?

V.P.: You see, the choral idiom is my favorite — and I'm talking about violin, oboe, or what have you. The literature is the greatest literature I know: it all started with voices and drums. It was so great to me that I felt

I could never write for chorus or solo voice. I tried as a kid, but ended up throwing everything out. One of the biggest hangups for me was the text. I read a lot of poetry, and I respect these texts.

One day, while I was doing one of my visitations to a university, I happened to be in the faculty lounge where several professors of the English department were discussing an interpretation of a poem by one of the master authors — and it hit me that they (the professors) were openly disagreeing as to the exact meaning of a poem. It suddenly occurred to me that I also had just as much right to my own idea of what the poem should say, and that I had the right to express my reaction in the idiom at my disposal: musical composition.

I had always felt that I dare not touch a text; I used to think "Why bother a good poem, it's so complete already?" I had to get over that hangup, also. You know, there IS something to that concept: why touch a poem — but then I realized that poetry is, in reality, a distilled concept full of implications that you can interpret many ways. So my composition is a statement of one of the implications of the poem, as I see it.

I guess I really got into working for the voice through Wallace Stevens. My song cycle "Harmonium" is based upon a book of poetry of his by the same title. I wrote him for permission to use his poetry, and he replied that his permission was not needed — for me to go ahead. I used nineteen of his poems, and the twentieth one in the cycle was to be another poem of his called "Thirteen Ways of Looking at a Blackbird." In this poem, I found that all of the previous nineteen poems were related in one way or another. And so I did this with all the music. I wrote Stevens about this, and he replied that he did not realize this connection.

R.P.: To me, you have hit upon one of the strongest points in artistic understanding: a significant work of art will project to the observer darts of implications which the author or composer himself may not realize.

V.P. I was so taken with Stevens' texts that we planned to do an opera together, but he died before this was an actuality.

R.P.: To me, your text awareness is strongly in evidence in both the *Stabat Mater* and the *Te Deum*, which we performed here in Philadelphia. There is a real care for the framing of the texts in both of these works. And when I heard your *Creation*, I was again touched by this close marriage of text and music as well as the essential religiosity and reverence of the mood as well as the meaning of the text. Would you care to speak to this?

V.P.: Yes. You see, I believe in my fellow human being; which means, in a way, that I believe what they believe. And if you like a certain tree, or a certain girl, or what have you — I like that tree or that girl, too. I mean that I respect you, and therefore what you believe in, I am touched by, and in a sense believe in it also. I am a very religious man, but not in a formal way. In the *Creation*, for instance, I used texts from many religions and cultures — and all of them had one thing in common: an awareness and a belief in some force that is above all. As a result, I don't see that much difference in a Christian, a Jew, a Hindu or what have you. I attempt, when I work with these different ideas, to become totally involved in that thought at that time: when I am working on an Episcopal *Magnificat*, my entire being is caught up in that — that's my whole world.

R.P.: Do you find it more difficult to expand or to delimit when you come across a poem or a thought? For instance, when you say that an Episcopalian *Magnificat* at that time is your whole being, it seems to me that that is automatically a small scope and that you must expand. Contrarily, when you discuss your *Creation*, you state that your idea is really a setting of the entire world — which would imply a tremendous delimiting process.

V.P.: I'm more comfortable in delimiting, I guess: to have the whole world but to put it in a frame for that particular work. This has a great implication, then, for the shaping of musical ideas and motives. I don't like to say a little about many things — I prefer to say much about less. And I think that this is what most composers aim for — take Bach or Beethoven, for instance. Otherwise you have the most talented music ever written — one gorgeous thing after another, winding up with beautiful experiences: a whole newsreel, but with no editing. You're not really saying anything, you are merely taking random shots of the landscape of Rome, or Venice, or London. Perhaps Shakespeare did more for the little section called England than a whole newsreel would or could.

R.P.: From a practical standpoint, when you have worked with the many conductors who have performed your works, do you find it difficult to project to them an attitude about the text which you have been describing?

V.P.: With some of them, I do have difficulty. The standard of choral performance has improved tremendously in the last 20 years. In my teens, I accompanied many choruses in Philadelphia and in New York, and I worked for a variety of conductors. Many were good musicians, but they had no idea of how to deal with a chorus: the phrasing, the rhythm of the choral idiom — it was foreign to them. Somewhere along the line (I'd say in the late Forties or early Fifties), the standard of choral conducting went skyrocketing up. Now it is possible to go into almost any state and into lots of communities and find an excellent chorus and a first-rate choral conductor; whereas when I was growing up, I was lucky to find even one in three states.

R.P.: To what do you attribute that change?

V.P.: It's hard for me to say; but believe it or not, I think that it has a lot to do with the rhythm of jazz that is in our blood. It's a rhythmic thing that the choral conductors finally could not escape. I'm talking about Lassus or Palestrina — a liquid line, but it has that inner rhythm or pulse — otherwise it falls apart.

R.P.: (Note: Dorothea Persichetti [the composer's wife] had been listening to the conversation, and contributed the following observation regarding the "choral happening," as she framed it):

D.P.: One of the things Vincent feels so strongly about is that the "choral happening" in this country probably came from the same thing that made the kids feel they can all make music even if they were lousy. You don't have to work as long to sing in a chorus as you do to play a fiddle. Then it grew — not just everyone was accepted into the chorus. The choral conductors began to respect themselves and they didn't have to learn to be orchestral conductors to be valid musicians. And my husband feels that in this country, the chorus is or will be as valid as the great orchestras. There are more people making choral music, but that is only part of the story. Vincent is strongly interested in the very best kind of choral music in his view, whatever that is. We've been to rehearsals where one of his works is being premiered, and on the program is another composition or two, placed on the program because it was "more effective," because there were places of shouting and parallel writing, things like that — which is much easier to do, and besides, it pleases the audience. Vincent has a strong respect for the choral idiom, and wants to give it the best of himself, even if it requires a little more from the audience to listen to, to hear, to meet — that's what he wants to do.

R.P.: One of the downfalls, yet one of the strongest points of the choral world is that it is possible to take an amateur singer and mold him into a respectable performing musician in a choral situation — yet the professional instrumentalist has little respect for the choral idiom because he senses that it is not composed of professional singing musicians

V.P.: Yes, it is difficult sometimes to interest a violinist or pianist or flutist in choral music. I think it has to be the choral conductor who does this.

R.P.: What suggestions would you offer?

V.P.: You must convince them of your love for the great music. It's as simple as that. You have to interest them in the music.

R.P.: Perhaps the most dramatic event of your life during the last calendar year was the incident regarding the commissioning of a work to be performed at the inauguration of President Nixon, and the subsequent withdrawal of the commission. Do you wish to comment on this?

V.P.: Well, all I can say is that is was really blown up out of proportion — and I was just doing what I wanted to do; I wrote my piece of music. You probably read all about it — but what really disturbed the Inaugural Committee, I believe, was that I didn't get disturbed about it.

R.P.: It is interesting to realize that it was the text that was objected to —
and in the light of our discussion this afternoon regarding your awareness
of poetry, of text, the incident takes on another aspect.

V.P.: When Dorothea and I were married in 1941, we absolutely had no
money — but that June 6, for my birthday, she came in with this big
package for me — it was the Sandburg Lincoln books — all of the volumes.
That cost a fortune — a fortune for us in those days, and I still don't know
how she did it — gave a few extra lessons, I suppose. I had read the second
inaugural address then, and was very impressed with it. When the Nixon
Inaugural Committee approached me on the phone about doing a work for
the inauguration, it suddenly clicked with me. What I told them was that I
don't take commissions: I can't work that way. The only time I take a
commission is when it coincides with what I am already planning to do. I
have had the luxury all my life of writing only what I wanted to write.

I told the Committee I would call them back the next morning, and since
it was my government asking me, I would consider the commission
carefully. I was up all night and reread this thing. I got involved again. You
don't "look" for a text — you don't search for a poem, you have to read all
the time, live with it, and suddenly it will mean something musical to you.
So I called them back and said that I could do it.

R.P.: I've never asked you this question before, but here goes: Where do
you place yourself in the overview of style in the 20th century?

V.P.: That's easy for me, as I've never been a part of an avant garde or any
particular camp. What I am, I guess, is an amalgamator — I use everything
that's around me. We're approaching a common practice era. For instance,
the Cowell clusters and the Penderecki textures — all of these ideas that are
around us contribute something to the total vocabulary of music — they
contribute some new element. But it is when it all comes together that really
counts. Take Bach, for instance — he was just a composer of great music
— he didn't invent the cantata form; he was a refiner.

When all of these ideas are synthesized they become the language of the
century. I think I'm part of the new Renaissance of music.

R.P.: In your music, I sense a completeness in the architecture of all you do and I confess that I sense a lack of flamboyance sometimes.

V.P.: As I say, we are free to write our music; and as "free," this kind of spontaneity without the overall design and something to contain it has no real value. It's just a momentary pleasure. But if in that whole design you can have this spontaneity, that's great — and I think I do achieve it sometimes.

R.P.: For whom do you write? For whose ears?

V.P.: For fellow human beings — like you and my wife.

R.P.: Does this imply that you write for an audience that brings a certain amount of awareness of what you might say to them through the music?

V.P.: Yes. I'm writing for those people. I'm not conscious of this, but I'm sure that's what I'm doing. I have no reason to try to please people or to entertain them or to have a big name or a big career. I know that I want to say something because it means something to me, and I know that you'd be interested in it, too ... like you would be interested in my woods, or my pictures, or whatever.

R.P.: You feel, then, that the people who listen to your music are on the same plateau with you, and that you're just conversing with them?

V.P.: I think so — and other composers who don't do this, CAN do this — I've seen it happen. The only thing that can be valid is what is right for you in your lifetime. I can't do anything else. It's a technique all of us have. You can only contribute if you are a valid human being (and everybody is — you're no exception), and you have to speak of yourself — that's the only chance you have in any art. If you don't "speak," you don't have the right to take my time — and I, as a composer, do not have the right to take the time of an audience. Anyone can write a work that will fail, or will be miscalculated. But I'm speaking of dishonest music: music that's conceived dishonestly. Not orally — it is a sound thing ... and it just is not "speaking." The pop field is way ahead of us in one respect, in that almost 100 per cent of the night club singers DO communicate. **What** they speak is something else. In our field (the piano and the choral conductor or composer), not everyone "speaks." I can show you twenty fine pianists who do not "speak."

R.P.: Perhaps it is because of the kind of training we have been taught to worship. We have trained performers who play notes beautifully but who do not see anything IN the notes. We have trained people who say "I must do only what is on the printed page" PERIOD, without the realization that the composer is hampered by the printed page himself.

V.P.: Exactly right. And in our world also, if the pianist doesn't "say" anything, the audience isn't going to boo him off the stage like the nightclub singer. I don't mean to draw a comparison as to the message that is being communicated — only that the communication itself is the important point to be made here.

R.P.: Of today's music — the music of "now" as you have referred to it — what are the schools of thought and the ideas which are strongest in your thinking?

V.P.: Elements of many composers: Penderecki — Berio ... but not only those living today, the classics are part of this. Many times composers promise, and they themselves don't deliver — it takes someone else to take the challenge and to complete the work. Honegger was a lot like this. There is a certain rawness about his writing — and there are in his music promises that are unfulfilled — and these implications or promises have helped other composers find and complete themselves.

R.P.: Have you done much with the electronic medium?

V.P.: No. I haven't gotten involved with it, but I have all kinds of ideas. I think about it, but I don't want to get involved with the media until it can be used more efficiently. I may never — I'm busy enough with what we have.

R.P.: You have not done anything a cappella since the *Mass* to my knowledge — is that correct?

V.P.: Yes. I really haven't written a major a cappella work since the *Mass*.

R.P.: That is a tremendously versatile work, and I've enjoyed performances of it at many different levels. Mary Brewer's Germantown Friends Choir, Mildred Beck with the Philadelphia All-City Junior High Chorus, and with my choirs at Temple.... It's a deceptive work, and I always use it in my conducting classes for problems in conducting non-metered rhythm.

V.P. Well, that's the secret: the conductor has to feel the quarters and dotted quarters, and a lot of very professional conductors just don't feel that. They slip in an extra beat that holds it back or something.

R.P.: The breaking down of all of these complex meters into essential twos and threes is the secret of it to me.

V.P.: That's what it is. Sometimes a composer can add a sixteenth to it, and that can throw the conductor a bit — but it's still basically twos and threes. It's Gregorian, after all.

R.P.: Is there anything on your heart that you would like to express to people who are in the choral field now? Things to watch for, or to look for, or to hope for? Or bad things that you have encountered that you'd like to draw our attention to?

V.P.: One of the things I encounter very often that really bothers me is a false respect for the composer's intentions. They try to be slaves to what the composer has written. There are some things that can be written: we can write ritards and accelerandos. But there are times when we **cannot** write accelerandos and ritards, but we mean them: when a phrase has to shape itself, and you must give and take. There has to be flexibility. Too many conductors are almost too afraid to show a disrespect for the composer.

R.P.: Is that a choral problem or is that a conductor problem?

V.P.: That's everything — not only choral.

R.P.: I am always aware in your writing that you have a tremendous respect for and a knowledge of basic healthy vocal tessitura. You never demand of a voice anything that that particular voice cannot do completely equitably. The most subtle use of this is in the *Celebrations*. I was so touched when I heard the Lowell Massachusetts State College Chorus and Wind Ensemble perform this under Mr. Gilday at an ACDA convention in Washington.

V.P.: I think that a composer has to be aware of this tessitura but then to press them beyond that as an exception, for certain kinds of effects, for certain moments.

R.P.: But you don't demand the extreme as being the norm.

V.P.: Never. I just can't do that. You know, you can write certain things that just don't "sound" with a chorus. An experiment we have done at Juilliard is to write contrapuntal and harmonic passages strictly from the standpoint of the compositional craft, not thinking of the medium that will perform it ... and then we have those played with different instruments and sung with a chorus (well-trained) ... and we find that some things simply do not work with voices.

R.P.: I agree: there is something in the matching of the vocal overtones that does not come out right when played with instruments, and vice versa. And many times, the composer simply does not know the vocal idiom.

V.P.: A lot of people write for chorus and orchestra as though "here is the chorus — the big mob coming in for the chorale." That shows no respect for the chorus.

R.P.: You have a marvelous gift for polytonalities that really work with a chorus — and in the *Stabat Mater* and the *Te Deum*, they are the most striking. The sonorities almost shimmer, and you almost always follow such a passage with a unison statement.

As a wind-up, do you have any specific projects in mind for this year of residence in Italy?

V.P.: No, I just plan to go to Italy and get lost. I requested from the Foundation simply time for personal reflection. Besides, Dorothea says I can only bring an inch and a half of manuscript paper with me. But I know you can buy manuscript paper in Rome!

But to tell you the truth, I am at the moment involved with a series of Parables for solo instruments. I wrote one for bassoon and one for oboe. Finally I wrote one for solo horn — you know, there is almost nothing in the solo literature for horn. I like doing these solo works, where the whole world is just you and your pipe. Maybe I should do one for solo voice.

R.P.: That's beautiful — "Where the whole world is just you and your pipe."

Robert Page, "In Quest of Answers: An Interview with Vincent Persichetti." *Choral Journal* 14 (November 1973), 5-8. © 1973 The American Choral Directors Association, P.O. Box 6310, Lawton, Oklahoma 73506-0310. Used by permission.

ROGER SESSIONS

AN AMERICAN REQUIEM by Andrew Porter
REVIEW: When Lilacs Last in the Door-yard Bloom'd (1977)

ROGER SESSIONS (1896-1985) was a child prodigy in music, completing his first opera, Lancelot and Elaine *at the age of thirteen. He entered Harvard a year later, studying with Edward Burlingame Hill and Archibald T. Davison. Sessions was awarded several fellowships and grants that enabled him to live and study abroad for a number of years, principally in Rome and Berlin. He returned to the United States in 1933 and began a series of teaching appointments at various schools, notably at the New School for Social Research in New York, at the Boston Conservatory, and later at the University of California at Berkeley and at Princeton, where some of his pupils included Milton Babbitt, Paul Bowles, David Diamond, Hugo Weisgall, and Andrew Imbrie.*

His primary compositional output was devoted to orchestra, although Sessions also wrote a large number of chamber works, a few works for piano or organ, three songs, and three operas (his best being Montezuma *(1941; rev. 1962). His important choral works include a unison Mass (1956), three choruses on Biblical texts (1971), and two works to texts by Whitman:* Turn, O Libertad *(1943) and, one of his most accomplished and profound works,* When Lilacs Last in the Door-yard Bloom'd *(1965). The history and genesis of the latter work, as well as its salient musical features, are well-amplified in the following review of the work's premiere, taken from* The New Yorker.

AN AMERICAN REQUIEM by Andrew Porter

In the central episode of "Alexander's Feast; or The Power of Musique," Dryden celebrates music's threnodial power: the composer Timotheus, seeing Alexander grow flushed and proud at the memory of his battles, chooses a mournful muse, soft pity to infuse, and soon the conqueror is moved to weep for his slaughtered foe, Darius great and good, fallen, fallen, fallen from his high estate. The sounds of mourning — the slow strong beat of a funeral march; the thud of muffled drums; full, solemn minor harmonies; the falling melodic motifs eloquent of grief — have often been shaped into noble music. Requiems usually rank high in their composer's oeuvre, whether the text is liturgical (Victoria, Cherubini, Berlioz, Verdi, Bruckner, Fauré), Biblical (Brahms), secular (Delius), or both liturgical and secular (Britten).

Whitman's "When Lilacs Last in the Door-yard Bloom'd" was written as an elegy for Lincoln. In 1946, Hindemith set it to music as an elegy for Franklin D. Roosevelt and for those who had fallen in the war; he entitled it "A Requiem 'for those we love,'" making plural the "for him I love" refrain of Whitman's first, tenth and eleventh strophes (or sections). In 1970, Roger Sessions completed another setting of the poem, as a cantata dedicated "to the memory of Martin Luther King, Jr., and Robert F. Kennedy." The work, commissioned by the University of California, Berkeley, in commemoration of the hundredth anniversary of its founding, was first performed on the Berkeley campus in 1971, conducted by Michael Senturia. In 1975, there were two performances at Harvard, conducted by Senturia. In 1976, Solti did it in Chicago. Last month, the Boston Symphony, under Seiji Ozawa, performed it. Next year, the San Francisco Symphony, also under Ozawa, will do so. It has not yet been heard in New York.

I attended two of the Boston performances. (It was done there four times in all.) Friends who had heard and got to know the piece at earlier performances had told me it was a major American composition, not to be missed. And they proved to be right. Some added that it is probably Session's masterpiece, and probably they are right in that, too; I do not know all of his late music well enough to say. At any rate, "When Lilacs Last in the Door-yard Bloom'd" is an inspired and stirring composition, one to set beside Delius's "Sea-Drift" (1903) and Vaughan Williams's "Sea Symphony" (1910) for its large, visionary presentation, with large forces, of Whitman's thought, and one to set above them for the way it makes music of the sounds and the movement of Whitman's actual lines. In

Session's cantata we find the rapture, tenderness, and poignancy of "Sea-Drift" and the energy, grandeur, and mystical, contemplative calm of the "Sea Symphony" together with a quality that can be more easily described than analytically defined as American. In part, at least, and especially to a British listener, the Americanness arises from the melodic inflections of the word setting. On the simplest level, it is a matter of pronunciation. Hindemith presumably learned British English as a boy: in his Requiem he scans the word "recesses," at the start of Whitman's fourth strophe, in the British way, with the accent on the second syllable, while Sessions puts the accent on the first; Hindemith gives "missiles" a long, and Sessions gives it a short, second syllable. (Musical setting throws such transatlantic differences into prominence. In the recent Manhattan School production of "Paul Bunyon" one heard Auden's "began/Cézanne" and "farmer/ melodrama" failing to rhyme, as in British productions they did; "later/ theatre" in "The Rake's Progess" and "myrtle/fertile" in "The Bassarids" point to a Chester Kallman, not an Auden, attribution for the relevant lines of these collaborative librettos.) But pronunciation is only a small part of it. National characteristics in melody have their origin in the intonations, inflections, and rhythms of national speech, which makes Mussorgsky's tunes Russian, Janáček's Czech, and Sessions's American. "When Lilacs Last in the Dooryard Bloom'd" calls for three soloists: soprano, contralto, and baritone. From a purely sonic point of view, the voices of Gundula Janowitz, Janet Baker, and Dietrich Fischer-Dieskau would provide an ideal cast. And yet those three beautiful singers would not be convincing interpreters of the work unless they had carefully studied American speech patterns. (Fischer-Dieskau's British English is good, as can be heard in Britten's "War Requiem"; his American English is unidiomatic, as can be heard in his record of Ives songs.) In an introductory note to the score, the composer instructs soloists to

> interpret the RHYTHMIC DETAIL, in terms of the
> unforced inflections of the English language, which the
> composer has used as the basis of his vocal conception.
> [The singer] should, therefore, on no account force himself
> into a mechanical rendition of the exact note-values as
> written, but rather interpret them freely in terms of natural

184

English diction, respecting the subtleties of rhythm and stress which are inherent in the words themselves. In this manner he will best realize the composer's intentions.

Whitman's lines spoken as a good American speaker might speak them form Sessions's starting point, and any discussion of his cantata can well begin by looking at the melody to which the first two of those lines are set. The work is above all a lyrical piece. The music, Sessions says, "is always to be sung in a full-voiced and lyrical manner; it contains no passages in which a preponderantly declamatory style is appropriate." And the music is always grateful, though often difficult, to sing. The first three bars present, in three-part writing, a gently insistent rocking figure, alternating between a consonant and a dissonant chord. Then the soprano soloist sings the opening lines ("When lilacs in the door-yard bloom'd, And the great star early droop'd in the western sky in the night") to a melody whose first ten moves are of either a third or a step; the eleventh move is a leap of a tritone, to sound the twelfth note of a note row. Without music type one would not venture on even the most perfunctory analysis of any two bars of the cantata. Perhaps not even with it, for Sessions does not compose schematic music. Forty years ago, he wrote of his antipathy toward "an intellectually determined basis for music," opposing to such a basis "the response of the human ear and spirit to the simplest acoustic facts," since music's "human meaning ... lies ultimately in the fact that such elementary phenomena as the fifth, and the measurably qualitative distinction between consonance and dissonance, are psychological as well as physical facts, out of which a whole language has grown, and which in music based on the twelve-tone system seem often more powerful binding forces than those inherent in the system itself." Some of the elementary musical phenomena in the opening melody of the cantata are readily perceivable; some of their simpler consequents became aurally apprehensible, as binding forces, at later hearings. The first nine notes are F-sharp, A; B-flat, D; E, C, A-flat; G, E-flat — a chain of adjacent or linked thirds, the first of them minor, the others major. The "tonal" implications are evident: notes one to four outline a D-major triad with an added note; notes five to eight, C major with an added note; notes six to nine, both A-flat major and C minor with an added note. The ear, even against contradictory harmonies from the rocking accompaniment, hears this, but enough else is happening to insure that (as Sessions remarks in his textbook "Harmonic Practice") "such quasi-tonal sensations are simply evidence that the ear has grasped the relationships between the tones, and has absorbed and ordered them." And "it is a mistake to regard such sensations as connected exclusively with the tonal system as such." Similarly, it would be a mistake to regard the end of the cantata as exclusively a D-major cadence (E and C; D and B-flat; then D,A, F-sharp — the first part of the row reversed, in pairs) over a dissonant pedal. The shape of this melody, thirds and steps (or, by inversion sixths and steps), makes it both singable and memorable; so one can hear a form of it return at the penultimate line, "Lilac and star and bird," and perhaps even hear the reversal of its first five notes at the very last words, "and the cedars dusk and dim." F-sharp and A seem to provide a recurrent still point, emphasized at the close of the first movement and at the very end. Thirds and sixths followed by a step often sound in the melodic line. In the first of his Juilliard lectures published, in 1950, as "The Musical Experience," Sessions laid it down that "a melodic motif or phrase is in essence and origin a vocal gesture," and proposed that "the basic ingredient of music is not so much sound as movement." The start of his cantata is a shapely gesture, and its movement is precise. The first five notes of the row, to which Whitman's opening line is set, rise. The next seven would fall did not an octave displacement convert a falling third to a rising sixth, leaping up to the words "great star," as the climax of this initial span. "Great" is on the A-flat above the staff; then the line drops, with a final plunge to the B-flat below it. Spoken in the rhythm of the music, and given a similar (though necessarily narrower) pitch contour, the words sound utterly natural. Not so in Hindemith's setting, where the first syllable of "lilacs" and of "western" and the last "in" are prolonged, and "star" is set to a higher note than "great."

Whitman, reviewing his own "Leaves of Grass" in the *Saturday Press*, wrote that "Walt Whitman's method in the construction of his songs is strictly the method of the Italian Opera." He was reported as saying in late years:

> My younger life was so saturated with the emotions, raptures, uplifts, of ... musical experiences that it would be surprising indeed if all my future work had not been

colored by them. A real musician running through "Leaves
of Grass" — a philosopher-musician — could put his finger
on this and that anywhere in the text no doubt as indicating
the activity of the influences.

The "musical" structure of "Lilacs," as of "Out of the Cradle Endlessly
Rocking" (from which Delius drew the text of his "Sea-Drift"), has often
been noted. Robert D. Faner's attempt to make "Lilacs" fit into sonata form
breaks down, I think but in a general — and sometimes in quite a specific
— way one can discern equivalents of recitative, aria, and chorus. The pace
and texture of the verses change as those of music might. Not surprisingly,
Sessions and Hindemith have allotted Whitman's lines between soloists and
chorus in much the same way. Both first bring in the chorus at "O powerful,
western, fallen star!;" both set the questions of the tenth and eleventh
strophes for solo voice, and the answers for chorus. The main difference is
that in Sessions the Death Carol, "Come, lovely and soothing Death," is a
long contralto solo, at the heart of the work, while Hindemith — rather
unsuitably for the song of "A shy and hidden bird ... Solitary ... The
hermit" — gives it to his chorus.

   In musical terms, there are three "themes" in "Lilacs": the Star,
representing Lincoln; the Lilac, representing spring and perpetual renewal;
and the Bird, the reconciler, singing of death with a beauty that makes death
"lovely and soothing." In a lecture on Lincoln's death, delivered fourteen
years after it, Whitman recalled that the season seemed to reflect the new-
won peace:

> Early herbage, early flowers, were out, (I remember
> where I was stopping at the time, the season being ad-
> vanced, there were many lilacs in full bloom. By one of
> those caprices that enter and give tinge to events without
> being at all a part of them, I find myself always reminded
> of the great tragedy of that day by the sight and odor of
> these blossoms. It never fails.)

The first, introductory strophe of his poem says the same thing —
prophetically, since it was written in 1865 before the lilacs had bloomed

again. The next three strophes form an "exposition" of the three principal themes, each of them stated independently. Sessions's cantata is in three movements, and these strophes form the first of them. The chorus sings of the Star, the baritone of the Lilac, and the soprano of the Bird. (Similarly in Hindemith, though he has only two soloists and the mezzo sings of the Bird.) Now Whitman moves into his "development section," where the themes are brought together. (Thus far, Mr. Faner's "sonata form" parallel works.) Like the Star, Lincoln's coffin moves westward, moves from Washington to its resting place in Springfield, moves through the bright burgeoning of Lilac and spring and through the sombre dirges and kneels of mourning. The Bird is singing, but the poet's attention is still on the national funeral. These strophes, five to thirteen, form Sessions's second movement: part funeral cortège; part hymn to Lincoln; part vision of broad-spreading America, peaceful now and plentiful. In the remaining strophes, which form Sessions's third, and longest, movement, the poet finds his "knowledge of death" and his "thought of death" beside him like two companions. The Bird begins its Death Carol, "with pure, deliberate notes, spreading, filling the night." And during the long, lovely song, the poet's eyes are unclosed to a vision of all those who fell in the war. They suffer not; only those who remain suffer. Hindemith, in his setting, inserts after this vision an orchestral interlude with a bugle playing "Taps." But in the poem something stranger happens. Vision, companions of death, the Bird's song, the Lilac, even the Star — all are left behind. Yet in some way they all form part of a transcendental experience: "Lilac and star and bird, twined with the chant of my soul, There in the fragrant pines, and the cedars dusk and dim." Sessions's music for this coda does seem to move into "a spiritual world in which 'the unattainable' in Goethe's words 'becomes event' and the fragments achieve a unity impossible in the real world." That, the composer said nearly forty years ago, is what art should strive to do.

Hindemith's setting, which is divided into eleven numbers, lasts an hour. Sessions's lasts about forty-two minutes. He has omitted a few lines, some with a recapitulatory function that the music itself can undertake, and others that describe what the music has already made manifest. ("Varying, everaltering song. As low and wailing, yet clear the notes, rising and falling"). Hindemith sets the poem complete — and, incidentally, both composers use the earlier, "Drum-Taps" text, not the revised version found in later editions of "Leaves of Grass" — but that does not wholly account for his greater length; it is due to the subordination of the words to his musical designs. Hindemith's Requiem opens with a slow instrumental prelude, a four-note tolling ostinato over a pedal point. Whitman's twelfth strophe is expanded as a choral fugue, with much word repetition and an insensitive forcing of the lines into a jigging 12/8 metre ("Mighty Man/-hattan with/spires — / *and* the/sparkling and/hurrying/tides"). The imitative entries, one voice after another breaking in with the tune, suddenly shift Whitman into the world of the Three Choirs Festival; the same thing happens in passages of the "Sea Symphony." There is nothing like that in Sessions's cantata: it is remarkable for being a completely natural setting of the words and yet a span of music so shapely and satisfying that those words might have been written expressly to fit the structure of the score. It has what Sessions has ever sought: a long line, a "total and indivisible musical flow the song." The composer Andrew Imbrie once concluded a close, subtle analysis of thirty bars of Sessions's Quintet with words equally apt to the cantata:

> It is true that all the details of line manipulation are not consciously seized by the listener: but the broad design is apprehended, and a sense of the rightness of the details in relation to this design cannot but be intuitively felt. In listening to this music, one is immediately made aware of the presence of a forceful musical personality at work, who has full command over his resources. Here is unconventional music in the great tradition; here is pattern made to sing; here is movement in sound, expressing that which is noble.

I found the cantata, like all Sessions's later music except the Concertine (which comes out to make friends at once), difficult to embrace at first acquaintance. Besides attending the two concert performances, I had the chance of hearing the piece in the close-up of recording sessions. (Bostonians were lucky, too; three of the concerts were broadcast.) I think that the execution became better and better as the singers, players, and conductor grew together into their interpretation; I am sure that I became a better listener. Only after the harmonies of a late Sessions score have been heard several times, I find, do they begin to make proper sense. What sounded like self-defeating density of texture is revealed as an energetic, lucid progress of lines, in which the movement of the main themes is clearly perceptible. Even the full-throated lyricism of the melodies is not evident from the start. It takes time to sort out background and foreground, to get one's bearings. When that is done, the scores disclose their merits — so clearly that one is amazed they could ever have been imperfectly perceived. But perseverance is needed; and champions are needed, too, to provide the opportunity for it. Sessions's music is not played as often as it should be; the public gets little chance of overcoming its possible first bafflement. Sessions's Third Symphony, completed in 1957, was played in New York that year, by the Boston Symphony, and then nineteen years passed before New York heard it again. His Sixth, completed in 1966, had to wait eleven years for a New York première; it was done last March, but the Juilliard Orchestra. The Eighth, a Philharmonic commission, was played by the orchestra in 1968, and not again. (It was a hit at an Albert Hall Prom last year, in a program with Sessions's Double Concerto, of 1971. Would that the forthcoming Fisher Hall Proms had concerts of that kind.) Still, a recording of the Eighth Symphony is available. And a recording of "When Lilacs Last in the Door-yard Bloom'd" will be; it was made by New World Records, and should be published by fall.

I have described the cantata as I finally heard it, and will do the same for its execution. By the third public performance, and after a long recording session (which gives artists a chance of hearing exactly what they do), the soloists had become precise, focussed their tones, refined their pitches, and got the lines surely into their voices. They were now able to sing expressively. Esther Hinds, the soprano, had just the kind of rapt, tender phrasing her music requires. Dominic Cossa, the baritone, sang his lyrical narratives clearly and firmly and his reflective passages with feeling. Florence Quivar, the contralto, made something wonderful of her long solo; the voice is unconventional, not equalized, but her use of it was affecting. The Tanglewood Festival Chorus, trained by John Oliver, sounded strong and confident. The orchestral colors, which at first encounter I had thought rather dense and dull, began to shine. Under Ozawa's baton, the work stood revealed.

Andrew Porter. "Musical Events: An American Requiem." *The New Yorker*, 16 May 1971, 133-40; reprinted in *Music of Three Seasons: 1974-1977*. New York: Farrar, Straus & Giroux, 1978. Used by Permission.

RANDALL THOMPSON

WRITING FOR THE AMATEUR CHORUS: A CHANCE AND A CHALLENGE (1980)

Probably no twentieth-century American composer was more attuned to the needs of, or met the desires and wishes of a choir than RANDALL THOMPSON (1899-1984). So many of his choral works — Alleluia (1940); the cycle Frostiana (1959) to words of Robert Frost; The Lark in the Morn (1940); the Mass of the Holy Spirit (1956); The Peaceable Kingdom (1936); The Testament of Freedom (1943) for men's voices — have become concert favorites, performed frequently and lovingly by choirs of all ages and abilities. An appealing, cantabile style permeates his writing, with beautifully crafted, soaring lines in each voice part, all set to thought-provoking, often profound texts. In the lecture below, first penned in 1959 and later revised in 1980 (those paragraphs set in italics), Thompson's advice to young composers, his strong feelings about the choral art and its practice, and his ruminations on beauty and appropriateness combine to form a strong statement from this preeminent American choral composer.

At the height of the Renaissance, Lorenzo de' Medici wrote a wonderful poem which opens with these words:

> Chi non è innamorato
> Esca da questo ballo.

It is easy in Italian, but a hard couplet to put into English. One might say it meant "Anybody not in love will now please quit the ballroom." Or: "Let anyone who is not lovesick leave the dance floor."

I quote this because, by analogy, if there is anyone here who is not in love with choral music, now is his chance to slip away. If he is not in love with choral singing, let him leave. I am a passionate devotee of choral music. I always have been. But as I set out to tell you what I think and feel about it, I must warn you: I'm on fire about it; and if you don't want to hear what a fanatic has to say on the subject, please go away.

These opening remarks of an address delivered before a meeting of the Intercollegiate Music Council at Yale University in May, 1959, had a curious effect: though written with the best intent, they were frowned upon by some of my distinguished listeners who had doubtless not expected such a tone. The discrepancy of opinion showed that choral music and choral composition had arrived at a crossroads in America, and this phenomenon had arrested my particular interest.

The history of music has taken many turns. Sociological factors, political events, historical incidents, philosophical ideas have changed its course, conditioned its content, brought about its popularity, enlarged its scope, determined its media, opened opera houses, closed churches, closed opera houses, opened churches, silenced — then released — singers, forbidden the intrusion of folk music, then made folk-music a rock on which to build.

It is only today that the latter remark might be construed as a pun. But if so, its truth holds: "Rock" has become one of the many new departures — one that is characteristic of the constant regeneration of music with which I was here concerned.

The ups and downs of music — and of the evolution of music — have been at once more violent and more abrupt than those of any other art. Sometimes it took centuries to effect any change at all; sometimes change was effected overnight. In the United States we have witnessed a mighty change — and a relatively quick one. What has happened in the last hundred years in this country is more rapid than ever happened in the Middle Ages, the Renaissance, or the Baroque. This, of course, has to do with the situation of a young country. But, as Oscar Wilde said, "People have been saying that for 300 years." And of course they are perfectly right.

193

It is natural that we should not, from the moment Columbus landed, have produced a "school" of musical composition. Columbus didn't stay very long; he didn't come here to teach music.

It is tempting to pause here and reflect for a moment upon what would have happened if Columbus had tried to share with the Noble Savage the art of music of that day — the mysteries of vocal counterpoint. He would have had a hard time, if my own experience in trying to teach the natives five hundred years later is any criterion.

Five hundred years is a long time. We made very little progress for about four hundred of those five hundred years. True, our early singing teachers gave us a modicum of musical literacy; true, there are fine documents of creative strength in early American choral music; true, the Handel and Haydn Society was founded in 1815, only a few years after Haydn's death.

By and large, however, we built our towns and our churches without any serious consideration of the music of Tallis, Byrd, Weelkes, Wilbye, Purcell — or of Monteverdi, Corelli, Vivaldi, Couperin, Rameau, Bach, or Handel. They lived and died without this country paying any attention to them. Thomas Jefferson's musical library extended from works of Purcell's father (also a composer) to Weber's *Der Freischütz*. But Jefferson was an exceptionally cultivated man. It would be unfair to expect many of his compatriots to have had such breadth of musical interest. Throughout the seventeenth, eighteenth and nineteenth century, the level of musical cultivation was extremely low, with only one or two exceptions and only two or three torchbearers.

Our debt to those torchbearers can never be repaid — how they fought and how much of the expansion of music in this country is due to them! I think of Oscar Sonneck, of John Knowles Paine, of Frank Damrosch, whose Oratorio Society at the turn of the century sang his editions of Lassus, Palestrina, Gabrieli. I think of Thomas Whitney Surette and of two outstanding leaders in twentieth-century college choral music: Marshall Bartholomew and Archibald T. Davison.

I could hardly hope to portray the struggle and the enlightened guidance that has brought about the present totally new state of choral music and through it, I believe, of all music in America. The truth is that while many a serious composer has been working in seclusion — doubtless producing fine works — a whole new medium of expression has come into being: nobody ever before had such a medium of communication as composers have today in the amateur chorus.

There are now an immense number of amateur choruses in this country — college and civic choirs, glee clubs and madrigal groups extend across the face of this continent. They have high musical ideals, high musical ambitions. They want to excel; excel in what they sing and in the way they sing it. This is a very special phenomenon of the twentieth century. An immense offering of work and great enthusiasm went into creating it. As a result, here is a new and a truly vast outlet for composers.

Now, composers are very special. They grumble about having no "market"; they grumble about being "unappreciated." Granted, they may be unappreciated. But *not* granted they have no "market." Nothing could be farther from the truth: boys and girls, men and women all across the country and around the world are ready and waiting, eager for new music to perform, fully as eager for it as an Esterházy prince ever was to have a new quartet!

In point of fact, the "outlet" for composers, their "market," is far larger than you and I could possibly estimate with any degree of accuracy. Great though it is, it will be much larger when capable leaders, desperately needed, move into hitherto silent, inert, potentially musical, vocal communities and "unlock their silent throats." This will have to come to pass. There are many more choral groups that want to sing well — and could sing well — than there are good choral conductors to lead them. And the end is not in sight.

Though written twenty years ago, this statement still holds true. The reason is in large part the greatly raised general level of musical education: while a new generation of choral conductors and while professional choruses have come into being, the demand for choral music continues to grow. But a principal reason is the quality of choral music itself. And this is a point that particularly occupied my mind at the time.

What do these people like to sing? Not an antiquated, trite repertory. They want to sing William Byrd, Bach, Beethoven, Berlioz, Brahms. Above all they want to sing more *a cappella* music.

Now there are two things about *a cappella* music. The first is that no chorus can really sing well with an orchestra, or even with piano or organ, until it can sing well by itself without accompaniment. The second is that if a chorus can sing well *a cappella*, a vast body of beautiful music is opened up to it. The whole *a cappella* literature from Dunstable to Monteverdi and extending into the nineteenth and twentieth centuries is the chorus's private domain.

For a long time we did not realize this. Much was done to bring great choral music to our attention, and it did a great deal of good. Men's colleges, taking the lead, sang many hitherto unheard masterpieces. But it was only a step in the right direction, as those responsible for it were the first to say.

I would defend the sensitive "arrangement" of great choral music — the transposition, the change of color and range. I would also defend the good arrangement of folk music — really, for centuries, a subdivision of choral composition. Arrangements can be very useful. But they have their limitations, and they can be carried too far. The chief value of choral arrangements was, and still is, that they enabled choruses of men's voices or of women's voices to enlarge their limited repertories and thus broaden their experience through acquaintance with a great literature. As co-education has spread in this country, the old-fashioned *Männerchor* organizations and ladies' singing societies have become far less common and far less popular.

In a way, this is a pity, for there is a fine literature for men's voices and for women's voices alone. It is to be hoped that this literature will never fall into disuse or neglect. The literature for mixed voices is infinitely larger, and greater; and the last hundred years or so have gradually put within easy reach a vast literature of music for mixed voices — sacred and secular — music of infinite variety, music of ineluctable beauty. Whole sets of musical monuments have appeared and are still appearing: English, French, Flemish, German, Spanish, Italian — chansons, madrigals, masses, motets. When I was in college, I procured with some difficulty a handful of Monteverdi's madrigals. Now his whole output is accessible to all. More and more octavo editions appear annually; more and more choral conductors prepare their own working editions. Indeed, I sometimes wonder whether it is co-education that is responsible for the increasing popularity of mixed choruses or whether the beauty of the literature has brought more and more co-educational choruses into being, nourished and sustained them. At any rate, this particular phenomenon — the proliferation of mixed choruses — did not occur, and could not have occurred, a hundred years ago. There would not have been anything to compare with the glory of the presently available literature, either in quality or in extent. Is it too much to say that the literature itself has been the dominant creative and sustaining force in the formation and flourishing of one mixed chorus after another?

Why, under these circumstances, with this unparalleled outlet within easy reach, *why* has there not sprung up in this country a *bona fide* school of choral composers? We hear about the "cultural explosion," but no such "school" has emerged. Of all the many possible reasons for this lack, I am going to select a few and elaborate on each one of them briefly.

1) *The tyranny of the Doctrine of Absolute Music.* This aesthetic fallacy has retarded choral composition in this country more than any other single factor. It has even done harm to the creation of absolute music, because an instrumental style unleavened by the knowledge and experience of writing for voices can become over-instrumental, even turgid, and in effect lose touch with the human spirit. Let me state at once that I consider, for example, Beethoven's C-sharp Minor Quartet one of the greatest achievements in music or, for that matter, in all art. It is, unimpeachably, absolute music. But think how much choral music Beethoven had written before he wrote the C-sharp Minor Quartet. Yet an absolute doctrine of absolute music persists in our day. It does infinite harm to choral music.

It may have been the matter of folk music arrangements, mentioned a little earlier, from which the division of opinion between some members of the audience and myself took its point of departure. But more likely it was this argument of a doctrine of absolute music. Though there was obviously no such intention, it might be applied to the orientation of some of my critics.

2) A second impediment to choral composition is the *difficulty of applying contemporary compositional techniques to writing for chorus.* Modern idioms — the insistence on dissonance and super-chromaticism, on fitful and irregular rhythms; the vogue for intensity and a pervading *martellato* style

(so accented throughout that there remains virtually no accentuation at all); the Romantic cultural lag that characterizes many a new work, a total absence of "inner check"; a ranting in tone or an equally excessive quietism — all such stylistic traits do not lend themselves *a priori* to the medium of the chorus. And as in writing for any medium, so in writing for chorus: it behooves the composer to understand the characteristics, the limitations and the capabilities of his chosen medium.

3) Certain other reasons have worked against the development of choral literature in this country. Writing for voices shows, for instance, quicker than anything else (except perhaps writing for string quartet) the *shortcomings in a composer's technique*; one reason why we have no "school" of choral composers (such as existed, in one period or another, in virtually every European country from the fourteenth through the twentieth century) may be that our young composers haven't acquired sufficient technical equipment. (Of course one never has!)

Meanwhile, many a composer — young and old — has a hard time earning enough to live on. In this I feel real sympathy for them. But my sympathy gives out when they shake their fists at a cruel world and say, "My art is not *wanted*; it is not *appreciated*; there is no *place* for the artist in contemporary civilization." As with Caesar and Brutus, the fault is not in their stars but in themselves. The acts of humility that they must undergo to enter "In diesen heil'gen Hallen" may be hard for them to submit to. But it would be wonderful if they would and did.

Let us consider what trials, what tests these young Taminos must undergo.

The first thing that they should realize is this: many of the greatest composers' greatest works are choral, and they can all be sung by amateurs. What would be the good of writing a choral piece that only professionals could sing? If a piece is too difficult for amateurs to sing, the chances are that it is not good enough. It would be a terrible indictment of contemporary schools of composition if, in this respect, they were accused of failing to do what their forebears did so well.

This is probably the hardest statement to maintain in my discussion now that another twenty years have passed. They have brought the developments of the modern professional chorus and of totally new choral idioms inspired by it. Perhaps the best comment I could offer is that these new idioms characterize the problem: they are predominantly developments of the Sprechstimme, *of sounds that the human voice can produce* besides *singing. The best way to restate my point might be: the farther we move from the natural limitations of the human voice, the farther we move from the nature-given laws of music.*

Writing for voices has been a passionate, life interest of mine. I warned you at the start: I am fanatical on the subject. Would it be decent for me to give you a feather or two out of my own cap?

Above all, choose a good *text* and not too long a text. Don't choose a mawkish, sentimental, obscure, problematic, eccentric text or any text capable of appealing only to a few. Choose a text of some universality, whether serious or comic, sacred or secular. And in choosing it, remember that (as Samuel Johnson said of the ideal prose) you want something "familiar but not coarse, elegant but not ostentatious." There is sometimes a real difference between what is popular and what is great; but there is no difference at all between what is great and what is widely popular over a long period of time.

A few suggestions in connection with your choice of text:

Read and re-read all the poetry you can — try to become a connoisseur of poetry. Do the same thing with prose. There is probably no richer source of beautiful, universal and poetic texts for choral settings than the Bible. A Concordance of the Bible can be enormously helpful in discovering texts.

Having found your text, commit it to memory. Sing it to yourself in a thousand different ways. Decide on the best, the most fitting melody for it. Don't worry about progressions; let the tune and the words determine the form. Let the music follow the *rhetoric* of your texts. Don't set a question in the text with a full cadence in the tonic. Don't place subordinate clauses in the very heart of the central tonality. Above all, place the voices where they will *sound*. Avoid inappropriate chromaticism. Avoid extreme ranges. Avoid unnecessary *divisi* in the individual parts. And finally sing the individual parts to yourself. If you *can* sing them, it doesn't necessarily mean that they are good; but if you *can't* sing them, there's something wrong, and you had better do some serious re-touching.

I have found it useful not only to search carefully for texts, but also to keep a file of poems or prose that might some day come in handy. My "file" has stood me in good stead. Years before I set it to music, I happened on the text of "The Last Words of David" in a Gideon Bible in a hotel room. When subsequently Koussevitsky asked me — at the point of a gun — to write a short choral piece for a documentary film on Tanglewood, I had the text in hand — and the gun never went off.

The first lines — the ones that set my mind to work — for a more recent large work written for a double chorus I happened to see on the front page of the *London Times*. In 1953 I wrote a little choral tribute (*Felices Ter*) to Dr. Davison on his seventieth birthday; the text was an inscription on a gate leading into Harvard Yard.

Don't worry about so-called ugly sounds in a text: difficult vowels or clusters of consonants, e.g., "make his paths straight." A good conductor will overcome any such difficulty. Just as there is, in the absolute sense, no "ugly" color, no "ugly" chord, so there is, in the absolute sense, no "ugly" combination of vowels or consonants.

Don't believe for a moment that, to be good, the musical setting must follow slavishly the natural declamation of the words. Naturally, one does not miscalculate words or syllables, except for very special effects; and naturally one does not stress unimportant words, especially prepositions. But neither does one have to follow the exact rhythm of the spoken word. Plainsong, noted for its natural declamation, is not always faithful to the normal accentuation of the text. But whether or not it is basically declamatory, it is supremely beautiful monophony. It has been said that Palestrina is a kind of polyphonic plainsong. This simply is not so. Here is a Palestrina phrase, a setting (chosen at random) of the word "Benedictus":

The beauty of the line makes us think nothing at all of the incongruity of the duration of the "i" in "Benedictus." But to return to our point, it is the syllable with the *tonic accent* that receives the melisma. This is good, though it cannot be made into a rule. Both plainsong and the polyphony of the Palestrina style place melismas on unaccented syllables. The most conspicuous example of this practice is the traditional *jubilus* at the end of the word "alleluja." But it works better with the final *a* than with most final unaccented syllables in English. We do not like to sing "beautifu-u-u-l." Above all, no one likes to sing a melisma on the inflected final syllable of a verb, e.g., "gazi-i-ing." This obscures the beauty and meaning of the word and accentuates instead the participial ending common to all verbs in the English language! No aspect of choral composition is harder to teach or to be specific about than choral prosody. There are virtually no hard-and-fast rules. The best way to acquire an instinctive feeling for it is to read poetry well and thoughtfully and, above all, to read it aloud. This is why it is a good idea to commit one's text to memory before starting to set it to music.

I have dwelt at some length on this point because composers are apt to be over-timid about "texting," or finicky, or careless. Ideally the music seems to grow out of the words. Certainly it must not be sacrificed to them. Music was never sacrificed to the words in Schubert's songs. How simple the problem can be is shown best of all in a traditional *ballad*. There the same music takes care of perhaps thirty verses or more.

Some strange prosody crops up in the stanzas of our hymns. On the other hand, consider the strophic ayres of Dowland or Ford, or the strophic choruses of Mendelssohn or Brahms. In "Marias Kirchgang" from the *Marienlieder*, Brahms used the same music for five or six stanzas; for one other he wrote special music, not because the prosody required it, but in order to suggest the church bells that, according to the legend, rang out miraculously.

The best rule remains: sing the words to yourself. If the melody brings out the feeling of the text and the significance of the important words and of the important syllables, then the prosody is good — then the musical rhythm and the rhythm of the poetry or prose are blended to create the rhythmic ebb and flow of the choral parts.

Some final technical observations:

In many contemporary works the time-signature changes every bar or so. This particular mannerism works rather badly with voices, especially with unaccompanied voices. Rather than differentiating rhythm, it distorts rhythm, and undistorted rhythm, whether slow or fast, is the singer's most important aid. Of course, occasional changes of meter are unavoidable. But constant or capricious changes (that perhaps just a fermata or an accent would render superfluous) make singers uncomfortable. The attacks become shaky; pitch suffers. Meanwhile, perhaps the whole passage could have been written in 4/4 time in the first place.

Repetition of words can be rhetorically highly effective: "Gloria! Gloria! Gloria!" or "Gone! Gone! Gone!". But "Full many a glorious morning have I seen, I seen" doesn't make sense to either singers or listeners. Words in any given line should never become meaningless fragments.

Be sure to check your syllabification by consulting a dictionary. Your editor may do it for you — or he may not. We sing "ligh-tning," but it must be printed "light-ning" (a very common type of error even in published music).

My last suggestion: I want to emphasize the great importance of learning to write well for unaccompanied chorus before trying to write accompanied works. Just as a chorus that cannot sing well *a cappella* cannot sing well with piano or orchestra, so a composer who cannot write well for *a cappella* chorus cannot hope to write really well for accompanied chorus.

In re-reading this passage, I am struck by the realization that more than three-hundred years ago Heinrich Schütz gave similar advice to the young composer of his day (preface for the Geistliche Chormusik, *1649). He called on the principles of the Renaissance to stem the tide of the Baroque. But such "Rebirth" will go through the ages as long as there are new generations of young composers.*

*   *   *

What, we might ask in the end, are the immediate advantages, what are the rewards of writing for chorus, men's, women's, mixed?

To cite perhaps the most direct advantage first: choral compositions can be an asset to a composer. At the beginning of his career, his *orchestral* works are often liabilities to him under our present musical economy. On the other hand, a good list of well-written choral works with good texts can supplement his annual income and perhaps enable him to keep on writing.

But far more important will remain the purifying and refining effect that writing for chorus will have on his musical style, both choral and instrumental. The individual parts of a choral piece must have character and interest if the singers are to be moved in any way by it; if they are not moved, they will not perform it well, their hearers will be apathetic, and the piece a failure. In order to succeed, a choral composer has to make his emotional intent crystal clear. A kind of fundamental simplicity is blessedly imposed upon him. But this should not make him feel constricted or thrown into chains. Fundamental simplicity is one of the outstanding characteristics of good music, of good art. To learn to be simple never did any artist any harm. True, the line between simplicity and banality is often only a thread. That pitfall obviously has to be avoided. But a composer who cannot do a simple thing well cannot be relied upon to do a complex thing well. Writing for voices may refine a potentially turgid style.

What gives me the greatest joy and the deepest inner satisfaction, and what I regard as the highest reward of all, is to know that the choral music I write is sung by boys and girls, men and women who are amateurs — and it is well to remember that the original meaning of the word is entirely positive. I put the notes on paper: they sing it; they are doing something they love to do, just as I have been.

Naturally a composer is pleased to have a Symphony Hall or a BBC performance of an orchestral work. But one can be just as much pleased by performances of a choral work of small choirs, choruses, glee clubs. One is pleased, too, and strangely affected when one hears that one's work has been sung by high-school students or by the choir of a little church in Kentucky, or by a naval college in Japan, a group of students in Korea, or a kind "Madrigal Society" in Bombay. Those are things that make one realize what writing music really means and what responsibility it carries with it; those are the things that make financial profit seem a very minor consideration; those are the things that lift up one's heart, that give one the courage to go on, the incentive to try and make it better the next time.

Haydn summed the whole matter up when he heard that *The Creation* had been performed on a small island in the Baltic Sea. From the little town of Bergen, capital of the island of Rügen in the Baltic, a society of amateurs wrote to thank him for the pleasure that performing his *Creation* had given its membership. Haydn replied:

> *Gentlemen:*
> *It was a truly agreeable surprise to me to receive so*

flattering a letter from a quarter to which I could never have presumed that the productions of my feeble talent would penetrate. Not only do you know my name, I perceive, but you perform my works, fulfilling in this way the wish nearest my heart: that every nation familiar with my music should adjudge me a not wholly unworthy priest of that sacred art. On this score you appear to quiet me, so far as your country is concerned; what is more, you give me the welcome assurance — and this is the greatest comfort of my declining years — that I am often the source from which you, and many other families receptive to heartfelt emotion, derive pleasure and satisfaction in the quiet of your homes. How soothing this refection is to me!

Often, as I struggled with obstacles of all kinds opposed to my works — often, as my physical and mental powers sank, and I had difficulty in keeping to my chosen course — an inner voice whispered to me: "There are so few happy and contented men here below — on every hand care and sorrow pursue them — perhaps your work may some day be a source from which men laden with anxieties and burdened with affairs may derive a few moments of rest and refinement." This, then, was a powerful motive to persevere, this the reason why I can even now look back with profound satisfaction on what I have accomplished in my art through uninterrupted effort and application over a long succession of years.

Randall Thompson. "Writing for the Amateur Choir." *American Choral Review*, 22, no. 2 (1980), 9-19. Used by permission of the American Choral Foundation. Haydn quote taken by Thompson from Oliver Strunk, "Haydn," in *From Bach to Stravinsky*, ed. David Ewen. New York: W.W. Norton, 1933, 85.

UNDINE SMITH MOORE
AN INTERVIEW by Carl Harris, Jr. (1985)

UNDINE SMITH MOORE (1905-1989) was a composer and teacher in the tradition of Harry (Henry) T. Burleigh and William Dawson, and like them, is most noted for her many settings of Negro spirituals. Her eventful life is described in the preface to the interview that follows, which finds the composer discussing, among other things, what it means to be an African-American composer, influences on her life and compositional style, and the choral works that are among her most important and favorite compositions.

Since January 1971 I have had the rewarding opportunities to have many informal conversations with Undine Smith Moore. We have discussed at length many subjects, particularly various aspects of music and the position of the black man in American music. I am grateful, proud, and honored that Dr. Moore has dedicated choral works to me and the Virginia State University Concert Choir. In 1974 the Choir, under my direction, devoted the third volume of its Afro-American Heritage Series to the compositions of Dr. Moore under the title *The Undine Smith Moore Song Book*. My association with her has led to these random thoughts about the unique world of Undine Smith Moore — pianist, composer, arranger, and educator.

Undine Moore was born on 25 August 1904 in Jarratt, Virginia. She graduated with top honors from Fisk University in 1926, receiving diplomas both in liberal arts and in performance, and won the first Juilliard Scholarship awarded for study at Fisk. In 1931 she received the M.A. degree and the Professional Diploma in Music from Columbia University, then later studied music theory and composition with Howard Murphy of the Manhattan School of Music and in workshops of the Eastman School of Music. She has performed as a concert pianist, organist, choral conductor, and lecturer.

For forty-five years (1927-1972) Professor Moore was a member of the music faculty at Virginia State University. During her later years she was co-director, along with Altona Trent Johns, of a project entitled "The Black Man in American Music" (1968-72), which was funded three times by the National Endowment for the Humanities and also by the Southern Educational Foundation. The aim of the project was to promote appreciation for the music of the black man in America through performances of, as well as study of, the music; it further attempted to elevate black music to a level commensurate with its influence upon other musics of the world.

After retirement from Virginia State University, Professor Moore taught at Virginia Union University as a Distinguished Professor, and has occasionally served as a visiting professor at Carleton College and the College of St. Benedict and St. Johns in Minnesota. During the academic year 1976-77 she returned to Virginia State as Artist-in-Residence. She has served as senior adviser to the Afro-American Arts Institute at Indiana University. She travels extensively, lecturing at colleges and universities throughout the United States.

Professor Moore has been honored with citations by many institutions, among them, Atlanta, Fisk, Huston-Tillotson, Morgan State, Norfolk State, Southern, Tufts, Virginia Union, and Winston-Salem State. Virginia State awarded her the Honorary Doctor of Music degree, *honoris causa*, in 1972; Indiana awarded her that degree in 1976; and in 1977 she was named Music Laureate by the Virginia Cultural Laureate Center. In 1975 she was honored as an outstanding music educator at the annual meeting of the National Association of Negro Musicians in Detroit; in 1980 she was similarly honored by the National Black Music Caucus; and in 1985 the Virginia Music Educators honored her.

Dr. Moore resides in Ettrick, Virginia, in an ultra-modern, contemporary-designed home, which was featured in a 1953 edition of the *Virginia Architectural Record*. Widow of the late James Arthur Moore, former chairman of the Health and Physical Education Department at Virginia State, she has one daughter, Mary Moore Easter, who is a professional dancer and dance professor at Carleton College.

Dr. Moore feels that her lifetime involvement in teaching, composing, and arranging was highly influenced by the Negro spiritual. She explains:

Both in my home life and in my life as a student at Fisk University, I was surrounded by these great musical expressions of the Afro-American people. As is frequently the case, that which is extremely familiar to us may temporarily escape our attention as the subject matter of creative effort. Thus, my early compositions at Fisk, and later at Columbia University, did not emphasize my background with spirituals.

After completing the master's degree, however, it suddenly dawned on me that the songs my mother sang while cooking dinner, the melodies my father hummed after work, moved me very deeply. I began to write down the melodies they sang for some vague, undefined, future use. We were all from "southside" Virginia, and I was struck by the fact that many of the songs sung there were not so commonly heard. It was these spirituals I wanted first to arrange for chorus.

In making these arrangements, my aim was not to make something "better" than what they had sung. I thought the spirituals so beautiful that I wanted to have them experienced in a variety of ways — by concert choirs, soloists, and instrumental groups. To attempt to do this has given me much musical pleasure and has strengthened the memories of the people who loved me and gave direction to my life.

Professor Moore has made many choral settings based on her personal collection of Negro songs and spirituals as recorded in "southside" Virginia. Often in contemporary arrangements of Negro spirituals, there is a tendency to move away from the original harmonies and characteristic old-time way in which the songs originally were sung. The traditional melodies and characteristic rhythmic vitality found in Dr. Moore's arrangements, however, assure us that it is possible to preserve the real import of the music and to realize authentic performances. She has pointed out that no one can reproduce these time-honored songs of sorrow, joy, hope, aspiration, and despair as well as those from whom the songs originally came.

Professor Moore believes that Afro-American music is a "house of many mansions"; her compositions reveal a blend of different traditions, made unique by her own black experience. Born of devoutly religious parents, who expressed their emotions in the singing of spirituals, she early realized that such expression could reveal the black man's truest character and disposition. Her association with John Wesley Work, Jr., at Fisk University deepened her awareness of the importance of this black heritage.

But she was also receptive to other kinds of music. As a student in New York City during the late 1920s and early 1930s, she vividly recalls the Harlem Renaissance, the influence of which is revealed in her settings of poems by Renaissance poet Langston Hughes. Other influences upon the development of her unique style were ragtime, blues, jazz, and gospel. In addition to choral works, her output includes solo music for piano and organ and chamber music for clarinet, flute, and cello.

Professor Moore is a master teacher, a beautiful woman who in expressing the joy and love of good music has enriched the lives of many. Several of her students have made outstanding contributions to the world of music in this country and abroad, and many are presently enriching the cultural environment in which they live through teaching and music performance. A citation presented in 1972 to this multi-talented individual at Town Hall by John Lindsay, at that time mayor of New York, reads, "To one who knows the true meaning of Service, Dedication, Beauty, and Love."

The following "conversation" with Undine Moore consists of excerpts from many memorable exchanges shared over Sunday brunches at the America House Restaurant in Petersburg, or in the spacious appointments of her home in Ettrick. As her next-door neighbor, I frequently dropped in to listen to a new piece of music or to a work-in-progress, to accept suggestions about the performance of one of her compositions, or simply to chat.

* * *

Carl G. Harris: *Dr. Moore, what is your definition of black music?*

Undine Smith Moore: Music is the most abstract of all the arts, and since it is completely non-verbal, it does not lend itself to a verbal definition. I gave a somewhat lengthy definition sometime back, which was published in

1978 in *The Black Composer Speaks*. Since that time, my definition has not changed, but there seems to be less tension over the use of the term and its meaning. Not every subject lends itself to a precise definition. This is one of them. Allowing for the imperfections and imprecisions of the English language, for me, black music is, in the simplest and broadest terms, simply music written by a black man.

What has been the greatest influence upon your compositional output?

Anyone who creates something creates it out of himself. From our earliest remembrances we are influenced by the things we hear when we do not even know what we are hearing, by the things we see when we don't know what we are seeing. I have had the advantage of being reared in my own culture. My training at Fisk University placed a great deal of emphasis on the musical traditions of blacks. We have profited from being forced into having two cultures, our own and that of the white man. As slaves and workers, black people have no other choice than to become deeply involved in the everyday, even intimate, lives of the whites. In our time, the exclusive culture of black people has been absorbed by whites.

Life is very complex, and it is difficult to isolate any particular influences upon my development. Perhaps that which I was born with, given to me by my family and community, had a bearing on my choices. You write out of yourself, your inner self — that part of man which is least understood. Then there was my education as a musician. Music is too rich and broad for one to pick "favorites," but the one absolutely indispensable composer is Bach. All composers have felt his influence. Then, too, I have always taught theory and counterpoint.

What compositional medium do you prefer in writing?

At one time I should have said that I most prefer writing for unaccompanied mixed chorus. Although I have written for a variety of media, I have written more music for chorus than for any other medium. When I came to Virginia State College in 1927, I was assigned to work with the chorus at the T. Webster Laboratory School on the campus. There was not always a lot of money for purchasing music, and often the vocal resources of the chorus were limited. As a result, I wrote and arranged music that would show off the best of these groups.

In later years I wrote and arranged choral compositions for the Virginia State College Choir under various directors, the Armstrong High School

Choir of Richmond, the choir at the Norfolk Division of Virginia State (now Norfolk State University), and the Children's Choir at Gillfield Baptist Church, among others. Publishers need music of quality to add to their collections. If one is writing all kinds of music, when something is published it gives one an enormous boost of encouragement to continue writing for that medium. However, at present, I feel a great need to make larger use of instruments.

If you had to make up a program of your three finest or best compositions, what would you include?

I might not want to accept that responsibility. It would be very difficult to separate some works from others. I suppose I would choose first my *Scenes from the Life of a Martyr*, To the Memory of Martin Luther King, Jr. (1978, 1981; text from Biblical, literary, and original sources), a cantata for large chorus, narrator, soloists, and orchestra. This work, which was nominated for a Pulitzer Prize, is being widely performed; the twelfth performance since 1981 will be given by the Oakland Symphony in February 1985. This follows performances in Haddonfield, Carnegie Hall, Richmond, Cincinnati, Detroit, Norfolk, Pomona, and other places.

I might include *Glory to God* (1974), a Christmas cantata written for TTBB chorus, narrator, flute, organ, and piano, with optional brass and percussion. Commissioned by the male chorus of the First Baptist Church (in Petersburg, Virginia), this work takes its text from St. Luke, St. Matthew, and the Book of Common Prayer. I might also choose the *Afro-American Suite* (1969), a four-movement, instrumental trio for flute/alto flute, violoncello, and piano, which was commissioned by the Trio Pro Viva.

It's hard to be objective about one's own compositions, but on the basis of what has been published and performed, I think that *Mother to Son* (1955, text from Langston Hughes) for alto solo with mixed chorus is one of my best works in terms of its utilization of vocal tone color and general writing. *Daniel, Daniel, Servant of the Lord* (1952, text from the Bible) is possibly my most frequently performed composition. The term "arrangement" is probably not an appropriate label for *Daniel*; considering the meager fragment from which it originated and was developed, one might more properly call it a theme and variations.

Another work that pleases me is *Lord, We Give Thanks to Thee* (1971), a festive choral setting that was commissioned by Fisk to celebrate the Centennial Anniversary of the "going-out" of the Fisk Jubilee Singers in 1871. This work gave me the opportunity to use such contrapuntal skill as I possess. It includes a fugue that is completely Afro-American in its subject; the rhythms are all black; and the climaxes call for the zest and intensity characteristic of black style. All three of these pieces are skillfully arranged in the technical sense.

Striving after God (1958) on a text by Michelangelo and *The Lamb* (1958) on a text by Blake are well written, which shows that size is not always a good measure of artistic worth. A song written for Jewel and Leon Thompson, *Love, Let the Wind Cry*, has been my most widely performed art song. All the things I do have value for me, for each of the pieces is different and is valued for its own sake. Well — it is fortunate that we do not have to make such choices.

How has your compositional style changed over the years?

We live in a world that is constantly changing. It would be very strange if the events of the world about us did not affect us. There are those who hang on to the traditional, and there are those who want to make or speak the new language. I hope — I should not want to be at the extreme end of either group. I do feel that, in any case, I must write with a sense of integrity; I must *not* write pseudo compositions, using the new language just to be in style.

In 1952 I wrote a *Romance* for two pianos; it was a romantic, Godowski-sounding piece. Recently, when a well known, piano duo-team asked for permission to perform it, I told them, "No, because it is filled with too many diminished-seventh chords." It was a perfectly honest piece when it was written in 1952, but it is no longer of worth in the mid-1980s.

Everyone's concept of tonality has been broadened a great deal since Schoenberg, Berg, and Webern experimented with the twelve-tone technique. I am a tonal composer who experimented with twelve-tone method in the Introduction and Allegro movements of my *Three Pieces for Flute (or Clarinet) and Piano* (1958). My basically tonal pieces frequently have strong modal references. In my use of twentieth-century techniques can be found varying levels of dissonance, which I believe I use for expressive purposes. With a very few exceptions, I believe my compositions to be largely dominated by black idioms. Often there are recitative-like passages and almost always strong contrapuntal influence. Counterpoint was one of my favorite subjects as both a student and a teacher.

Other than composing, what do you consider your most significant achievements?

It is hard to separate one's life — all the things we are, all the things we do — into compartments. Teaching has always been a wonderful, tremendously important part of my life. My experiences as a composer and as a teacher are totally intertwined. To teach is a privilege, for a teacher learns as much from his students as his students learn from him. I have had the pleasure of teaching many outstanding artists and composers — for example, Billy Taylor (the jazz pianist), the late Leon Thompson (conductor), Jewel Taylor Thompson (concert pianist), Camilla Williams (opera singer), Robert Fryson (gospel singer), and Phillip Medley (composer) — as well as many of the nation's leading music educators and administrators. A number of my former students who do not necessarily have national reputations, but whose work I nevertheless respect just as highly, are raising the level of music appreciation and understanding in many places, from large urban areas to small rural communities,

Perhaps next to teaching my most significant accomplishment was the establishing of the Black Music Center at Virginia State in 1968 with the late Altona Trent Johns as co-director. Supported by three grants, from NEH, Title III, and the Southern Educational Foundation, the Center was designed to disseminate information about and appreciation for the contributions of the black man to the music of the United States and the world. It included the offering of a three-hour course for graduate or undergraduate credit. Although the Center no longer exists, its vitality still endures in this course, which enrolls approximately two-hundred students each semester. (The present interviewer had the honor and privilege of teaching this course from 1972 through 1984).

Herbert McArthur of NEH said of this project, "You certainly accomplished a great deal with your grant, and you have every reason to be proud. The collection of materials which you sent speaks eloquently of your hard work and your imaginative approaches." It is one of my deep regrets that Virginia State did not build on our pioneering work.

I have been enormously fortunate because of the circumstances of my personal life. I am justifiably proud of my personal achievements as a mother and wife. My late husband, Dr. James Arthur Moore, a scholar of many talents, provided me with the security that permitted me a personal freedom denied many wives of my generation. My talented daughter, dancer Mary Moore Easter, and grand-daughters Allison and Mallory, along with their varied talents, have been my pride and joy.

What commissioned works have you written, and how do you approach such compositions?

As is apparent in my output, there is little difference, if any, between my approach to commissioned works and my approach and procedure in sitting down to write a new composition on my own initiative or inspiration. I will give a great deal of thought to the commissioned assignment, then let it alone until it is ready. I have read so extensively in so many sources that I know the better, if a work is required that the words will come to me out of the past rather than my having to search for them. The specific details of the commission naturally will determine such matters as the medium, length, size of forces required, etc.

I have been commissioned to write some two dozen or so works, primarily for choral groups, some of them college groups and others, church choirs. Let's see, to mention a few — there were works written for the Fisk Jubilee Singers; Spelman College Glee Club; Bennett College, Winston-Salem, and Virginia State College choirs; and the Wentz Presbyterian Church choir. Some things have been written for student senior recitals and for concert artists, and I recall at least two vocal compositions written for weddings and one memorial piece.

You were a student at Fisk University and a young teacher at Virginia State when the era known as the Harlem Renaissance swept the country. How were you affected, and what are some of your reflections on this period?

To answer that question fully would require a book! We were not aware at that time that we were living in a period that later would be called the Harlem Renaissance. I was young and eager to experience life. Being young and a part of the times, my experiences were not viewed from afar. Besides, a highly developed cultural life was a part of everyday existence at Fisk. I can now look back on my experiences with the kind of assessment that comes afterwards when one is not necessarily a conscious part of the experience.

When I was at Fisk, several well known students were there. I should not try to list names, but I must say that the poet Lucy Ariel Williams was one of my close friends. Yolande DuBois, daughter of W.E.B. Dubois, was also there, but little attention was given to students simply because of their celebrated parents. At Virginia State I had contacts with Langston Hughes through Alston Waters Burleigh, son of the composer Harry T. Burleigh and a young faculty member at the college. Mr. Hughes had autographed a copy of *The Weary Blues* for Alston, and had said that he wanted me to have the book. On occasion, Langston Hughes spoke at Virginia State. Many of us who were fortunate enough to live during that unique era were very much involved with the arts and with fads and tempos of the times. Our attitudes did not necessarily reflect the manner in which these experiences came to be valued in later years.

During the academic year 1971-72 you went to Africa with Altona Trent Jones. What are your strongest recollections of the trip?

It was a tremendous experience. My feeling about it then, and now is that if I had been younger, I should have wanted to go to West Africa to live — in a place where everybody looked like me, or I looked like everybody else. I saw so many people who looked like relatives of mine — Uncle Berry, my cousins Louis and Johnny, other members of my family. I felt a tremendous surge of joy when I saw these people, and I was strangely reminded of so many of my relatives. To see Africans working in all the high positions, Africans *in control* of the activities was inspiring to me.

Whatever difficulties the people of West Africa have experienced, it is true that there is not a single child who did not grow up in a situation where he was of a majority group. These people have just not experienced on a day-to-day basis what it means to be members of a minority. I was particularly impressed by the way the arts are integrated into life — not regarded as something for the museum. And oh, the beauty of the people! I remember especially the Senegalese; the women walked more beautifully than any I have ever seen. We were given a private performance by the National Ballet of Senegal, an arrangement made for us by Ambassador Rudolph Aggrey.

On the other hand, I found myself distressed — and angry — when we visited the slave-trading centers of El Mina in Ghana and Gorée in Dakar, Senegal. At Gorée, the largest of the old slave markets, to see the House of Slaves was heartbreaking. It is a small, underground, closet-like place where the men were weighed in order to determine their value, while their families huddled into separate corners. Pregnant women had their abdomens slit and were thrown into the sea. The marks of human heads can still be seen on the walls. The full experience of slavery is brought down upon me whenever I think of those slave markets.

To return to more pleasant recollections. I think among the most memorable were the performance and lecture Altona and I gave at the Nigerian embassy and the many hours we spent just observing the everyday living activities of the "ordinary" people, especially those living away from the great urban centers. Altona, my most inspiring friend, was a marvelous traveling companion; she added much to my appreciation and enjoyment of the trip.

Dr. Moore, I want to thank you for your generosity in sharing your rich experiences with me. May you always make beautiful music!

Carl Harris, Jr. "Conversations with Undine Smith Moore, Composer and Master Teacher." *Black Perspective in Music*, 13, no. 1 (Spring 1985), 79-90.

KIRKE MECHEM
AN INTERVIEW by Leslie Guelker-Cone (1987)

Born in 1925, KIRKE MECHEM has composed an intriguing body of over forty choral works that demonstrate an eclectic approach to materials and procedures. Mechem can be serious, although many of his pieces are witty and display a keen sense of humor. Among his more popular shorter compositions are the American Madrigals *(1976), a set of five works with funny texts and an audience-pleasing style, belying their compositional complexities; the handful of madrigals called* Five Centuries of Spring *(1968); and the* Seven Joys of Christmas *(1964). His longer works include the cantatas* The Children of David *(1974);* The King's Contest *(1962, rev. 1974); and* The Winged Joy *(1964) for women's voices.*

Kirke Mechem is the composer of over 150 published vocal and instrumental works, a majority of them for the choral medium. He has received commissions from numerous choruses, orchestras, and universities throughout the United States. His "Dan-u-el," commissioned by [the American Choral Directors Association], was premiered by the Texas All-State Choir at the National Convention in March 1987.

Educated at Stanford and Harvard, Mechem has taught and conducted at both Stanford and the University of San Francisco. He now composes full time. Recently I had the opportunity to talk with him at his San Francisco home as he shared some thoughts about composition and the choral art.

L.G.: I've heard you didn't intend to be a composer. What happened?

K.M.: My father was an historian and a writer. My mother was a pianist — she studied in Germany and gave us all piano lessons. I was crazy about sports when I was a kid and I really didn't do more than get the rudiments of piano. I was going to be a writer, and at Stanford I was an English major. But in high school I started to play popular songs by ear, started to write songs without ever having seen a harmony book. When I was a sophomore at Stanford I decided to take a harmony course just to see what it was like, and it was a turning point. My first harmony teacher was Harold Schmidt, the Stanford choral director. He insisted that everybody in his harmony class sing in the chorus. I told him I couldn't sing — I had never sung in a chorus before in my life. So he said, "Fine, then go stand in the tenor section. Even if you don't sing you've got to come every time." I guess he knew that I would start singing — which I did. It was a thrilling experience for me to be surrounded by all the wonderful strands of music. Before, I had just written my terrible songs at the keyboard and my concept of harmony was strictly black and white. Here all of a sudden was technicolor. So I continued taking harmony and counterpoint — my English courses seemed dull by comparison — and I decided to major in music. I thought I would probably be a teacher — a choral conductor, because I was hooked on choral music. Then Harold Schmidt said I should go to Harvard and study with Randall Thompson and Walter Piston, so I did. When I came back I was Harold's assistant for three years at Stanford, but I kept composing all the time — mostly for chorus at first, but then branching out, writing piano music, chamber music. It almost seemed that every time I wrote a piece it was to see whether I could do it or not.

L.G.: What is composition for you — a driving force, a more methodical working out of ideas or a combination of both?

K.M. Sometimes one, sometimes the other, but never very methodical. Sometimes I use the piano more than at other times. Some pieces I write without the piano at all — like the *Seven Joys of Christmas*, which I wrote at home in my library. (I had to come up with something easy for a women's chorus I was conducting. It was simpler to composer something than to find the right piece.) But sometimes I wake up in the middle of the night with ideas and I want to go right down and work on them. Other times I have to generate the ideas. When you are a professional, you work every day and you learn tricks for priming the pump. Reading scores sometimes helps, sometimes taking a walk, listening to music, or just sitting down to work out sketches.

L.G.: What is your compositional process? What comes first — melodic fragments, colors, or rhythms?

K.M.: Again, sometimes one, sometimes another. You never know — I'm grateful for anything that comes the easy way. So much of it is a process of trial and error. You get an idea and start working and find out something isn't right, so you try to determine what is the thing that IS right — and what you need to do with it that you haven't done. And sometimes you have to live with it for awhile. I've had pieces that seemed to write themselves — "The Shepherd and His Love," for instance, I wrote quite fast and it's one of my best pieces. Sometimes I'll work very hard at a piece and when I look at it years later it doesn't seem quite right, it sounds labored. Other times, the piece that came hard sounds as if it all came in a flash. There doesn't seem to be any rhyme or reason to it.

L.G.: Which teachers and composer have influenced you most profoundly?

K.M.: Harold Schmidt was by far the most important person in my development as a choral composer and conductor. And it's because of the success of my choral music early in my career that I was able to get my other music published. It made all the difference in my life. Another teacher at Stanford, Leonard Ratner, was my principal theory teacher. Studying Bach chorales and singing in the chorus gave me the concept that music wasn't just blocks of sound, but melodies, and that the way a singer judged a piece of music was by his own part. Was it interesting to sing and how did it fit together with the whole? Leonard Ratner was an excellent theory teacher — he had a fine, analytical, musical mind. These two were an excellent balance — Schmidt with his great enthusiasm and love for choral music, and Ratner with the ability to teach harmony and counterpoint in a non-academic way — through the music itself. At Harvard I did have a composition class and also a course in Handel's music from Randall Thompson. He of course had a great influence on me, and I admired Walter Piston very much, too. I also had classes with him but as I never studied composition privately with anybody, there's really no one you can fix the blame on. In that sense, I am self taught as far as my compositional style goes, but of course I have learned from all the composers I have studied.

L.G.: How would you describe that compositional style?

K.M.: I think it's hard for anybody to describe his or her own style. In fact, it always makes me uneasy when I hear anyone describe my style because I don't like to be pigeon-holed. Some of my music is easy, some is hard, and it bothers me to hear of conductors who think all my music is too difficult for them. Even worse is to hear of a good choir which thinks that I write only light music, that I'm not a very serious composer. So I don't like to categorize my own style. It depends on the piece, on what I'm trying to do at the time. I've tried to do many things, and of course sometimes I've been more successful than others.

L.G.: Though you have written numerous instrumental works, including two well-received symphonies, a major portion of your output has centered around choral music. What draws you to the medium?

K.M.: Choral music is, I think, the healthiest sector in the classical area because it is in touch not only with professionals but also with enthusiastic, gifted — sometimes not so gifted — amateurs. It's like the art song was in the nineteenth century. All composers wrote songs then and everybody, whether they were professionals or amateurs, bought and sang them at home for each other. Today, every decent high school, junior high school, college, and community has a lot of choral music. And much of it is *new* music. A composer can write as imaginatively as he likes and there always seems to be a market. It's great to feel that somebody really wants what we're producing. And singing is a very healthy thing for people to do together. The twentieth century has often been called the age of alienation — big cities are so anonymous. But choral music is a great socializing force that brings people together with something beautiful and meaningful.

L.G.: How do you choose texts? What do you look for?

K.M.: Text is very important to me. Sometimes a great poem will not attract me musically because there is something about it that is too intellectual or so philosophical that I wouldn't feel comfortable singing it myself. It has been pointed out that I tend to use texts with simple language. The King James Version of the Bible, for instance, is far superior to any of the revised versions. ("House" is better to sing than "edifice" or even "dwelling.") Singing should be a natural process. The singer should feel that he is expressing something from the innermost part of himself in forceful, direct language with the same words he would speak. Also important, of course, is that the imagery, the poetic quality, must seem to invite music. The extra life of some intellectual poems is in the mind, is in the resonance they have in our thinking — maybe it's a different half of the brain. They don't seem to want that extra life outside of you, to have you express it, to somehow be part of the air, of the sunshine and the light. I have set dark texts, I've set poems that are poignant, sad, or profound, but even there they must have the force of natural, direct expression.

L.G.: How does your choral conducting experience affect the way you compose?

K.M.: I would give the same advice to any young composer that Randall Thompson gave to me. "Conduct your own works." He said it would make me a better composer, and he was absolutely right. When I compose, I'm thinking not only of the singer — and I sing almost everything that I write — but I also think of the conductor. I try to make my intentions as clear as possible, always keeping in mind the fact that music does not come alive until someone performs it.

L.G.: How much control over the performance process would you ideally like to have? Does the conductor add a desirable new dimension?

K.M.: When I was a young composer, I wanted to tell performers exactly how to do every detail and if it didn't sound just the way it sounded in my head, it was wrong. But when I started hearing groups who have never worked with me do my published music, I saw that gifted performers/conductors often had ideas about making the music live that I hadn't thought of

— shadings of tempi, phrasing, dynamic contrasts. I have learned a lot from performers, and I have learned that if you try to tell them exactly how to do everything, they feel like automatons. They give up and say, what's the point in putting any creativity or energy into this — all I'm supposed to be is a phonograph record and copy everything exactly the way he says. To get a creative performance the composer has to trust the performer's musical instincts. I want the performer to be conscientious in figuring out exactly what I want and why I notated the piece as I did, but then I want him to go beyond that. If something doesn't work or if he sees what I mean but he's not getting it, I want him to figure out a way that does work.

L.G.: You were commissioned to write a piece that was premiered at the 1987 National ACDA Convention in March. Can you tell us something about the piece?

K.M.: I have been turning down commissions because I must write my new opera about John Brown, and it takes everything I've got. But when the ACDA commission came along, it meant a lot to me and it would have been foolish to refuse. I wanted to use the opening of Act II of the opera because it is basically a choral piece, and the ACDA, through Dave Thorsen, was kind enough to agree. It's based principally on the spiritual words, "Didn't my Lord deliver Daniel." My piece is called "Dan-u-el." (In some renditions of the text, that's the way it's given.) It draws on the great spiritual tradition, but the music is original. After a first act full of conflict and tragedy, it's a moment of jubilation. You see, John Brown is such a controversial figure that a lot of people's initial reaction to him is extremely negative — that he was crazy, or just a religious fanatic, or a murderer. But he was a lot more than that, and I want to show him as he really was. To many people he is a great hero — he certainly was to those he recused from slavery. In this chorus, I try to show John Brown from the point of view of a man he risked his life to save.

L.G.: What kind of effect do you think the commissioning process has on the composer and the choral art?

K.M.: It's a great encouragement to composers — particularly to young ones. Even a successful choral composer doesn't make that much in royalties, so regular commissions are regular income. I would certainly encourage groups to commission works and to consider two things when they do — to commission a composer whose style they know and like, and not to ask the composer to write essentially the same piece that he's already written, which often happens.

L.G.: You presented a session at the convention dealing with your music. What did that cover?

K.M.: I tired to arrange that so it was just a sampling, a retrospective of what I've tried to do in choral music from Opus 1, #1 to the latest piece, which is "Dan-u-el." Two excellent choruses from Northern California, the San Jose State Choraliers, directed by Charlene Archibeque, and the Peninsula Women's Chorus, directed by Patty Hennings, were selected to perform the music. They kept hinting that perhaps we were trying to cover too much music, so I cut back somewhat. They said that people wanted to hear me talk more than they wanted to hear the music, but it was hard for me to abandon the conviction that a composer speaks best through his music.

L.G.: What do you think are the most significant choral works by Kirke Mechem to date? Which are your favorites?

K.M.: Significant — I wouldn't know. Most people believe that a piece has to be long to be significant, and there is something to that. Favorite pieces — even that's hard. It's like asking a parent which of his children is his favorite. But I do have some favorite pieces. "The Shepherd and His Love" has always been one, and I think it's one of my best. But there are certain pieces that are only done a lot because they're so accessible, like the *Seven Joys of Christmas*. I like the *Seven Joys*, and I think it's well written, but it's certainly not as "significant" as, for example, the *Songs of Wisdom*, which is, I think, one of my best works. It's not terribly difficult, but it's a thirty-three minute a cappella piece, so it doesn't get done very much. It's really a set of five motets; anybody with a good church or college choir could do individual pieces and then at the end of the season perform the work as a cantata. They're quite accessible pieces with strong and varied texts from the Old Testament — the search for meaning in life. Another cantata, somewhat shorter and with eleven instruments (or big orchestra), is *The King's Contest*. It's also one of my favorites. It's very popular whenever it's done, but not many conductors know about it because it's not divisible into smaller pieces. Another work with instruments that is done a little more often is *Singing Is So Good a Thing (An Elizabethan Recreation)*. Again, it's always as much a hit with singers and audiences as anything I've ever written. I would like to see conductors take a little more interest in these more substantial works. When I attend a choral concert I groan when I see that the whole evening is going to be little bits and pieces. I really think the time goes faster for the audience if on one half of the program there is something that sustains the interest. So that is the one small disappointing aspect of the choral scene for me personally: too many conductors (even those who perform a lot of my music) do not know my best work.

L.G.: What is in store for us from you in the future? Where are you headed?

K.M.: Opera is the main thing in my life now, but I'm sure there will never be a time when I don't write something for chorus. *John Brown* is full of choral writing and I'm sure that I will extract from it a number of other choruses. After that, perhaps a big oratorio for chorus and orchestra. There will always be a special place in my heart for choral music.

Leslie Guelker-Cone. "Kirke Mechem ... An Interview." *Choral Journal* 27 (April 1987), 19-24. © 1987 The American Choral Directors Association, P.O. Box 6310, Lawton, Oklahoma 73506-0310. Used by permission.

223

SELECT BIBLIOGRAPHY
FOR FURTHER STUDY

GENERAL WORKS

Boulton, J.F. "Religious Influences on American Secular Cantatas." Ph.D. dissertation, University of Michigan, 1965.

DeVenney, David P. *American Masses and Requiems*. Berkeley, Calif.: Fallen Leaf Press, 1990.

_____. "From Billings to Ives: American Choral Music on Record." *Research Memorandum Series* of the American Choral Foundation, No. 152 (April, 1989).

Dox, Thurston J. *American Oratorios and Cantatas: A Catalog of Works Written in the United States from Colonial Times to 1985*. Metuchen, NJ: Scarecrow Press, 1986.

Ellinwood, Leonard. *The History of American Church Music*. New York: Morehouse-Gorham Co., 1953.

Harris, Carl Gordon, Jr. "A Study of Characteristic Stylistic Trends Found in the Choral Works of a Selected Group of Afro-American Composers and Arrangers." D.M.A. dissertation, University of Missouri-Kansas City, 1972.

Jackson, G. P. *White Spirituals in the Southern Uplands*. Chapel Hill: University of North Carolina Press, 1933.

Jacobs, Arthur, ed. *Choral Music*. New York: Penguin Books, 1963.

Jones, Maurice Allen. "American Theater Cantatas." Ph.D. dissertation, University of Illinois, 1975.

Kent, Ralph McVety. "A Study of Oratorios and Sacred Cantatas Composed in America before 1900." Ph.D. dissertation, University of Iowa, 1954.

Lorenz, Ellen J. *'76 to '76, a Study of Two Centuries of Sacred Music*. Dayton, Oh: Lorenz, 1975.

Metcalf, Frank. *American Writers and Compilers of Sacred Music*. New

York: Abingdon Press, 1925.

Stevenson, Robert M. *Protestant Church Music in America.* New York: W.W. Norton, 1966.

Swan, J.C., ed. *Music in Boston: Readings from the First Three Centuries.* Boston: Boston Public Library, 1977.

Taylor, Jewel Annabelle. "Technical Practices of Negro Composers in Choral Works for A Cappella Choir." Master's thesis, University of Rochester, 1960.

Ulrich, Homer. *A Survey of Choral Music.* New York: Harcourt Brace Jovanovich, 1973.

White, E.D. *Choral Music by Afro-American Composers.* Metuchen, NJ: Scarecrow Press, 1981.

Wienandt, Elwyn A., and Young, Robert H. *The Anthem in England and America.* New York: The Free Press, 1970.

Young, Percy. *The Choral Tradition.* New York: W.W. Norton, 1981.

BEFORE 1830

Anderson, Gillian. "Eighteenth-century Evaluations of William Billings: A Reappraisal." *Quarterly Journal of the Library of Congress*, 35 (1978), pp. 48-58.

Barbour, James Murray. "Billings and the Barline." *American Choral Review*, 5/2 (Jan. 1963), pp. 1-5. Reprinted 18/4 (1976).

———. *The Church Music of William Billings.* East Lansing: Michigan State University Press, 1960.

Belcher, Supply. *The Harmony of Maine*, ed. H. Wiley Hitchcock. New York: Da Capo Press, 1972.

Blakely, L. G. "Johann Conrad Beissel and Music of the Ephrata Cloister." *Journal of Research in Music Education*, 15/2 (1967), pp. 120-138.

Crawford, Richard. "The Moravians and Eighteenth-century American Musical Mainstreams." *Bulletin of the American Moravian Foundation*, 21/2 (Fall-Winter, 1976), pp. 2-7.

Crawford, Richard, and McKay, David. "The Performance of William Billings' Music." *Journal of Research in Music Education*, 21/4 (1973), pp. 318-330.

Curtis, G.H. "G.F. Bristow." *Music*, 3 (1893), p. 547.

Daniel, Ralph T. "The Anthem in New England before 1800." Ph.D.

dissertation, Harvard University, 1955. Evanston: Northwestern University Press, 1966.

David, Hans T. *Musical Life in the Pennsylvania Settlements of the Unitas Fratrum.* Winston-Salem: Moravian Music Foundation, 1959.

DeVenney, David P. *Early American Choral Music: An Annotated Guide.* Berkeley, Calif.: Fallen Leaf Press, 1988.

_____. "An Early American Mass Setting." *American Choral Review*, 34/2 (Summer/Fall, 1992), pp. 1-2.

Dooley, James Edward. "Thomas Hastings: American Church Musician." Ph.D. dissertation, Florida State University, 1963.

Doran, Carol Ann. "The Influence of Raynor Taylor and Benjamin Carr on Church Music in Philadelphia at the Beginning of the Nineteenth Century." D.M.A. dissertation, University of Rochester, 1970.

Drummond, Robert Rutherford. *Early German Music in Philadelphia.* New York: D. Appleton and Co., 1910.

Garrett, Allen McCain. "Performance Practice in the Music of William Billings." *Journal of the American Musicological Society*, 5/2 (Summer, 1952), p. 147.

_____. "The Works of William Billings." Ph.D. dissertation, University of North Carolina-Chapel Hill, 1952.

Grider, Rufus A. *Historical Notes on Music in Bethlehem, Pennsylvania, from 1741-1871.* Philadelphia: Martin, 1873. Reprinted Winston-Salem: Moravian Music Foundation, 1951.

Kaufman, Helen Stewart. "John Cole's 'Rudiments of Music': Performance Practice in Early American Church Music." *American Choral Review*, 18/4 (1976), pp. 50-65.

Keenan, Joseph John. "The Catholic Church Music of Benjamin Carr." M.M. thesis, Catholic University of America, 1970.

Kroeger, Karl. "Dynamics in Early American Psalmody." *College Music Symposium*, 26 (1986), pp. 97-105.

_____. "The Moravian Choral Tradition: Yesterday and Today." *The Choral Journal*, 19/5 (1979), pp. 5-9.

_____. "A Singing Church — America's Legacy in Moravian Music." *Journal of Church Music*, 18 (March, 1976), pp. 2-4.

Leaman, Jerome. "The Trombone Choir of the Moravian Church." *Moravian Music Foundation Bulletin*, 20/1 (Spring-Summer, 1975), pp. 2-6.

Lowens, Irving, ed. "Performance Practice in Early American Choral

Music." *American Choral Review*, 18/4 (1976), entire issue.

MacDougall, Hamilton C. *Early New England Psalmody: An Historical Appreciation*, 1620-1820. Brattleboro, Vt.: Daye, 1940. Reprinted New York: Da Capo Press, 1969.

McCorkle, Donald M. "The Moravian Contribution to American Music." *MLA Notes*, 13/4 (1955-56), pp. 597-606.

_____. "Moravian Music in Salem." Ph.D. dissertation, Indiana University, 1958.

McKay, David P., and Crawford, Richard. *William Billings of Boston, Eighteenth-century Composer*. Princeton: Princeton University Press, 1975.

Murray, Sterling E. "Performance Practice in Early American Psalmody." *American Choral Review*, 18/4 (1976), pp. 9-26.

National Society of the Colonial Dames of America. *Church Music and Musical Life in Pennsylvania in the Eighteenth Century*. Philadelphia: privately printed, 4 vols., 1926-47.

Osterhut, Paul R. "Note Reading and Regular Singing in Eighteenth-Century New England." *American Music*, 4/2 (1986), pp. 125-144.

Rau, Albert F. "John Frederick Peter." *The Musical Quarterly*, 23 (1937), pp. 306-313.

Roberts, Dale Alexander. "The Sacred Vocal Music of David Moritz Michael: An American Moravian Composer." D.M.A. dissertation, University of Kentucky, 1978.

Robinson, Albert F. "Choral Music and Choirs in Early America." *Journal of Church Music*, 18/2 (Feb. 1976), pp. 2-5.

Sabin, John T. "Analysis of Selected Works of the Moravian Composer Johann Peter." M.A. thesis, Illinois State University, 1967.

Sachse, Julius Friedrich. *The Music of the Ephrata Cloister*. Lancaster, Penn.: privately printed, 1903. Reprinted New York: AMS Press, 1971.

Schnell, William E. "The Choral Music of Johann Friederich Peter." Ph.D. dissertation, University of Illinois, 1973.

Seeger, Charles. "Contrapuntal Style in the Three-Voice Shape-Note Hymns." *American Choral Review*, 18/4 (1976), pp. 66-80.

Smith, Ronnie L. "The Church Music of Benjamin Carr (1768-1831)." D.M.A. dissertation, Southwestern Baptist Theological Seminary, 1970.

Smith, Timothy Alan. "Congregational Singing in Colonial New England: Problems Addressed by the Singing School." *Journal of Church Music*, 26

(Sept. 1984), pp. 10-15ff.

Sprenkle, C.A. "The Life and Works of Benjamin Carr." Ph.D. dissertation, Peabody Conservatory, 1970.

Temperley, Nicholas, and Manns, Charles G. *Fuging Tunes in the Eighteenth Century.* Detroit: Information Coordinators, 1983.

Van Camp, Leonard. "Dynamics in Performing Early American Choral Music." *The Choral Journal,* 26/4 (1985), pp. 13-25.

1830-1920

Allwardt, Anton Paul. "Sacred Music in New York City, 1800-1850." S.M.D. dissertation, Union Theological Seminary, 1950.

Block, Adrienne Fried. "Why Amy Beach Succeeded as a Composer: The Early Years." *Current Musicology,* 36 (1983), pp. 41-50.

Campbell, Douglas Graves. "George W. Chadwick: His Life and Works." Ph.D. dissertation, University of Rochester, 1957.

Chadwick, George W. *Horatio Parker.* New Haven: Yale University Press, 1921. Reprinted New York: AMS Press, 1972.

DeVenney, David P. "A Conductor's Analysis of Mass in D by John Knowles Paine." D.M.A. dissertation, University of Cincinnati, 1989.

_____. *Nineteenth-Century American Choral Music: An Annotated Guide.* Berkeley, Calif.: Fallen Leaf Press, 1987.

_____. "Romantic American Choral Music." *International Choral Bulletin,* 11/3 (July, 1992), pp. 31-2.

Dwight, John Sullivan, ed. *Dwight's Journal of Music: A Paper of Art and Literature.* Boston: Ditson, 1852-81. Johnson Reprint Corp., 1967.

Foote, Arthur. *An Autobiography.* Norwood, Mass.: 1946. Reprinted with new introduction by Wilma Reid Cipolla, New York: Da Capo, 1979.

_____. Boston Public Library, Music Division. Programs and clippings from 1 Feb. 1879 — 17 April 1937. Compiled by the B.P.L. music division, 1942.

Gallo, William K. "The Life and Church Music of Dudley Buck." Ph.D. dissertation, Catholic University of America, 1968.

Gray, Arlene Elizabeth. "Lowell Mason's Contribution to American Church Music." Master's thesis, University of Rochester, 1941.

Hastings, Thomas. *Dissertation on Musical Taste.* New York: Mason Brothers, 1853, second edition.

Howe, M.A. DeWolfe. "John Knowles Paine." *The Musical Quarterly*, 25/3 (July, 1939), pp. 257-267.

Kauffman, Byron E. "The Choral Works of William Henry Fry." D.M.A. dissertation, University of Illinois, 1975.

Kearns, William Kay. "Horatio Parker, 1863-1919: A Study of His Life and Music." Ph.D. dissertation, University of Illinois, 1965.

Krehbiel, H. E. *Notes on the Cultivation of Choral Music and the Oratorio Society in New York*. New York, 1884.

Ledbetter, Steven. *George W. Chadwick (1854-1931): A Bibliographical Source-Book*, 1983. Typescript. Available at the New England Conservatory of Music, Boston.

Lowens, Margery M. "The New York Years of Edward MacDowell." Ph.D. dissertation, University of Michigan, 1971.

Mason, Daniel Gregory. *Music in My Time*. New York: MacMillan, 1938.

Mason, Henry Lowell. *Lowell Mason: An Appreciation of His Life and Work*. New York, 1941.

Mason, William. *Memories of a Musical Life*. New York: Century Company, 1901. Reprinted New York: AMS Press; Reprinted New York: Da Capo Press, 1970.

Matthews, W.S.B. "German Influence upon American Music as Noted in the Works of Dudley Buck, J.K. Paine, William Mason, J.C.D. Parker, and Stephen A. Emery." *The Musician*, 15 (1910), pp. 160ff.

McKinley, Ann. "Music for the Dedication Ceremonies of the World's Columbian Exposition in Chicago." *American Music*. 3/1 (1985), p. 42-51.

Merrill, E. Lindsay. "Mrs. H.H.A. Beach: Her Life and Music." Ph.D. dissertation, University of Rochester, 1963.

Messiter, A.H. *A History of the Choir and Music of Trinity Church*. New York, 1906. Reprinted AMS Press, 1970.

Miller, John. "Edward MacDowell: A Critical Study." Ph.D. dissertation, University of Rochester, 1961.

Osgood, G.L. "St. Peter, an Oratorio." *North American Review*, 117 (1873), pp. 247-250.

Paige, Paul Eric. "Musical Organizations in Boston: 1830-1850." Ph.D. dissertation, Boston University, 1967.

Paine, John Knowles. Boston Public Library, Music Division. Letters, scrapbooks, programs, etc., compiled by the B.P.L. music division.

_____. Cambridge, Mass.: Harvard University, Eda Kuhn Loeb Music
Library. Letters, scrapbooks, programs, etc., compiled by the Harvard
music library.

Perkins, C.C., and Dwight, J.S. *History of the Handel and Haydn Society of
Boston, Massachusetts.* Cambridge: Harvard University Press, 1934.

Roberts, Kenneth C., Jr. "John Knowles Paine." M.A. thesis, University of
Michigan, 1962.

Rogers, Delmar Dalnell. "Nineteenth-Century Music in New York City as
Reflected in the Career of G.F. Bristow." Master's thesis, University of
Michigan, 1967.

Root, G.F. *The Story of a Musical Life.* Cincinnati: John Church Co., 1891.
Reprinted New York: Da Capo Press, 1970.

Salter, Sumner. "Early Encouragement to American Composers." *The
Musical Quarterly*, 18 (1932), pp. 76-105.

Scanlon, Mary Browning. "Thomas Hastings." *The Musical Quarterly*, 32/2
(1946), pp. 265-277.

Schabas, Ezra. *Theodore Thomas: America's Conductor and Builder of
Orchestras, 1835-1905.* Urbana, Ill.: University of Illinois Press, 1989.

Schleifer, Martha Furman. *William Wallace Gilchrist (1846-1916): A Moving
Force in the Musical Life of Philadelphia.* Metuchen, N.J.: Scarecrow
Press, 1985.

Schmidt, John C. "The Life and Works of John Knowles Paine." Ph.D.
dissertation, New York University, 1979. Ann Arbor: UMI Research
Press, 1980.

Semler, Isabel Parker. *Horatio Parker: A Memoir for His Grandchildren.*
New York: G.P. Putnam, 1942. Reprinted New York: Da Capo Press,
1973.

Thomas, Theodore. *Theodore Thomas: A Musical Autobiography*, ed. George
P. Upton. Chicago: A.C. McClurg & Co., 2 vols., 1905.

Tuthill, Burnet C. "Mrs. H.H.A. Beach." *The Musical Quarterly*, 26 (1940),
pp. 297-306.

Upton, George Putnam. *The Standard Cantatas: Their Stories, Their Music,
and Their Composers, A Handbook.* Chicago: A.C. McClurg, 1889.

_____. *The Standard Oratorios: Their Stories, Their Music,
and Their Composers, A Handbook.* Chicago: A.C. McClurg, 1886.

Upton, William Treat. *William Henry Fry: American Journalist and Compo-
ser-Critic.* New York: Thomas Y. Crowell Co., 1954. Reprinted New

York: Da Capo Press, 1974.

Van Camp, Leonard. "Nineteenth-Century Choral Music in America: A German Legacy." *American Choral Review*, 23/4 (1981), pp. 5-12.

Walters, R. *The Bethlehem Bach Choir*. Boston, 1918.

SINCE 1920

Amman, Douglas D. "The Choral Music of Ross Lee Finney." Ph.D. dissertation, University of Cincinnati, 1972.

Anagnost, Dean Z. "The Choral Music of Virgil Thomson." Ph.D. dissertation, Columbia University, 1977.

Andre, Don Alan. "Leonard Bernstein's Mass as Social and Political Commentary on the Sixties." Ph.D. dissertation, University of Washington, 1979.

Arvey, Verna. *William Grant Still*. New York: J. Fischer, 1939.

Ashizawa, Theodore Fumio. "The Choral Music of Vincent Persichetti." D.M.A. dissertation, University of Washington, 1977.

Baker, David, Belt, Lida M., and Hudson, Herman C. eds. *The Black Composer Speaks*; a project of the Afro-American Arts Institute, Indiana University. Metuchen, NJ: Scarecrow Press, 1978.

Barham, Terry J. "A Macroanalytic View of the Choral Music of Vincent Persichetti." Ph.D. dissertation, University of Oklahoma, 1981.

Barnard, Jack Richard. "The Choral Music of Vincent Persichetti: A Descriptive Analysis." Ph.D. dissertation, Florida State University, 1974.

Bender, James F. "Three American Composers from the Young Composers Project: Style Analysis of Selected Works by Emma Lou Diemer, Donald Martin Jenni, and Richard Lane." Ph.D. dissertation, New York University, 1988.

Bergman, L. *Music Master of the Middle West: The Story of F. Melius Christiansen and the St. Olaf Choir*. Minneapolis: University of Minnesota, 1944. Reprinted New York: Da Capo Press, 1968.

Berry, Wallace. "The Music of Halsey Stevens." *The Musical Quarterly*, 54/3 (1968), pp. 287-308.

Bloch, Suzanne. "Ernest Bloch — Student of Choral Music: Some Personal Reflections." *American Choral Review*, 10/2 (1968), pp. 51-4.

Bloch, Suzanne, and Heskes, Irene. *Ernest Bloch, Creative Spirit: A Program Source Book*. New York: National Jewish Council, 1976.

Broder, Nathan. *Samuel Barber*. New York: G. Schirmer, 1954.

Brookhart, Charles E. "The Choral Works of Aaron Copland, Roy Harris, and Randall Thompson." Ph.D. dissertation, George Peabody College for Teachers, 1960.

Brown, Cynthia Clark. "Emma Lou Diemer: Composer, Performer, Educator, Church Musician." D.M.A. dissertation, Southern Baptist Theological Seminary, 1985.

Browne, Bruce S. "The Choral Music of Lukas Foss." D.M.A. dissertation, University of Washington, 1976.

_____. "The Choral Music of Lukas Foss." *The Choral Journal*, 16/8 (1976), pp. 12-13.

Brunelle, Philip. "Dominick Argento and His Music for Chorus." *American Organist*, 22/5 (May, 1988), pp. 178-80.

Brunner, David L. "The Choral Music of Lou Harrison." D.M.A. dissertation, University of Illinois, 1989.

Bumgardner, T.A. *Norman Dello Joio*, Boston. Twayne, 1986.

Carnine, Albert, Jr. "The Choral Music of Howard Hanson." D.M.A. dissertation, University of Texas at Austin, 1977.

Christiansen, Larry A. "The Choral Music of Daniel Pinkham." *The Choral Journal*, 9/2 (October, 1968), p. 18.

Cooper, Paul. "The Music of Ross Lee Finney." *The Musical Quarterly*, 53/1 (1967), pp. 1-21.

Copland, Aaron, and Perlis, Vivian. *Copland: 1900 through 1942*. New York: St. Martins Press, 1984; and *Copland: Since 1943*. New York: St. Martin's Press, 1989.

Cottle, William Andrew. "Social Commentary in Vocal Music in the Twentieth Century as Evidenced by Leonard Bernstein's Mass." D.A. dissertation, University of Northern Colorado, 1978.

Cox, Dennis Keith. "Aspects of the Compositional Styles of Three Selected Twentieth-Century Composers of Choral Music: Alan Hovhaness, Ron Nelson, and Daniel Pinkham." D.M.A. dissertation, University of Missouri-Kansas City, 1978.

Creigh, Robert Hugh. "Stylistic Characteristics of Randall Thompson's Choral Music." M.Ed. thesis, Central Washington University, 1970.

Davis, Deborah. "The Choral Works of Ned Rorem." Ph.D. dissertation, Michigan State University, 1978.

_____. "An Interview about Choral Music with Ned Rorem." *The Musical*

Quarterly, 68/3 (1982), pp. 390-7.

Detweiler, Greg Jeffrey. "The Choral Music of Elliott Carter." D.M.A. dissertation, University of Illinois, 1985.

DeVenney, David P. *American Choral Music Since 1920: An Annotated Guide*. Berkeley, Calif.: Fallen Leaf Press, 1993.

Downes, Edward. "The Music of Norman Dello Joio." *The Musical Quarterly*, 48/2 (1962), pp. 142-72.

Evett, Robert. "The Music of Vincent Persichetti." *Juilliard Review*, 2/2 (Spring, 1955), pp. 15-30.

Forbes, Elliot. "The Music of Randall Thompson." *The Musical Quarterly*, 35/1 (January, 1949), pp. 1-25.

Foss, Lukas. "Inaudible Singing." *The Choral Journal*, 13/1 (1972), pp. 5-6.

Fulton, Alvin W. "Ernest Bloch's Sacred Service." M.M. thesis, University of Rochester, 1953.

Fusner, Henry. "Sowerby's *Forsaken of Man*: A Forgotten Masterpiece?" *American Organist*, 16 (May, 1985), p. 48.

Gardner, Effie Tyler. "An Analysis of the Technique and Style of Selected Black-American Composers of Contemporary Choral Music." Ph.D. dissertation, Michigan State University, 1979.

Garofalo, Robert J. "The Life and Works of Frederick Converse." Ph.D. dissertation, Catholic University of America, 1969.

Goodwin, Joscelyn. "The Music of Henry Cowell." Ph.D. dissertation, Cornell University, 1969.

Gorelick, Brian. "Movement and Shape in the Choral Music of Roger Sessions." D.M.A. dissertation, University of Illinois, 1985.

Gottlieb, Jack. "The Choral Music of Leonard Bernstein: Reflections of Theatre and Liturgy." *American Choral Review*, 10/4 (1968), pp. 156-77.

_____. "Leonard Bernstein: *Kaddish* Symphony." *Perspectives of New Music*, 4/1 (1965), pp. 171-5.

_____. "Symbols of Faith in the Music of Leonard Bernstein." *The Musical Quarterly*, 66/2 (April, 1980), pp. 287-95.

Gradenwitz, Peter. *Leonard Bernstein, the Infinite Variety of a Musician*. London: Berg Publishers, 1987.

Gray, Arlene E. *Listen to the Lambs: A Source Book of the R. Nathaniel Dett Materials in the Niagara Falls Public Library*. Crystal Beach, Ontario: A.E. Gray, 1984.

Griffen, Malcolm J. "Style in the Choral Works of William Schuman."

D.M.A. dissertation, University of Illinois, 1972.

Griffith, M.J. "William Schuman's *Carols of death* — an Analysis." *The Choral Journal*, 17/6 (1977), pp. 17-18.

Griffiths, Richard Lyle. "Ned Rorem: Music for Chorus and Orchestra." D.M.A. dissertation, University of Washington, 1979.

Haar, James. "Randall Thompson and the Music of the Past." *American Choral Review*, 16/4 (October, 1974), pp. 7-15.

Haas, Robert B., ed. *William Grant Still and the Fusion of Cultures in American Music.* Los Angeles: Black Sparrow Press, 1972.

Hadley, Richard T. "The Published Choral Music of Ulysses Simpson Kay — 1943 to 1968." Ph.D. dissertation, University of Iowa, 1972.

Harris, Carl Gordon. "A Study of Characteristic Stylistic Trends Found in the Choral Works of a Selected Group of Afro-American Composers and Arrangers." D.M.A. dissertation, University of Missouri-Kansas City, 1972.

_____. "Three Schools of Black Choral Composers and Arrangers, 1900-1970." *The Choral Journal* 14/8 (April, 1974), p. 11-14.

Hausfield, Susan Elizabeth. "A Study of Mass by Leonard Bernstein." M.A. thesis, The Ohio State University, 1977.

Hawthorne, Loyd F. "The Choral Music of Gordon Binkerd." D.M.A. dissertation, University of Texas at Austin, 1973.

Hayes, Laurence M. "The Music of Ulysses Kay, 1939-63." Ph.D. dissertation, University of Wisconsin, 1971.

Heinz, William, Jr. "New Light on Samuel Barber's *Reincarnations.*" *The Choral Journal*, 25/3 (1985), pp. 25-7.

Herrema, Robert D. "The Choral Music of Ulysses Kay." *The Choral Journal*, 11/4 (1970), pp. 5-10.

Hinds, Wayne B. "Leo Sowerby: A Biography and Descriptive Listing of the Anthems." Ed.D. dissertation, George Peabody College for Teachers, 1972.

Hines, R.S. *The Composer's Point of View: Essays on Twentieth Century Choral Music by Those Who Wrote It.* Norman, OK: University of Oklahoma Press, 1963.

Hitchcock, H. Wiley, and Perlis, Vivian. *An Ives Celebration.* Urbana, Ill.: University of Illinois Press, 1977.

Hobbs, Odell. "A Study of Selected Outstanding Negro College Choirs in the United States of America." M.M. thesis, Catholic University of America,

1966.

Holmes, James. "A Guide to the Sacred Choral Music of Ned Rorem."
American Organist, 23/5 (May, 1989), pp. 66-8.

Hoover, Kathleen, and Cage, John. *Virgil Thomson: His Life and Music*.
New York: Yoseloff, 1959.

Jenkins, Gwendolyn N. "The Choral Style of Randall Thompson." M.M.
thesis, University of Rochester, 1955.

Johnson, Craig R. "An Examination of Dominick Argento's *Te Deum*."
D.M.A. dissertation, University of Cincinnati, 1989.

Johnson, Marlowe W. "The Choral Music of Daniel Pinkham." Ph.D.
dissertation, University of Iowa, 1968.

_____. "The Choral Writing of Daniel Pinkham." *American Choral
Review*, 8/4 (June, 1966), pp. 1, 12-16.

Johnston, William R. "Choral Settings of Walt Whitman by Norman Dello
Joio." Master's thesis, Louisiana State University, 1970.

Jones, Raymond D. "Leo Sowerby: His Life and His Choral Music." Ph.D.
dissertation, University of Iowa, 1973.

Jones, Robert E. "Skyscrapers: An Experiment in Design." *Modern Music*, 3
(Jan.-Feb., 1926), pp. 21-6.

Kelley, Kenneth B. "The Choral Music of Leslie Bassett." D.M.A.
dissertation, University of Illinois, 1976.

_____. "The Choral Music of Leslie Bassett." *The Choral Journal*, 19/4
(1978), pp. 16-17.

Kimberling, Victoria J. *David Diamond: A Bio-Bibliography*. Metuchen,
N.J.: Scarecrow Press, 1987.

Knapp, Alexander V. "The Jewishness of Bloch: Subconscious or
Conscious." *Royal Musical Association Proceedings*, 97 (1970-71), pp.
99-112.

Kumlien, Wendell C. "The Sacred Choral Music of Charles Ives: A Study in
Style Developments." Ph.D. dissertation, University of Illinois, 1969.

Kummer, Randolph F. "An Analysis of the Compositional Techniques
Employed in the Requiem by Randall Thompson." M.M. thesis,
University of Wisconsin, 1966.

Lamb, Gordon H. "Interview with Robert Shaw (on the Music of Charles
Ives)." *The Choral Journal*, 15/8 (1975), pp. 5-7.

Larson, Robert M. "Stylistic Characteristics in A Cappella Composition in
the United States, 1940-53: As Indicated by the Works of Jean Berger,

David Diamond, Darius Milhaud, and Miklos Rozsa." Ph.D. dissertation, Northwestern University, 1953.

Latta, John Arthur. "Alice Parker: Choral Composer, Arranger, and Teacher." Ed.D. dissertation, University of Illinois, 1986.

LePage, Jane W. *Women Composers, Conductors, and Musicians of the Twentieth Century: Selected Biographies*. Metuchen, N.J.: Scarecrow Press, 3 vols., 1980-88.

Loessi, John. "The Choral Works of Randall Thompson." M.M. thesis, University of Cincinnati, 1955.

Loucks, Richard N. "Arthur Shepherd." Ph.D. dissertation, University of Rochester, 1960.

_____. *Arthur Shepherd, American Composer*. Orem, Utah: Brigham Young University Press, 1980.

MacNeill, Roger M. "Secular Choral Chamber Music in America since 1950, as Represented by the Music for This Genre by Samuel Adler, Jean Berger, Eugene Butler, and Kirke Mechem." D.A. dissertation, University of Northern Colorado, 1986.

Mann, Alfred, ed. *Randall Thompson: A Choral Legacy*. Boston: E.C. Schirmer, 1974.

McBrier, Vivian Flagg. "The Life and Works of Robert Nathaniel Dett." Ph.D. dissertation, Catholic University of America, 1967.

McCray, James. "Lukas Foss' *A Parable of Death*: Comments on Structure and Performance." *American Choral Review*, 18/3 (1976), pp. 12-13.

_____. "Norman Dello Joio's Mass Settings: A Comparative Introduction." *Diapason*, 80 (September, 1989), pp. 14-16.

McGilvray, Bryan Wendol. "The Choral Music of Randall Thompson, an American Eclectic." D.M.A. dissertation, University of Missouri-Kansas City, 1979.

Mechem, Kirke. "Alienation and Entertainment, Continued: Choral Music and Its Effect on Audiences and Students." *The Choral Journal*, 13/7 (1973), pp. 9-10.

_____. "The Choral Cycle." *The Choral Journal*, 10/7 (1970), pp. 8-11.

Meier, Ann. "An Interview with Norman Dello Joio." *Music Educators Journal*, 74 (October, 1987), pp. 53-6.

Merritt, Susan. "Text and Tune: Back to Basics with Alice Parker." *The Choral Journal*, 25/1 (1985), pp. 5-9.

Miller, Donald Bruce. "The Choral Music of Kirke Mechem: A Study and

Performance of Representative Works." D.M.A. dissertation, University of Southern California, 1981.

_____. "The Choral Music of Kirke Mechem." *American Choral Review*, 12/4 (1970), pp. 163-71.

Mize, Lou Stem. "A Study of Selected Choral Settings of Walt Whitman Poems." Ph.D. dissertation, Florida State University, 1967.

Moe, Orin. "The Music of Elliott Carter." *College Music Symposium*, 22/1 (Spring, 1982), pp.1-31.

Mosher, Lucinda. "Children's Choral Corner: Alice Parker on Composing for Children's Voices." *The Choral Journal*, 24/6 (1984), p. 23.

Mottola, Gail Louise H. "A Survey of the Choral Works by Thea Musgrave with a Conductor's Analysis of the *Five Ages of Man* and *Rorate coeli*." D.M.A. dissertation, University of Texas at Austin, 1986.

Muilenburg, Harley W. "A Study of Selected Unpublished Choral Compositions of Leo Sowerby." M.S. thesis, University Wisconsin-Eau Claire, 1976.

Murphy, James L. "The Choral Music of Halsey Stevens." Ph.D. dissertation, Texas Tech University, 1980.

Musselman, Joseph. *Dear People ... Robert Shaw: A Biography*. Bloomington: University of Indiana Press, 1979.

Newman, William S. "Arthur Shepherd." *The Musical Quarterly*, 36/2 (April, 1950), pp. 159-79.

Olmstead, Andrea. *Conversations with Roger Sessions*. Boston: Northeastern University Press, 1987.

Osborne, William. *American Singing Societies and Their Partsongs*. Lawton, Ok.: American Choral Directors Association, 1994.

Parks, O.G. "A Critical Study of the Works of Leo Sowerby." M.M. thesis, North Texas State University, 1941.

Perrison, Harry D. "Charles Wakefield Cadman: His Life and Works." Ph.D. dissertation, University of Rochester, 1978.

Pinkham, Daniel. Papers, 1949-1972. Houghton Library, Harvard University. Contains manuscripts and printed scores of Pinkham's compositions, concert programs, and miscellaneous items.

Plum, Nancy. "A Conversation with Composer Ned Rorem." *Voice*, (Nov.-Dec., 1985), pp. 1ff.

Pollack, Howard J. "Walter Piston and His Music." Ph.D. dissertation, Cornell University, 1981.

Powers, Harold S. "Current Chronicle [Sessions's *Lilacs...*]." *The Musical Quarterly*, 58 (1972), pp. 297-307.

Restine, James H. "The Choral Idiom of Randall Thompson." M.A. thesis, West Texas State University, 1959.

Revicki, Robert K. "A Study of Recent Settings of the Mass by American Composers." Master's thesis, Brown University, 1960.

Riegger, Wallingford. "The Music of Vivian Fine." *American Composers Alliance Bulletin*, 8/1 (1958), pp. 2-6.

Robinson, Ray. "Gian Carlo Menotti's New Mass." *The Choral Journal*, 20/5 (January, 1980), pp. 5-7, 21.

_____. "John Finley Williamson: His Contribution to Choral Music." *The Choral Journal*, 22/1 (1981), pp. 5-10.

Roma, Catherine. "The Choral Music of Thea Musgrave." *American Choral Review*, 21/1 (Winter, 1989), pp. 5-13.

Rosner, Arnold "An Analytical Survey of the Music of Alan Hovhaness." Ph D dissertation State University of New York at Buffalo, 1972,

Ryder, Georgia A. "Another Look at Some American Cantatas." *Black Perspective in Music*, 3/2 (May, 1975), pp. 135-140.

_____. "Melodic and Rhythmic Elements of American Negro Folk Songs as Employed in Cantatas by Selected American Composers between 1932 and 1967." Ph.D. dissertation, New York University, 1970.

Saladino, David A. "Influence of Poetry on Compositional Practices in Selected Choral Music of Gordon Binkerd." Ph.D. dissertation, Florida State University, 1984.

Schiff, David. *The Music of Elliott Carter*. New York: Da Capo Press, 1983.

Seigle, Cecilia Segawa. "The Choral Music of Vincent Persichetti." *American Choral Review*, 7/3 (March, 1965), pp. 4-5.

Shackelford, Rudy. "Conversation with Vincent Persichetti." *Perspectives of New Music*, 20/1-2 (1981-82), pp. 104-34.

_____. "The Music of Gordon Binkerd." *Tempo*, 114 (September, 1975), pp. 2-13.

Simpson, Ralph R. "William Grant Still — the Man and His Music." Ph.D. dissertation, Michigan State University, 1964.

Smith, Gregg. "Charles Ives and His Music for Chorus." *The Choral Journal*, 15/3 (1974), pp. 17-20.

Smith, James A. "Charles Sanford Skilton (1868-1941): Kansas Composer." M.A. thesis, University of Kansas, 1979.

Smith, Julia. *Aaron Copland: His Life and Contribution to American Music.* New York: E.P. Dutton, 1955.

Somerville, Thomas. "Some Aspects of the Choral Music of Halsey Stevens." *The Choral Journal*, 14/5 (1974), pp. 9-13.

Southern, Eileen. "Conversation with William Grant Still." *Black Perspective in Music*, 3/2 (May, 1975), pp. 165-75.

Sowerby, Leo. Sketchbook of holograph scores for various choral works, in the Music Division, the Library of Congress, Washington, D.C.

Sparger, A. Dennis. "A Study of Selected Choral Works of Randall Thompson." M.A. thesis, Eastern Illinois University, 1965.

Spencer, Jon Michael. "The Writings of Robert Nathaniel Dett and William Grant Still on Black Music." Ph.D. dissertation, Washington University, 1982.

Stallings, Valdemar L. "A Study of *Forsaken of Man*, a Sacred Cantata by Leo Sowerby." M.S.M. thesis, Southern Baptist Theological Seminary, 1956.

Stehman, Dan. *Roy Harris: A Bio-Bibliography.* Westport, Conn.: Greenwood Press, 1991.

_____. *Roy Harris: An American Musical Pioneer.* Boston: Twayne Publishers, 1984.

Strimple, Nick. "An Introduction to the Choral Works of Roy Harris." *The Choral Journal*, 22/9 (1982), pp. 16-19.

Studebaker, Donald. "The Choral Cantatas of Daniel Pinkham: An Overview." *The Choral Journal*, 29/5 (1988), p. 15-20.

_____. "The Sacred Choral Music of Norman Dello Joio." *Journal of Church Music*, 28 (October, 1986), pp. 10-12.

Swan, Howard. *Conscience of a Profession: Howard Swan, Choral Director and Teacher*, ed. Charles Fowler. Chapel Hill, N.C.: Hinshaw Music, 1987.

Thompson, Randall. "On Choral Composition: Essays and Reflections." David Francis Urrows, compiler. *American Choral Review*, 22/2 (1980), entire issue.

_____. Papers, 1917-1978. Houghton Library, Harvard University. Contains manuscript scores, some with annotations; printed scores; photocopies of scores; and preliminary drafts of Thompson's choral and non-choral works. Also, miscellaneous printed and photocopied scores by other composers from his library, as well as his own pencil sketches and other fragments of compositions.

_____. "Requiem: Notes by the Composer." *American Choral Review*, 16/4 (October, 1974), pp. 16-32.

Tircuit, Heuwell. "Alan Hovhaness: An American Composer." *American Choral Review*, 9/1 (1966), pp. 8, 10-11, 17.

Tortolano, William. "The Mass and the Twentieth-Century Composer: A Study of Musical Techniques and Style, Together with the Interpretive Problems of the Performer." D.S.M. dissertation, University of Montreal, 1964.

_____. "Melody in the Twentieth-Century Mass." *Diapason*, 60/5 (April, 1969), pp. 18-19.

Tuthill, Burnet C. "Leo Sowerby." *The Musical Quarterly*, 24/3 (1938), pp. 249-64.

Urrows, David Francis. "The 'Lost' Choral Work of Randall Thompson." *American Choral Review*, 23/1-2 (Winter/Spring, 1990), pp. 8-16.

Van Allen, Janice Kay. "Stylistic and Interpretive Analysis and Performance of Selected Choral Compositions by Three American Composers: Vincent Persichetti, Virgil Thomson, and Daniel Pinkham." Ed.D. dissertation, Columbia University, 1973.

Vanderkoy, Paul Arthur. "A Survey of the Choral Music of Halsey Stevens." D.A. dissertation, Ball State University, 1981.

Voorhees, Larry D. "A Study of Selected Vocal-Choral Works of Samuel Barber." M.A. thesis, Eastern Illinois University, 1965.

Waring, Fred. *Tone Syllables*. Delaware Water Gap, Penn.: Shawnee Press, 1945.

Willoughby, Dale E. "Performance Preparation of Various Choral Works Representing Selected Periods of Music History." D.M.A. dissertation, University of Miami, 1971.

Wilson, J.H. "A Study and Performance of *The Ordering of Moses* by Robert Nathaniel Dett." D.M.A. dissertation, University of Southern California, 1970.

Yancy, Henrietta Miller. "The Contribution of the American Negro to the Music Culture of the Country." *School Musician*, 41 (March, 1970), pp. 60-1.

INDEX

Musical works are listed alphabetically by title, with the composer's name following.
Numerals in italics indicate a full article by that author; bold numerals indicate an illustration.